MY LIFE STORY: MY JOURNEY THROU

MW01172838

TABLE OF CONTENTS (Since I have constructed a "living" document it is possible that page numbers and percentages will be off from time to time-but, thy should be close enough to be representative.)

FOREWARD ABSTRACT

The entire purpose of this book was to share with my children my missed opportunities along my life's journey…to this point. It is my hope that they would know my missed opportunities and have insight to take advantage of the opportunities that come along for them in their lives. I realized that my parents had not put down in any formally documented way the things that happened in their lives. I really wanted to share with them the experiences of my ancestors. Those are things that influenced me and led to the possibilities that I had afforded to me.

I also realize that along the way my sister had done work to document my family's history, and I would know some things because of the work that she did. I would also know things about my family because of what my grandmother, great aunts and uncles told me about my family. Much of what they told me has been documented in census records, death and birth notices and records housed at the Great Salt Lake City Mormon Temple.

But even more than that, I want my children to know the things that I had done, the things that I had participated, and some real missed opportunities in my life. Such as: my opportunity to become a professional model, a professional athlete, my opportunity to become a naval aviator, my opportunity to become a school principal or administrator, and my opportunity to become a college department head.

Along the way I will discuss each of those opportunities as they interrelate with the rest of the events of my life, which should thereafter be documented.

I also want to provide this "Coxism", this proverb, this old country saying: "If you throw a rock into a pack of dogs the one that it hits will yell." I am including this disclaimer at the beginning because some people who read what is in this document might take offense to the statements. I intentionally used initials in the recounting of certain events. You have to know the initials and the events to be able to put yourself in a position to be disgruntled. No one else could know these details – BUT, if they do know themselves in these events, they will know that I am telling the truth.

THE DECISION TO SELF-PUBLISH

As I move forward in the development of this book, I think it is also important that those people who would come along and read this should understand that initially I really had created this document to be a journal of my life for my children. It was my way for them to get to know little something about their dad.
The reason I determined to self-publish this book was mostly because The Christian publishers that I had encountered:
One – Wanted a lot of money to produce every process of the book. An expensive proposition.
Two – They all wanted me to redact the section on my sexual escapades.

These two factors were large indicators that it would be best for me to self-publish the book and publish it electronically with Amazon.

A lesson I also embraced from M.C. Hammer came to mind. When the major record labels began to approach Hammer about signing meager, miniscule contracts; where the costs for promotion and studio time would come out of the already paltry fees, Hammer told them "I am already making a ton of money, selling my own CDs and cassettes out of the trunk of my car. Everything I get is mine to keep. Why would I sign with you and make little to know money when everything is said and done?" The lesson within those words have always stuck with me. Sometimes, the cost of publishing, and trying to find an agent, are in many ways, far more costly than just going ahead and publishing it yourself. Give your work a reasonable price. Then see where the financial chips fall. But, wherever the chips fall, they all belong to you.

Another consideration was that even Christians have lives and pasts. They have lives that are kind of all over the place. They have "isms" and they have "schisms". They have "psychosis" just like everybody else. Christians also have vices, addictions and challenges just like everyone. Some are addicts and have various addictions. So, in the long and short of it, we may as well be honest, and not try to act like life is pristine and unblemished. That's not the way it works. There is redemption, forgiveness and recovery from all forms of addiction; including the one that I had for sex. In fact, I don't call my sexual desire and addiction. I thought it was very natural.

A LIVING DOCUMENT

This book is a "living" document. I will continue to make updates as long as I have this Amazon publishing account. In the theatre, and with traditional publishing, you run into deadlines, and the document is set. With this document, I know from time to time I will have another remembrance or have another noteworthy life event take place. I want to leave things as open as possible to make those interjections.

CONVERSATION WITH MARC

I remember having a conversation with my good friend and brother Marc Taylor one morning. We were discussing our life's pathways and choices. Even things that could have been eventualities or occurrences based on our choices. I remember talking to him about the opportunity I had to go to New York City. I was told by the representatives of every major modeling/talent agency in New York City that if I came to New York one of the agencies would sign me. They all told me that if it were not their agency one of the other agencies would sign me. That included agencies like Ford, Wilhelmina, Elite, John Casablanca's... all their men's divisions.

I told him that I had my car packed ready to leave Denver to go to New York, but subsequently I was encouraged to come back to Nashville and teach at Tennessee state University. I commented on the notoriety I would have gained, and the amount of money I could have earned. I commented on the kind of things I could have done to help family and friends. Marc was insightful enough to share this perspective with me: The only thing that we know for sure is that what we are doing right now is the result of the decisions that we made, to be where we are right now. Marc went on to say I had no idea of what would happen if I had struck out for New York. Even with all the opportunities: the apartment above my aunt and Uncle's house free of rent. Even with the train station just five blocks away from their home... you do not know what would have happened. You do not know... you could never know. You will never know. Hell, on your way to New York you could have incurred a bad accident; perhaps even a fatal accident. You do not know that once you were in New York or going into New York City you could have traveled down the wrong blocked or the wrong street. You do not know. You do not know what randomly just could have happened. It is all based on the decision that you make. It may have been a good decision, but fate always intervenes, and the bottom line is: The only thing we know for sure is for sure that we are alive right now. The way things have turned out up to this point is all we know, because it is all based on a decision. It is based on now decision and we have no idea how a decision we COULD have made would have resulted.

As I thought about that I thought: I am going to pass that advice along to others. We make the best decision that we can make in the now and hope and pray that it turns out to be a favorable decision. In most cases clear, rational thinking and planning does give way to good results. But we must never forget the randomness of the intervention of fate; and that in life things that should not pop up, pop up for no rhyme or reason. There is no reason for them to pop up and yet they do. Every day we leave home thinking that we are going to return home. Yet so many things happen that are unexpected, unplanned, and unprepared for.

Example: A gentleman left his home to go to an auto parts store to pick up a part. Apparently, he needed the part to work on a vehicle. In those intervening moments, a young man had stolen a car. He had wrecked the car once and continued down the street to escape from police pursuit. The young man struck the car driven by the elderly gentleman even before the elder could pull out of the parking lot. The innocent elderly man was killed. The person who had stolen the car survived. The point is: You never, ever know.

EAST NASHVILLE / WHERE I WAS BORN

I was born in Nashville, Tennessee. My parents lived in East Nashville on Straightway Avenue. They had recently married. My dad had served four years in the Navy, in Korea. He served on the USS Brush; a ship named after an army field marshal. I believe my mother and father were students at Tennessee State University. My mother is from Birmingham, Alabama, and had just become good friends with my aunt Tommie. My dad was my Tommie's brother. After dating for, I do not know how long, they were married. Along came the first child. A daughter who did not live very long. When she died in the hospital my dad was hot with the doctors because he said the doctors did not do enough to try to save her. According to my dad, the doctors did not try to save her. They were out playing golf when they should have been at the hospital seeing about his daughter. Then my brother Carl was born. Carl had the spend time in an incubator. He was born in General Hospital. I was next to be born. I was born in Riverside Seventh-day Adventist hospital, in the North Nashville area, across from American Baptist Theological Seminary (as it was known at that time). American Baptist Theological Seminary is now known as American Baptist College. I can't tell you too much about these Nashville and what it was like growing up in East Nashville because I was really too young to remember What I know is what I have been told by my parents and that is we lived on Straightway Avenue when Carl was born and when I was born, and we moved shortly after Kenneth was born.

PROVIDENCE

As I said, my parents lived on Straightway, and sometime around the time that the next sibling came along, my brother Kenneth, my parents moved us back out to the village of Providence. The village of Providence is in the southern part of Nashville, close to the Williamson County line. My first remembrance of Providence was that we stayed in the lower part of a home right on Nolensville Pike. When it rained it did flood our neighbors to the South. Our neighbors to the south were the Youngs. Roy Young, and Anne his daughter. They lived across the creek from us, and every time the creek flooded it got both families and properties. The next home I remember in Providence was on Providence Heights. When you go there, even now, it is one of the steepest hills in the village. During the spring, summer and fall Providence Heights was a land mine of boulders, deep holes, and loose gravel. If you did not know how to navigate a car up Providence Heights you could easily tear out the transmission or the oil pan. In the winter we would get sleds, and we would ride on sleds down the slope of Providence Heights. When I was four or five it actually snowed in Nashville. We would have plenty of snow to ride sleds to the bottom of the Heights. Sometimes we go nearly out into Nolensville Pike. It is a wonder that none of us ever went out into Nolensville Pike. Honestly! The house on Providence Heights was not the height of luxury. There was an outhouse; and under the bed in our room we kept the slop jar. There were bugs. There were rats and mice. The home was heated by firewood and a coal stove oven set close to the center of the house. In the kitchen when it came time to take a bath, there was a large, galvanized tub. The water was heated on (if I remember this correctly) a wood burning stove. We took our turns in the tub. The boys: me, Kenny, and Carl, would take baths in that galvanized tub. Heaven could only help you if you were the second, and then the third person into that tub. I said we kept a "slop jar" under the bed. For those of you who do not know what a "slop jar" is, it was a porcelain or ceramic pot. When you had to go to the bathroom you either peed, or you took a dump into that pot. Before the pot got way too full one of us would have to take it to the outhouse and dump it. Using the outhouse was not an uncommon occurrence. The neighbors slightly up the hill from us where the Grays. Across the street directly from us were the Shelton's. I remember my brother Carl learning to ride a bike. The way the hill sloped, and the natural contours lent themselves to a quick trip down. It was quite a steep drop from the top of our property to the yard: and if you missed the yard there was about a five foot drop off where the driveway was established. One day as Carl was learning to ride. He came from the top of our hill, maybe he was on the Grays property. This time he could not get the bike stopped in time before he flew over across the yard, over the top of the car, into the bushes. It was quite festive, but I'm sure Carl would think of it that way.

After we had lived on Providence Heights for a couple of years my parents began to have a house built on Winston Avenue. I must address, at this point, to help you understand. My grandmother owned a great deal of property that started at the end of Nolensville Pike and went up to our present 4413 Winston Avenue. It is my understanding that my parents never intended to live in Providence. My uncle Joe and aunt Cora Scales came along and wanted to move to Providence. My father sold them his half of the land that my grandmother owned that would be his. and Aunt Cora and Uncle Joe lived at 4409 Winston Avenue. They had a rather large yard with a fabulous garden adjacent to it. When my mom and dad decided to become permanent residents of Providence I don't know if they bought the property back or if they still had a parcel of this land; but the part they did not sell to aunt Cora and uncle Joe is where they built the present 4413 Winston Avenue home. When we lived on Providence Heights, from time to time we would walk through the woods to see how they were coming along with the house. As they were framing the house, I remember my dad and Mr. Percy using what they called a plumbing tool to balance the points where the four main posts of the house needed to go in order to create a sturdy foundation. Plumbing… that's old school, and I'm sure they don't build houses that way anymore. I cannot remember the year, but finally they got the house finished. There was hardwood throughout the house. It was not an especially big house, but it did have three bedrooms, one bath, a kitchen-slash dining room, and a living room. The four boys would sleep in one room. My sister Angela had a separate room and my parents, of course, have their room. This home put us in a line with Granny having the first house that you encountered on Winston Avenue, and the white house of Aunt Cora and Uncle Joe was next. Then came the garden of Uncle Joe and Aunt Cora. 4413, which was the home where we lived. Later, Aunt Cora and Uncle Joe would sell half of their property to aunt Cora's sister, Willoughby Cantrell. Mrs. Willoughby, as we called her, and her husband Elvin Cantrell, will be our neighbors for several years - well into our adulthood. As I said, it is never talked about, but Mr. Elvin was the chief, or head groundskeeper at Cheekwood. Much of the success of the gardening during that time was due to the effort on Mr. Elvin Cantrell.

Providence, I can tell you, was a truly amazing experience for a young boy growing up. Providence was the "country". Those that know or remember Mayberry R.F.D. or the Andy Griffin show will understand when I say that Providence was more rural than Mayberry. It was a quiet community where we did not see much crime. I think the main reason for that is because the people of Providence held everyone accountable for what happened in the community, or in the village. In a strange but delightful kind of way we were all related somehow. It really took my grandmother to explain it to me. At times I wondered who this person in the neighborhood was, or who was that person in the neighborhood. My grandmother could explain the family relationship. If anyone ever said this is your cousin so and so, and you did not know or understand their explanation for the relationship you get always go to Granny. Granny would be very precise in knowledge; but at the end of her unraveling of the knowledge, you felt like your brain had probably been warped because of the amount of detail that she went into for her explanation. However, as a young child, it could not be in a safer place to grow up. I have already said that the people of the community held each of them accountable but the actions of everyone else. Any type of news spread at lightning speed through the neighborhood. Say, for instance, if anything untoward had happened at school the people of the community would know even before you left the school grounds what you had done, and that in some crazy way it had been broadcast to the community. The elders of the community would sit on their porches. Some would say "boy, you gon' be in trouble when you get to yo granny's house", or an elder came off their porch and smacked you upside the head and said "I heard what you did at school. You are gonna get it again when you get to your grandmother's, and when your parents get home you really gonna get it." That was true. By the same token, the elders would let anything happen to any child of that village. The elders had the responsibility to mete out consequences. The same responsibility they took to protect us like fierce lions and lionesses or mama bears. Vicious attack dogs had nothing on the elders of Providence when it came to protecting every young person who either lived in the village or who happened to be in the village. As a young boy I could walk through the woods… the dense woods that surrounded Providence, with never a fear of anything happening except the occasional tick, the bouts with chiggers, the bugs that make your dick swell up. It is interesting to note that battles of the Civil War were fought all the way from Franklin Tennessee into Nashville Tennessee. These skirmishes course took occurred through the woods of Providence, Mount Pigsby, and the fields of the Croft farm (now, the Nashville Zoo location). My grandmother said that as a boy, my father had a great collection of Civil War artifacts, which included Civil War caps, muskets, and bayonets. My dad's collection also included butterflies and moths. All his collections were categorized and assembled with great care. My father said that as a boy he would roam the woods around Providence. He said that Civil War artifacts lay on the ground exposed to human sight, to the elements, to everything. That is why he could just walk through the woods as a boy and pick these items up. My dad was born in December 1931. That is not even 60 years after the end of the Civil War. Many soldiers died on those fields between Franklin and Nashville. There is also a cave system that runs under the area of the village. I know this to be true for because of two distinct reasons: anytime there is any amount of blasting in the area the echoes from the blast reverberate through the caverns or the chambers. My dad also told me he used to be an amateur spelunker. He knew where the entrance to these chambers were, and he never told us. My grandmother said that my dad did go into the caves, and that there were days he would come home muddy as all get out because he had been crawling through the caves. So, to this day, there is no telling what other Civil War artifacts might be found in those caverns. My dad never told us how to get into them although I think they are somewhere near the property of the Redd family. None of us ever had the fortune to go down into those caves. There must be an underground stream or lake under the area; as well, because our back yard neighbor, Mrs. Lilly had a hole bored through the rock, and she had a container she could lower through the hole, through the rock. When she would pull up the container it would be filled with fresh water. There were times when it rained that I literally saw the streams of water run through the rock formations.

Now, when we grew up in Providence you had to be a tough, stand up for yourself, individual. The boys of the community were being raised on farms, for the most part, in a very rural environment, a very Spartan kind of life. We were born to be tough and resourceful. Born to lookout for yourself and to stick up for yourself. My father (Korean Navy U.D.T. man) made it clear he did not want us fighting, and if there was an opportunity to walk away from a fight, to walk away; but if there came that time where you could not walk away my father's expectation was that you hold up your end of a fight. Because if you didn't, and he found out about it, you would have to fight him (and believe you me I was not going to let that happen) so the skirmishes that I had I did pretty good, because in the back of my mind I didn't want to have to tangle with Washington Dobbins, senior. The thing was, all of us young men/boys became very close; and it only took one or two scraps to let everyone know that you would take up for yourself. Then, that would be the end of that, and your fighting days were few. One of my earliest remembrances was when we moved to Winston Avenue, and my oldest brother Carl and I were both attending the Providence community or village school, which was located on the same property that Southern Hills hospital now sits. We would walk along the Seven Mile Creek bed (and I would like to say at this point I believe that the part of Seven Mile Creek that ran through our community was dug out. The reason I believe this is because the bed was stone lined. As we walked alongside the creek, we would see the life cycle played out. Whether it was birds hatching from eggs and growing and developing. We saw baby chicks doing the same thing. Whether it was the snake that could pop up anywhere, at any time. Whether it was beavers who dammed the creek in different places. Whether it was the tadpoles and minnows that you watch develop out of the eggs in the creek. Whether it was frog gigging at night in the pond that was up the street, (and those of you who do not know frog gigging - you have a stick with a nail. At night, when the bullfrogs come out you spike the bullfrogs with the nail, cut the legs off and throw the rest back. You could have a really good meal of fried up frog legs, but the thing I remember is that if I had an issue, it always seemed to be with "D". I believe that M.T. and I had traded blows at the school enough to know that each other would take up for ourselves and that pretty much settled it. But somehow, I always seemed to have an encounter with "D" (I am not saying that "D" was the neighborhood bully but I believe "D" liked to good scrap all the time.) We would walk to school with our lunch sacks, and whatever lunch money we had to buy something extra, like a pudding or cake, or an ice cream double-cream sandwich. "D" wanted my extra money. The first couple of times I went against the "Washington rule". I was intimidated and gave in, and let me say, my brother did not jump in to meditate because we all learned early on you had to stand up for yourself and fight your own battles. Because if you did not you never would. Well, there did come the day - and it came after around the second or the third time when I was going to go to school without my extra money. I told "D" he would have the square it up right there; and we did have one good round of fisticuffs. "D" did not get my money, and this did not happen again. I made the decision to stand up for myself. After that "D" did not try to take my money anymore; although he could still be very aggressive and try to intimidate you. The other time would be when we would play sports, and "D" would try to intimidate you to get what he wanted. In the end everyone wanted to know whether you would stick up for yourself or would you let somebody pick on you. I know all of us boys and young men were determined that we were not going to let anyone take advantage of us, and in the end we all had each other's back. That is a great testimony. One of the things that we used to do for fun is play dodgeball with Osage oranges. Now, again I am using a lot of country terminology and expressions. We also used to call them "milk balls." The Osage orange is the fruit of a thorny tree and depending how long they were allowed to stay on the tree they get really big and develop a green pebbly outer covering with a white, milky, liquid substance on the inside. As boys (and I do not know why most of us are not dead) we would pile up our arsenals of milk balls and we would then take turns hurling them at each other. We were all fair game, and some were pretty good at the aim game. For instance, "J" and "M" were "country strong". They were deadly accurate with the milk balls; and you could get hit upside the head. You could have easily ended up with broken ribs, broken arms, broken bones, and contusions. As a boy you learned early to man up. You could not go home crying about getting hit in the head with the milk ball. You toughed up, went home, and came back, and did the same thing the next day. Hopefully, your aim was better, your strength was better, and all of us became very proficient in playing "Dodge the Milk Ball."

Another special event that took place were the Nights of Fun which took place every Friday or Saturday night on Nolensville Pike. I do not remember whose property it was held on, but we used to walk right down from Providence Heights, across Nolensville Pike to the yard where they had strung up all kinds of lights, and someone had brought a record player. They played records, people danced, people bought and ate fish sandwiches, hot dogs, hamburgers; and just as a village (and I use that term so much) we just had a really good time. The closest thing now that I can even remember or call an equivalent of the Night of Fun is that the relatives of Mrs. Lillie (our backyard neighbor) who purchased the property - the Bryant King family, have parties outside and they do string up the lights, they do play the music, they do cook out, they do dance and socialize. That is about the closest that I can think of that takes place now that would be like the old-fashioned Nights of Fun that we had in Providence. Again, I do not remember any violent activity, any law enforcement that ever had to be called in that people just did not look out for each other and were totally respectful of each other. I am sure… I did not know, but I am sure it happened that people snuck off and did things that adults would do. They were human, very earthy people. We were very rural people. We all knew each other; we were very comfortable with each other. People from the community often married people from the community; and so, I am sure that there were adult things that went on that I was not privy to at the time.

JUNIOR PRO FOOTBALL

Another example of growing up tough in Providence is that my brothers and I played Junior Pro Football. We were not the biggest children in the world, so we had to be pretty tough. I remember that all of us were not afraid to take on the biggest of the kids; either on our team, or the opposition. Providence did not lend itself to being frightened. We were supposed to be scrappy and tough; and if we sustained a heavy blow from the opponent on the field our parents did not move. Doris and Washington Dobbins stayed put. They were not like the parents of today who want to go and check up on their child who's stumped his toe and tripped on himself. No, if you got hit hard and went to the ground hard, Doris and Washington Dobbins did not move a muscle. The thing was, you'd better get up, and you'd better learn that you have to get up for yourself, because they wouldn't be helping you to get up. And don't embarrass us. So, you'd better get up. What better lessons to learn for life: When you were knocked down, you're going to have to pick yourself up. Don't wait for someone else to do it. Don't let someone else do it. That was a great lesson, and the lesson that has served me well in many endeavors, and many turning points or opportunities of life.

One of the young men who made the community proud was the one beautiful Dejuan Buford. Dejuan was a member of the Buford family and a spectacular athlete, who was not only a high school star but a college star as well. Dejuan had his pathway to a professional football career cut short due to an injury. I shared a note on Facebook, after I recalled seeing a picture of him in his Mcalhaney insurance football uniform. The picture reminded need that his father would bring him over to watch the Dobbins boys at their various football games. My father and mother did the very same thing after we boys finished playing, or before we played. Either way we watched as much as we could games that featured other young men from Providence, including Dejuan Buford and Gary Hockett. I will try to recall as much of that exchange as possible, but in essence, it starts with me seeing the picture of Dejuan that he posted on Facebook. It is the team photo of Mcalhaney insurance which featured his image. I replied to him Mcalhaney insurance brought back a lot of memories.

Dejuan replied: "Now Wash, you know you were my hero back in the day. My daddy would always make sure we either watched you at practice and in your games. We would be in the stands and he used to always say keep your eyes on him. Son, he is about to score. We literally thought you might score every time they handed the ball to you! Let me make one correction at this point, Dejuan was actually referring to my brother Joel. Later Dejuan would make the correction. My response to Dejuan was "Thank you! That is a great compliment coming from a tremendous athlete like you. Joel was a far more proficient scorer than I. Growing up in Providence generated priceless relationships. After our games, my mom and dad brought us over to watch you and Gary play. My dad said the same thing about watching y'all light up the opposition. Providence always showed up for

Providence. A lot of men of Providence played in the softball league at the park near Chestnut and the train tracks. Those were the days. (I could not remember the name of that park so I just gave a description.)

Dejuan replied with a great compliment; especially considering the talented athlete that he had become. Dejuan said: "You and Joel were my idols. I have also told Joel this a million times, as well. I will always remember him having the nickname back then, OJ." I replied Dejuan, Thanks, Dejuan, I believe it was your dad who established that nickname. I like to bust heads. Antioch high school football standouts Tony Glover and Ron Adelot were my Junior Pro Football teammates. They got to feel the fury in practice. I want to say you have made my day! All the citizens of Providence groomed us to be people of the highest integrity! I love your dad, your uncle Dewey Hockett, and Baby Watson! The list is long!

A NEST OF HORNETS

One of my other remembrances of growing up in Providence is being stung by a nest of Hornets. When we lived on Providence Heights, we went down the street to a neighbor's house. This neighborhood had fabulous outdoor furniture on her lawn. Being just being a little boy, and just being neighborly, I sat down when one of her outdoor couches. Before I knew it felt like I had caught on fire. I had no idea what was going on; however, my dad saw immediately that I had been attacked by a swarm of hornets, and that they were stinging the living daylights out of me. Some of the stingers were still imbedded in me and still wiggling. Washington Senior whipped out his pocketknife, began to grab the stingers between the thumb and the knife blade, and pulled him out. Once he was successful at that (since my dad was a chain smoker, I will mention this again: he lit one Pall Mall red package filter less cigarette from the prior one. He could go through two packs a day of those filter less cigarettes easily.) On this occasion he took out a cigarette and he shook all the tobacco out put it in his mouth, chewed it up, and then took that tobacco and spread it over those places where I had been stung. It was sort of a modern-day triage. The pain subsided quickly. I'm told it was the content of nicotine that counteracted the venom of the hornets.

LAKE PROVIDENCE MISSIONARY BAPTIST CHURCH

I start out by telling pastor Bruce Maxwell (and sometimes I just say Bruce because we grew up together in Providence) Lake Providence Missionary Baptist Church was the center of everything that happened in the Providence community. The Providence community itself was established 1868 (which was two years after the civil war, or I think after Lincoln's second Emancipation Proclamation) by a group of newly freed slaves who came to this area where there was generally what was regarded as a lake at its' center and began to hold church services and settle the area. The church, I often tell pastor Maxwell, or at least the present church, because there were three or four different versions of Lake Providence Missionary Baptist Church. There was the original building, then the first real substantial structure was the building they called the 1950 building. Then came the more modern Lake Providence church, which was erected somewhere around 1990 after my dad's funeral. Next came the present Lake Providence church edifice, which is located about 5 miles from where the original Providence community existed. Everyone in the community attended the Lake Providence church. My family was a little different in that we sort of had dual church membership; because my mother was a member of Pleasant Green Missionary Baptist Church (I will talk more about this great church later) and my dad and grandmother-Granny Mary, were members of the Lake Providence church. I have to say loosely that my dad was a member, because there was some controversy regarding his membership when he enlisted in the Navy and was gone for four years. However, this was the church where we did attend regularly. We went to Sunday school practically every Sunday at Lake Providence; and every Sunday there were many activities: the Christmas program, the Easter program. We learned our little Easter poems that we presented with our Sunday school classes at the church.

AN EASTER EGG HUNT NOT EVEN TOPPED BY THE WHITEHOUSE

There was also the epic Easter egg hunt. The Easter Egg Hunt usually took place about two blocks South of the church, on the Buford property. The Buford's had a beautiful front yard with trees, shrubs, and various grasses. All of the eggs were made by the people of the community, and the Golden eggs, the silver eggs, the yellow eggs, the colored eggs which contained prizes of money, or a very special treat were all hidden. All the people of the community and their relatives came and hunted Easter eggs. I could tell you it is probably one of the best Easter egg hunts ever assembled. No one worried about anyone contaminating the eggs or doing anything to harm any of the children. It was one of those events which made the Lake Providence area so special.

I talk to my pastor and friend, Reverend Bruce Maxwell, a lot. When we have the opportunity to talk, I remind him that the people of our village; our elders: my grandmother, his parents, and the other elders of the community prayed over us, sacrificed for us, generously poured into us. They had a vision and they prayed for things they never got to see on this side of life, but I know that they are looking down from their places in glory to see where their prayers and their sacrifices lead. One example is of a church that cost $22 million dollars to build. It took strong and prayer and through the leadership of Reverend Bruce Maxwell, the deacons, and trustees that $22 million dollars was paid off in 15 years. I look about the sanctuary, the grounds, the campus, and I tell Reverend Maxwell that this is what my grandmother prayed for. It is what she envisioned, it's what she knew was possible. I believe that she also knew it was not meant for her to physically enjoy; and I know that she realized that even at the time she was praying, giving, and sacrificing that her prayers would be answered. (My grandmother's answered prayers apply not only to the church, but for her children and grandchildren.) so, this whole discourse does hold part of the book is home part of my life was generated by 20 mins him missing it transcript that was meant for my dad and I am glad that I have it and watching a scene from the movie saying God does work in mysterious ways.

TWO CHURCH FAMILIES

When I talk about being blessed, I mean I was really blessed to have not one, but two distinct church families. I talked about my church family at Lake Providence where I grew up, but I also have to talk about my church family at Pleasant Green Missionary Baptist Church. I had sort of a country family and a city church family type of existence. I was also influenced by a high level of accountability. In other words, I could not just do the types of things that I wanted to do, or things that were socially unacceptable because not only did I have the family at Lake Providence to answer to, but I also had the family at Pleasant Green to answer to. Having to answer to either of those families would not be a day at the beach.

Pleasant Green is where I was baptized. I was baptized by Reverend Andrew L Porter. My baptism really came at the insistence of my great aunt, Drucilla Pair Edwards. I give "Tee" the credit more than anyone else because she really talked to me about being baptized; far more than my parents or anyone else had talked to me about being baptized. My brother Carl answered the call to give his life to Christ and made his public profession of faith before I did and was baptized. One Sunday, as I was sitting with my great-aunt Drucilla Edwards in church, my knees started to jump because I really wanted to go forward and make my public profession of faith, but you know you sit there and you're kind of glued to the seat. My great-aunt just kept urging, and kept urging, and finally I stood up. Once you stand up, you kind of have to go through with it. I made my way to the front and soon after that I was baptized. Whoa!!! That pool that they had upstairs was freezing!!! Later on Pleasant Green would add a heater or heating unit to the pool, but when I got baptized that water was like being immersed in a block of ice. I don't think I could do a Polar Ice swim, an Ice Water Challenge, or the athletic ice bath! Heck now!!!

My pastor, Reverend Andrew L. Porter was really a super cool guy who was very, very smart. Reverend Porter was very biblically intellectual (he was just a very intelligent person). I could not have had a more solid biblical and religious foundation then I got at Lake Providence and Pleasant Green Missionary Baptist Churches. The way that Pleasant Green Missionary Baptist Church happened to become such an important part of my development is that my dad had a period of time where he really did not attend Lake Providence church; even though he maintained his church membership there. My mother came from Birmingham, Alabama and united with Pleasant Green because that is where my great aunt and great uncle, and my mother's brother and sister-in-law were members. There were families that were so instrumental and influential in my development. I always had additional mothers and additional fathers at Pleasant Green. There were the Taylors: Estes and Virginia. The Taylor children were like our sisters and brothers. There were the Lannoms, the Otey's; and of course, we were like sisters and brothers. There were the McAllisters, the McKays, and countless other families. At Pleasant Green young people's music was a very big part of the religious experience. There was the Imperial Choir, which really were the older (and by older, I mean people who were in my parent's peer range group and above) members of the church, but we also had a very strong youth musical program. Practically all of us young people at Pleasant Green played some type of instrument and performed in various musical organizations in school and at the church. We were a musical bunch led by Lornetta Taylor. Lornetta was attending Fisk University. Lornetta was a Fisk Jubilee Singer. Lornetta was a tremendous, tremendous singer herself.

Being a very musical youth department in the church we would team up or align with Riverside Seven-Day Adventist Church. I don't know how this came about, but I do know that they, too, had excellent musicians at their church. Their young people performed many of the same pieces that we did at Pleasant Green. So, on occasion, it was very easy to team with them for concerts and things of that nature to perform these really good musical numbers again I just feel extremely blessed that I was put in the midst of such a musically talented group of young people there at the church.

Pleasant Green paid for its young people to attend church camp each summer. They would send us down to Linden Tennessee, on the Buffalo River. This was every summer. We would meet and travel with young people from other churches in Nashville. We would then gather with other church youth groups there at camp Linden. We stayed there for an entire week. We had all of our meals there (and the meals were pretty darn good). We would have Bible studies during the day; and then at night we mostly had some type of preaching/music program. Different church groups, preachers and choirs would lead the evening programs, and afterwards we would just kind of all hung out together there in the country in Linden Tennessee. That was quite an experience.

The Rabbit Feast

Every year the men of Pleasant Green Missionary Baptist Church held what was known as the Rabbit Feast. The men would hunt rabbits all during the season and freeze them. Then, one weekend in the fall they would bring all of their harvested rabbits to the church. They would barbeque them, they would fry them, they would bake them. This gathering was known as the Rabbit Feast. One thing that you had to be careful about was chomping down on a buckshot pellet in the rabbit. As well as they tried to clean the rabbit, they could still miss a piece of buckshot in the rabbit. I can tell you now biting down on a piece of buckshot when you're eating really well-prepared rabbit does not end very well. But, the rabbit was great, and the rabbit feast was one of those things that I do really, really remember.

The Emergence of Deacon Dobbins

Pleasant Green Missionary Baptist Church is also where I was ordained as a Deacon. Reverend Forrest Harris was the pastor. I have been recommended as a candidate to become a Deacon at Pleasant Green. The first time I was asked to take this responsibility, I actually turned it down. At first, I was afraid. Second, I really didn't think that I had the wherewithal to be a Deacon, or that I was spiritually sound enough to be a Deacon. But the second time that it was presented to me I accepted it and entered into the Deacon training program. I was ordained by Reverend William Buchanan from 15th Avenue Baptist Church, under the direction of Reverend Forrest Harris. I was selected to become the head of the Deacon Ministry. I had the privilege of leading Pleasant Green Missionary Baptist Church at a time when the church was without a pastor. I tried to follow one of the most basic Boy Scout tenants: Leave something better than the way you found it. I prayed that I would do nothing to damage the precious gem that Pleasant Green Missionary Baptist Church meant to my life. I remember having to be tougher as a leader than I had ever been in my life. It is not a light responsibility that the shepherd must protect the sheep from the wolves. I had to stand up to a lot of wolves. The overwhelming number of wolves were inside the church family. Many of them were opportunists who felt because I was a nice personality (a people person) I would let them get away with certain things like picking on members who did not have the wherewithal to fight back. They could not have been more wrong about me. The part of my father came to the surface. I had to be careful about the language, but definitely not the attitude. I am proud to say that I "lit up" the wolves who needed "lighting up" without always using the Navy language of my father. I always spoke in "no-uncertain" terms. I developed the belief that if you sometimes try to speak tactfully people will act like they didn't really understand what you said, or they will try to misinterpret what you said. When the message is clear-sometimes course (But, not vulgar) there is clarity. There were times when I had to address the congregation in "no uncertain terms" that some members that had actually mentored me (and who I was close to) called me and called to my attention that I had been a bit abrasive at the meeting. I did my best to thank them for their observations and that. Because it was their request that I would make every attempt to be more diplomatic without sacrificing my convictions. Sometimes it worked. Sometimes…not so well.

The Decision to Leave the Membership Of Pleasant Green Missionary Baptist Church

As things would go; eventually there would come a time when I would leave the membership of Pleasant Green and formally become a member of Lake Providence. It's kind of hard to say sometimes why you do things or why things happen; but in the end I want to say that it was God-inspired. This decision put me back in direct contact with the community where I grew up, with a church where I had also grown up but never became a member. It really put me back in touch with my heritage; meaning it was one of the churches I grew up in. The funerals of both my father and grandmother were at Lake Providence. I can't tell you how I felt after I formally walked down the aisle to join Lake Providence. I often tell people I have not had as much fun, or that I did not believe a person could have as much fun being a Christian as I have had being a member - and that I am having being a member at Lake Providence. I have never forgot the foundation and the stability of my family, and the support of the people of Pleasant Green Missionary Baptist Church. Pleasant Green is a vital part of my life and my history. There are just so many memories and friendships. Brotherhoods and sisterhoods. Pleasant

Green was an extended family. Being a member there made it one of those things that just lets you know how charmed of a life that you have lived. It let me know how blessed I was. They're just some things you could not asked for, but that God alone provides. God does provide.

FRAMMIN' AND JAMMIN'

I like to call this section "Framing 'n Jammin. So, this is the story behind this. One night my dad took us out in the car. We rode with him to some friend of his house to pick up something. I cannot really say what it was because I don't know. Well, what happened is that while my mother and us kids waited out in the car, my dad went into the house and came out with some other men. These men and my dad carried out guitars. I can say now because of my experience in music, and my limited knowledge of musical instruments - guitars specifically, that these were rather fine instruments. There were three of us boys at the time. My dad handed each one of us one of these guitars. It was a short drive back to our house. I believe at that time we were living on Providence Heights. Me, Carl, and Kenneth all began to stram, strum, and fram those guitars for dear life. It was a short ride back to Providence Heights... just a couple of blocks really, but with the commotion of those three guitars being frammed to death, my dad turned the car around, went back to those men's house, took those guitars from his sons and they have not been seen since. This, however, was to foreshadow the musical talent (especially for stringed instruments) that the Dobbins boys and my sister actually had. It would be years later (I would actually be a grown man) I was having conversation with my Aunt Fannie, that she disclosed the curiosity she had as she watched from afar the musical development of the Dobbins children. Aunt Fannie went on to say that our great-grandfather was known as Professor Davis. He was a Fisk graduate, and an outstanding violinist. All those years, even after the reclaiming of the guitars, in which we were thrust into the world of music in elementary school and on.

Washington Dobbins – The Navy Years

I guess I'm really on a tear now about my dad and his personality, but I remember my dad talking about his Navy experiences. Realize, again, that this is a man whose father died when he was eight, who practically, in many senses raised himself. A young man who graduated high school and immediately enlisted in the United States Navy, serving during the active Korean conflict, and returning home after that. My grandmother and my aunt Tommy both reflected that when my father returned to Providence, he was not the same person who left little old Providence. They both say my father came back from Korea a different person. I've often reflected on that and thought how you can stay the same person, when at age eighteen you enlist in the Navy and become a member of the underwater demolition team. You see things and do things that an eighteen-year-old should never see or have to do. I believe you will become a changed person. My father told stories about Long Beach California. When he was in the Navy they would come back into San Diego. I suspect they would have shore leave, being young sailors, they did what young sailors do …they went out and raised hell.

THE LONG BEACH INCIDENTS

My father tells the story: they would go into the bars in Long Beach, and my father would order a drink (and, yeah, he would order a drink) the bartender would refuse to serve him a drink. Well, that infuriated the men that he served with – who, by the way were pretty much all white. It was his white shipmates who would tell the person behind the bar (running the bar, or who owned the bar) that if they did not serve my dad, they would tear that bar apart. Their reasoning was that my dad serve right alongside them, put his life in the same danger that they did, and they weren't having it that you are gonna tell him that he couldn't be served when his buddies were being served. According to my dad many a bar got torn up in Long Beach California. One would think that California, being one of the most liberal places in the world, that there would not be that type of prejudice, but there was. Ironically, my dad wanted he and my mother to settle in California, but my mother said "no" because her entire family was in Birmingham, Alabama. So, my dad followed her lead, and we grew up in Nashville Tennessee.

POLYNESIAN SHIPMATES

My father served with Samoan Americans, or men from America Samoa. He talked about how proficient swimmers that they were, and that they pretty much swam before they walked. My dad also told the story of getting really drunk one night. On this particular night of drinking, carousing, and hellraising one of his Samoan buddies decided that he was going to swim back to the ship. My father told him no, that's not possible, I'm not gonna let you do that. He jumped on the man's back to keep him from swimming back to the ship. My dad said the only thing that was accomplished was that he learned how truly strong swimmers the Samoans were. The man swam all the way back to the ship with my dad on his back. Again, that is one of my dad's stories, and I'm going to stick to it.

MY MOM'S FAMILY IN BIRMINGHAM AND MY DAD

When I talk about my dad, I would be remiss if I did not talk about how, he loved family. I know that he loved my mother, my grandmother, his mother, and his sister, because she was his only sibling. But I know that he loved my mother's people; especially my mother's mother - my grandmother. Of course, I wasn't around when all of this took place, but I remember my dad saying that when he started dating my mother that there was a time that he had had way too much to drink, but he still got in the car to drive to Birmingham to see my mother. When he arrived in Birmingham he was totally inebriated, and it was my grandmother who made him go get in the bed, lay down and sleep off the alcohol. From that point I can't tell you how much he appreciated and love them. I remember the times; especially when my grandmother was very ill (I would come to find out that she had cancer) that on many a Friday evening my dad would rush home from work, pack us all up in the station wagon, and we would set off to Birmingham. In those days, when you went to Birmingham most of it was on Highway 31, which was an old-school, two-lane highway from Nashville to Birmingham. We would go and we would not even stop by my grandparents' home. We would drive directly to the hospital. If my grandmother (and later when my grandfather became ill) my father would go and roll up his sleeves without hesitation to give blood. Whatever they needed he would be the donor for whatever the amount was.

THE DRIVE TO LOS ANGELES

I was sixteen when our family took one of the most memorable trips ever. I remember the age sixteen because I had just earned my driver's license. I drove every night on the way to Los Angeles and back to Nashville. We drove from Nashville to Los Angeles California, and then on down to San Diego, where my dad had been stationed in the Navy. From San Diego we crossed the border and went into Tijuana Mexico. A great example of his love for my mother's family is that my mother had three sisters who lived in Los Angeles. The three sisters were at odds with each other and someone mentioned that they did not want us to visit the other two sisters. My dad was firm but clear in a way that only my dad could be clear. He didn't curse or use bad language to speak his mind, but he let it be known that we had come all the way from Nashville to Los Angeles; and that he loved all three of them. His family was going to see all three sisters and their families, and no one was going to stand in the way of us doing that. That's just the way it was and we went around to see all three sisters and their families. It was a great trip. It was a memorable trip. It is a trip I say all families should take by motor vehicle at least once in their lifetime. Families can take either Route 66, or by going the route the lower part of the country that that we took. A highlight of this trip is that I recall a story that I probably share once a year with my family. When we reached the Painted Desert - which gets you into the Grand Canyon area - my father walked down to the edge of a cliff and the drop looked like it could have been a mile or two to the bottom. My dad walked straight to the edge of the cliff, turned around with this unbelievable backdrop at his back, and told someone to take his picture. I guess you know no one was holding the camera at the time; and we had to rush to the car and get the camera and take his picture, because we were so afraid if he slipped it was going to be curtains. That picture is somewhere in my mother's house. The next time I'm there I will find that picture. I'm going to take a picture of it with my phone camera so I can have it in my archive.

THE TRIP TO NEW YORK CITY

I guess the other memorable trip was when we drove to New York. We took my grandfather (my mother's father) with us on the trip (I should note at this point that my paternal grandfather died at age 40 when my dad was age eight, so I never knew my father's father). So, this was my mother's father – again, who my dad revered. We left Nashville and went by way of Bristol, in the Tri-Cities area of Tennessee. Bristol is where you get to see Bristol Virginia and Bristol Tennessee. One on each side of the street. You get to see the Blue Ridge Mountains. We passed by Washington, D.C. and headed on into New York. My Grandfather smoked (the as the best I can describe) green cigars. I believe the car we were in was a Buick LeSabre. It could have been the Buick Electra 225, but in any case, it was a big roomy car that that eight people could ride in comfortably. We were still young children at that point. I remember that they had a plastic trash container attached or fitted along the window seal. My granddad had a propensity for spitting into napkins. He piled the napkins up in that plastic trash container; and as he smoked those green cigars, he also dumped the ashes into that same container. We were riding along the interstate; probably close to ninety or one hundred miles per hour. In a frenzy, we all started to look about the car to see where the smoke was coming from. We realized it was coming from that plastic trash container. By the time my dad could slow the car down, pull it over to the side of the road and lay hands on that trash container, it had erupted into full flame. Luckily, we got the container out the window; avoided certain disaster and drove on to New York City. My uncle Robert and aunt Louise, and cousin LaVergne lived in Jamaica Queens

New York City. I don't know how many of you have ever had the opportunity to drive in New York City; but that was the first time I had ever been to New York. The trip was also memorable for some negative reasons; but my dad did a masterful job of navigating New York. There was, however, a mistake in navigation. We ended up going the wrong direction on the Verrazano Narrows bridge. Persons from New York will understand what I'm saying. At this point we are on the Verrazano Narrows bridge. First, there is nothing narrow about the Verrazano Narrows. We were going the wrong way, and probably headed into New Jersey, and literally we stopped at some point in the middle of this bridge. I don't remember what was said to the bridge officer, but he stopped traffic, and literally we turned the car around and headed back in the other direction. We finally did make it to aunt Louise, uncle Robert and Laverne's house. New York was memorable because there was so much to do and to see. The New York city zoos and museums are pretty impressive and pretty amazing. I remember uncle Robert drove us into the heart of the city… into Manhattan… downtown, and parked the car. We made our way along the streets of New York City - downtown Manhattan. We went into Macy's, and I don't know which other large stores. I remember as we were about to go into Macy's a young black man on a bicycle when tearing past us, and as we just thought this was another day in New York City, a limousine - a big black limousine pull over to the curb. A huge white man jumped out of the limousine. The man popped the trunk of the car and pulled out a tire tool. He chased the young man down the streets of New York City. Well, we went into Macy's, and when we came back out the white man had the bicycle and was giving it back to a young lady who was in the car. I think what scared me most is that I don't know what became of the young black man who I had initially seen riding the bike. And I still don't know. The next thing I remember about New York City is that my dad was the world's biggest fan of westerns, or "shoot 'em ups", as he was so apt to call them. We went to Radio City Music Hall and we saw the John Wayne movie True Grit. You don't really appreciate a trip like that at the time. You know it's pretty cool, but you don't really appreciate being in Radio City Music Hall watching True Grit on the giant screen, featuring John Wayne, Kim Darby, and Glen Campbell. But that's the stuff memories are made of.

On our way home from New York City, I believe my dad and my mom had made an agreement to stop in Washington DC to view the monuments and to take in the city. I want to stop right now and give my parents a lot of credit …a lot of credit, because young black children being able to take those kinds of trips to see the kinds of things, and to be exposed to the locations - and all the things that these locations had to offer as children was super …absolutely super. Well, this is what happened as we made our way into Washington DC. I believe we had left New York later then our anticipated schedule. The traffic in Washington DC was horrendous; and even though we can look out the car window and see the monuments as we rode along my dad did not stop in the city. Consequently, we did not see things like the Washington Monument, the Lincoln Memorial, The White House, the Capital up close and personal. It broke my mother's heart and I just remember her "boo-hoo" crying as we continued back to Nashville. My Grandfather had to have had a difficult time. It took a different kind of strength that told him, correctly, to stay out of the business of his married children. He never said a word. I don't know how he felt, except that he was blessed to have been able to have made that trip with us, and that he had the opportunity to visit New York City to see his daughter, son-in-law and granddaughter. So, then when my grandfather became ill, mostly to due to the insistence of my dad, we spent a lot of time going back and forth to Birmingham Alabama. My dad his usual thing: whatever my grandfather needed, if my dad could supply it, he was determined to do it. Now, as I reflect upon it, it may will be why my dad appreciated my mother's family so much. The loss of his own dad robbed him of so much. It was so great a loss that when he had the opportunity to add a loving family like my mother's to his world and life he committed that he would take the opportunity to do all that he could for my mother's family. My father valued and understood family in ways that those of us who have complete families our entire lives never know.

I also want to interject here (because I might not remember), my dad did one hell of a job being a father and being a husband. I say that because, as I said before, my dad did not have a father to bring him along in the ways that a son learns through observation, how a father should act and what a father should be. I don't know about my brothers, but I feel that whatever you could have thought about my dad he did a good job - not having a clear example day in and day out. I know that I am a much better person because if I didn't like some of the things that he did, I didn't do those things. If you liked certain examples that he exhibited, then you followed those. But he had to be a tremendous person to be as caring and concerned as he was. He was a person who would give his children the literal shirt off of his back if we asked him, and he never really had a father to example that for him. It's easy to be critical will you have so much going for you because so much is being given to you. I just hope that I was able to take from him all of the good things that I saw, and try to improve upon those things, and try to avoid doing the things that I didn't like, or that I thought were horrendous. And I will tell you there were many of those incidents.

THE CAR TRIES TO PASS US / THE WOMAN OPENS HER DOOR

Here is another story about my dad. When we were young my parents had taken us to the mall known as 100 Oaks, which was not too far from our house. When I say my dad didn't take crap off of anyone at any time that is not an understatement. I know he felt that way because he expressed it, as he says, he served in the military in the Navy in Korea. During active conflict time he had seen death, come close to death, and put his life on the line in duty for this country. He was outspoken … he had an "A" personality …and he told white men, black men, white women, black women, police officers, firemen, whoever what he thought as he thought it, when he thought it. He said "as much hell as he went through for this country, no one had the right to treat him like a second-class citizen, and he never allowed it, no matter what anyone thought.

OK I started out getting ready to tell you about the 100 Oaks incident. The family had been to 100 Oaks mall; and were returning home. I think the name of the little two-lane highway is Sidco Drive (and it is two-lane to this day). As we were returning home a car with two young white men pulled out around us. They were going to pass us on the two-lane highway. Well, Washington Dobbins, senior, was a person who had a lot of attitude…and I say because of his Navy experience. He looked in the sideview mirror as the car was approaching us. My dad stepped on the accelerator of the old station wagon, and he would not let that car go past. as we looked up that two-lane highway, there was on-coming traffic. Now, a real game of chicken had commenced. My dad did not blink. He did not look at the occupants of the other vehicle. But, I could hear them yelling "Let us in! Let us in!" And, there was I'm coming traffic! The situation was going to be very bad. At the last possible moment, the car that was trying to pass us hit his brakes and swerved back in behind us. Never mind my mother pleading "Wash, let them go by." And, I am sure Wash was cursing under his breath that he was not about to let them go past him. Well, that could have been enough excitement for one day, but it wasn't. We reached Nolensville Pike, and the Providence community produce stand the Pratt family had always maintained. They had all manner of produce… fruits and vegetables of all kinds, and people from everywhere would stop and buy produce from the Pratt family. This one particular extra-fateful day the entire world was determined to trample the last good nerve that Washington senior had that day. A white woman pulled over to the side in front of the fruit market, and as we approached, she threw the driver side door open. It was everything my dad could do the stand on the brakes and not take that door off that woman's car...and take her along with it. When he finally got the station wagon stopped in the middle of Nolensville Pike, it happened that my mother's passenger side window was down, and my father gave that woman a cursing like you cannot believe existed. I am sure the woman didn't know what do, because number one, she had never been cursed like that, number two: she had never been called names like that, and three: because of the way my dad put together the cursing words, I'm sure she had never heard anything like that in her entire life. My mother didn't say a word. The Pratt family members who were standing there didn't say a word. The woman who had been cursed proficiently and thoroughly did not say a word. When Washington was done, he simply drove us on home to Winston Avenue.

My Dad Coaches

I recall my dad at work at Third National Bank. He was more than just a porter. He was a highly trusted individual who transported sensitive bank documents, and copious amounts of cash money to banks branches, and the Federal Reserve Treasury. As a side note, it is interesting that my wife's uncle (who was more her father) worked at the Federal Reserve Bank in Nashville. My father knew Mr. Bridgewater and my mother also knew Reverend Bridgewater and his wife, because they had both attended American Baptist Seminary, where she was secretary to the president of the college. However, I digressed a little but let me get back on track with this part of the story. My father coached the basketball team at Third National Bank in an industrial sports league. On occasion they would play another company who had a predominantly black or African American team. The games always took place at the YMCA downtown, close to the state Capitol. My dad would take us to the games. My dad took us to a lot of places. Our dad took us to the Crescent Theater, where we had to go in through the back way. I will come back to that. On this occasion at the YMCA, my dad's Third National Bank basketball team was playing a predominantly white team. I don't remember the company that they represented. What I do remember is that my dad's team was being hit with penalties; with foul calls left and right. Wow! The white team set out to execute exceedingly hard fouls. The referees were not calling any of those hard fouls. As we, me and my brothers, walked on the track above the action I heard one of the players tell my dad that he was becoming frustrated about the fouling situation. My dad instructed this player to take the knife edge of his hand and whack the opposing player underneath his nose. My dad also told him that you cannot hit him hard or you will kill him which was interesting to hear. When play resumed There was of course the next hard foul; and the white player was struck as my father had instructed. Blood went everywhere! I don't remember if there was a near fight or what, but the game ended. Needless to say, Washington Dobbins, Sr. was not a person who took stuff from anyone and did not expect his players or his sons to take stuff from anyone.

MY MOTHER

So, I probably don't have a lot to write about my mother the way I've written about my dad, but I think the reasoning for this is because my mother was not the colorful personality that my dad was

My mother, strong suits were being practical and being steady. There's nothing wrong with that it just is the way it is and I don't know that you could really go through life with too many colorful personalities like my dad running around.

My mother graduated high school at the age of sixteen from Parker High School in Birmingham, Alabama. She was skipped twice. I know what an accomplishment that is. When I was in high school, I was not motivated enough to spell "skip". I just wanted to make sure I graduated with my class. Another great accomplishment for my mother was that she was able to teach school for 38 years now you ask me how many people are able to teach school for 38 years because I would have to ask you how many people could go into a classroom for one week or for one day and contribute meaningfully to the development of young American minds Challenge you to say that one day or one week would be easy let alone 38 years so that is quite an accomplishment.

My mother was also a fiscally and financially responsible person. She manage money well enough to have a great retirement, a great pension to be able to own two homes and have both completely paid for so in terms of intelligence and my mother also graduated at age 16 from high school, so in terms of intelligence, my mother does not take a backseat to anyone

It is true as we were growing up my mother was more of the disciplinarian drill instructor. That's not to say that my dad could not have done that or that, but my dad's whole approach the discipline was totally different than my mother and he was a disciplinarian, so let there be no doubt to it but I remember, for the most part is that it was my mother, who was the disciplinary

CARL AND JOEL

I thought this would be a good opportunity to talk about my brothers, Carl and Joel. They are both super talented, musicians, songwriters, musical theorists and technicians.

Joel is a very proficient bass player and songwriter, but I think his strongest talent is in being able to take a piece of musical equipment or device, analyze it to the nith degree and be able to tell you what the technical specifications and limitations of that particular device happened to be. In minute detail, Joel could tell manufacturers the kind of things that their equipment will do that they didn't even know it would do. I don't know if there is anyone Joel doesn't know. Joel's connections in the music industry are nearly without limits. Not only is he acquainted with countless celebrities, they have a deep and abounding respect for Joel, and his wealth of music knowledge.

My oldest brother, Carl, is a fantastic bass player. Recently, Carl told me a story that I thought was funny. The event happened about forty years ago. I guess I had never heard this story until a few weeks ago.
Carl, Guy Spells, Rod Bronough, and a couple of other guys whose names I can't remember (I can't even remember the name of the group) all went out to Los Angeles California to seek fame and fortune. I think they had a record deal. As a group, they ended up playing in one of the largest nightclubs in Los Angeles, The Total Experience. The club was located in Crenshaw. Carl said you never knew who you would see sitting in the front row of the club: Gladys Knight, Earth, Wind, and Fire, Verden White and many others sitting on the front row.

One night Carl said, technically, things were going really bad. The mixing of his bass…everything was really poor. The sound of his instrument; the whole mix was bad. After the show, Carl and the group were back in the greenroom. Carl said he blew a gasket! Now, let me say this is unusual for Carl, because Carl is about the most even-tempered, mild-mannered person you will ever meet in this natural life. But Carl said he blew a gasket and was cursing and fussing. He was going through a lot of changes when a lady walked up to him and said, "Young man, young man with that attitude, you will not go far in the music business." The woman he would go onto to say, was Martha Reeves. Yes, the famous Martha Reeves of Martha Reeves, and the Vandellas. Carl was taken to task by Martha Reeves of Martha Reeves and the Vandellas. That was his story of one of his encounters with stardom.

I think I've already related the story about the time Carl was playing for a Greek show at Tennessee State University. Some guys came to me after the show. They said they wanted to meet the bass player. They asked me if I knew him. I said yes, I know him, but why do you want to meet him? They kept on talking. One of them said, "My name is Razor Sharp." The other guy said "My name is Catfish, Catfish Collins." Catfish said, "We're with Bootsy's Rubber Band." Catfish went on to say "We just wanted to meet him because we know good bass playing when we hear it. He's a really good bass player." Finally, I said "Well, that's MY brother that's playing bass." I asked why they were in town, and they said we come to Nashville all the time just to hang out. Needless to say, I made sure I introduced them to Carl.

KEN DOBBINS

My brother, Ken, is a Tennessee University Architectural Engineering graduate. Ken Dobbins is one of many Tennessee State University engineering majors hired by Proctor and Gamble. Ken was a high-echelon engineering manager in research and development. Ken guided not only the virtual computer building of a plant that was physically constructed in Belgium or Holland (I apologize for not knowing which country). Ken had to make a trip to that location to make sure all construction aspects we met accurately and completely. Ken was such an effective executive for Proctor and Gamble that the company offered him early retirement; then discovered that they had a special project they needed him to spearhead. Ken understands global product development, marketing, and financial strategies. Ken was still able to retire early when they offered him the opportunity the second time.

ANGELA AND MY MOTHER

It's always interesting to me because when I talk about my mother then I also talk about Angela. Their existence was very intertwined.

Angela pledged Alpha Kappa Alpha Sorority, Incorporated. Mind you, when Angela pledged, my mother had not, at this time gone through the intake process for Delta Sigma Theta Sorority, Incorporated. The reason my mother did not pledge Alpha Chi undergraduate chapter at Tennessee State University is because Alpha Chi got itself kicked off the yard. I was just laboring under the impression that my mother felt her days of becoming a part of the Greek letter world had gone past. Well, as it turns out, my mother still had a huge desire to become a member of Delta Sigma Theta Sorority, Incorporated. Angela had pledged Alpha Kappa Alpha Sorority, Incorporated. I was not aware at the time, however, that there was a bit of negative excitement on my mother's part about Angela's sorority choice. My mother had always wanted Angelo to pledge Delta Sigma Theta Sorority, Incorporated so that they could celebrate sorority things together. I'm saying all of this with the convenience of "20/20 hindsight."

I remember after she had become a member of Alpha Kappa Alpha Sorority, Incorporated she and I kind of randomly kick stories around about Greek life. This is when I found out that my mother was very upset about Angela pledging Alpha Kappa Alpha Sorority, Incorporated. It was also during the course of pledging Alpha Kappa Alpha Sorority, Incorporated that Angela borrowed a dress from my mother. One of Angela's "big sister's", J.C., I guess was being tough specifically on Angela. J.C. may have been evil and mean, as Angela referred to her, because she was of dark complexion. I'm not getting into the "paper bag test" now. I'm sure that dark complexion, along with her combative personality, had made it extra hard for J.C. to make Alpha Kappa Alpha Sorority, Incorporated. J.C. told Angela she was going to take that dress that belong to my mother from Angela. Ooops! Angela grew up in Providence with four brothers. Angela told her they would be rolling in the floor; because she was not gonna let J.C. get her hands on that dress. Angela told J.C. "I am not going back to my mother, with her already being mad at me, and have to explain that the dress got taken from me by an Alpha Kappa Alpha. That was not gonna fly!" Angela told her they'd have to fight. I think that ended that one.

I'm trying to make a long story short. Years later (and this was after Angela had passed away) my mother finally expressed her disappointment that Angela had pledged Alpha Kappa Alpha Sorority, Incorporated and not pledged Delta Sigma Theta Sorority, Incorporated. I kind of looked at my mother, and I said "Well, I don't know how you would have expected her to have pledged Delta. My mother said "why do you say that?" I said "you were the one who allowed her to go to all those Lambda Iota Theta events and activities. Every weekend Lambda Iota Theta was having some type of training for courtesy, decorum and etiquette, and all of these things." I said "you never once said anything in opposition to all this indoctrination. You took her or had one of us take her to those activities." I said, "you had to know that L.I.T. was being sponsored by Alpha Kappa Alpha Sorority, Incorporated. Their colors were pink and green. Not only that, but you also knew that every little girl in Lambda Iota Theta would eventually end up pledging Alpha Kappa Alpha Sorority, Incorporated. They were being indoctrinated in that way." I said "you never took her to anything that was being sponsored by Delta Sigma Theta Sorority, Incorporated consistently or anything that would have indoctrinated her to Delta Sigma Theta. None of her friends were going the Delta route, so when she got to college what else was she going to pledge?" I guess my mother thought about it for a second and she said "you know you're right."

It is important to note that Angela probably bought more Delta things for my mother; and my mother probably brought more Alpha Kappa Alpha things for Angela than they bought for themselves. I always have to laugh about that. I know when my mother would go to the conventions and events for Delta Sigma Theta they were always someone selling paraphernalia of all of the "Divine Nine." My mother did not hesitate to pick me up things up things for Alpha Phi Alpha Fraternity, Incorporated, or things for Angela's Alpha Kappa Alpha. So, no need for me to complain. That's how that story went. In the end they were both happy. My mother was happy that Angela was an Alpha Kappa Alpha, and Angela was happy that my mother finally got her opportunity, and did successfully, get through the intake process into Delta Sigma Theta Sorority.

To add to everything, Angela and my mother were traveling buddies. Many of the events, especially with Third National Bank, the awards, the honors and everything that Angela was receiving through Bank of America, she and my mother would travel together to these destinations to attend these events. They traveled to Las Vegas Several times. They traveled to Los Angeles to visit my aunt, uncle, and cousins. So, to type everything off, they were big traveling mates.

ANGELA/THIRD NATIONAL BANK

I will take a moment to talk about Angela and her success. As Angela would say "All Dobbins's children were highly accomplished, and highly successful - all of us. We were accomplished in terms of in our individual pursuits and interests. It was Angela that said that "Our parents had five children, and that each of the five children had their own distinct personalities, interests, and strengths.

Obviously, Angela had a skill for math, and for banking. Angela talent was quickly recognized by the men who owned Third National Bank, Mr. Cook, Mr. Fleming, and Mr. Clay. Angela was working as a teller at the downtown Third National Bank, with the main office located at Fourth Avenue and Church Street. Third National Bank was bought by SunTrust Bank. SunTrust later became Truist Bank. But, as it was Third National Bank, the owners remembered my father. They came across Angela's name. They asked if she was related to the Washington Dobbins who had worked there. She told them he was her father. Mr.'s Clay, Cook and Fleming began to closely monitor Angela's performance. They immediately determined she had far more potential than to just be a teller. They felt she had great potential to be upwardly mobile, so they put Angela on a fast-track management program plan.

Angela moved up into management at the Bank that would become SunTrust. Angela was hired from SunTrust by Bank of America, where she rose to the rank of vice president. It was doing the course of her tenure at Bank of America. that Angela was transferred to manage many, many locations. Angela was often sent to help locations that were not making various Bank of America business quotas. Perhaps one of the most impressive moves was when they relocated Angela to Smyrna Tennessee. She had also been out in Lebanon Tennessee, but they relocated her to Smyrna Tennessee. When we went down with her to see this new location it was pretty much on a dirt road. What is now known as Sam Ridley Parkway looked like a" cow path." This Bank of America, which is still there, was one of the most technologically advanced Bank of America's in the country. It was already pre-wired for technical upgrades that Bank of America would be implementing in the future. Who could have guessed!

BOA/ SALT LAKE CITY, UTAH OLYMPICS

Angela was a highly decorated Bank of America manager/vice-president. This is one opportunity for me to talk about what I feel is one of Angela's peak experiences.
Bank of America held a nationwide performance contest among all of its managers to select the management staff for the Bank of America branch located within the Olympic Village during the Salt Lake City Utah Olympics. Angela was one of the managers who was fortunate enough to be a winner of the contest. Of course, Angela bought us pins, which she said the athletes traded with other athletes from other countries. She was able to trade Bank of America pins with the athletes to get pins from their countries, as well as general Olympic pins. I still have the ones that she gave me. Angela said it was interesting flying in and out of Salt Lake City

because as the commercial airliner came in on final approach, they were shadowed by fighter aircraft. When her commercial aircraft left Salt Lake City, they were also escorted out by US military fighter aircraft.
It was quite an honor and quite an accomplishment for Angela, but it was more of a reflection of what it meant to be a Dobbins.

ANGELA AND THE SOUNDETTE UNIFORM ADVENTURE

My sister is a very pretty girl. Angela audition; tried out for; or however you want to see it, for the Nashville Sounds. They were not cheerleaders, they were hostesses, and Angela was selected to be one. After the selection came the onboarding. Angela bought her uniform home. It was fashionable for the day: halters and shorts. I say again, it was fashionable for the day, but kind of skimpy all the same. But, again, to be a hostess, it was the uniform.

Angela was showing us the uniform. My dad came in and she showed him the uniform. He looked at it for a minute or two, and then he said "Well, where's the rest of it?" And as only Angela could, especially with my dad, in true Angela fashion she rolled her eyes until they almost popped out of her head! She took her skippy little uniform and left the room. She went to her room and closed the door. Actually, you had to be there to see it; but it was kind of funny (although I dared not laugh at the time. I thought being supportive would be far more beneficial for me in the future). Knowing my scandalous background, I think it was kind of ironic that I could call anything skimpy – but hey, that's my sister!

THE HOUSE IN BIRMINGHAM

There was a little house in Birmingham called Cottageville. The address was 34th Way North. I recall This little house from the days of my infancy. My mother thinks that I don't remember things that happened at that house when I was one and two. She thinks I was way too young to remember some of the things that happened to me. I remember having the chicken pox. I remember walking out onto the front porch of this house only wearing a diaper and no shirt. I remember getting my first haircut at this house. My uncle Bob took a chair outside and placed it near the fence that separated their yard from the neighbor's yard. I remember Uncle Bob cutting the plats off of my head and giving me my first haircut. My mother says I'm too young to remember any of this, but I do; and many other things that would come about during my growing up. I remember my grandparents having a formal living room, or parlor. The furniture in this room was always covered with plastic. I don't think I remember seeing the plastic off the furniture. The house was not an amazingly large house. There was a nice front porch, there was the parlor, there was the forward bedroom which my grandparents shared. There was a large living room dining room and a formal dining room. Next to the dining room was the kitchen; and the kitchen had a eat-in dinette set. Next to the dining room was the only bathroom in the house, which I can tell you could become a very busy place. I remember our mother, her siblings their husbands and children all converged into this one house, with one bathroom. To the back of the house was a medium-large bedroom. On the opposite side of the house next to the kitchen was another bedroom area, which is where my uncle Bob and aunt Annie Mae slept. Next to their bedroom, near the back of the house was another room which was used as a bedroom by Alvin and Lester. There was a small back porch and sheds where cars and tools were kept. My family in Birmingham kept a sizable garden with all manner of okra, purple hull peas, corn, squash, tomatoes and other assorted fruits and vegetables. The yard also contained peach trees and a fig plant. There was a spacious yard on the north side of the house; which provided an area for the boys to play. Our playing often spilled out in 34th Way North. This house was amazingly close to Sloss steel mill or foundry. Birmingham is known as the Pittsburgh of the South. I remember at night, to the north there would be a tremendous red orange yellow glow, which was the glow from Sloss foundry. I understand that my grandfather worked at Sloss. It is probably where he contracted emphysema. You had to be a tough individual to do that kind of labor. It was dangerous. It was hot. The fumes that were emitted from the molting steel were harsh on the lungs. My Grandfather did that work. I always knew when we had got close to the house because the smell of sulfur (which was used in the making of steel or, as a byproduct) filled the air. There was no escape. Cars had to be kept under sheds In Birmingham because the ash created by the foundry was constantly falling from the air, and if your car was white when you got there, it was black when you left. I remember they did not allow the boys to stay in the house during the day. You had to go out and play and be out of the house …there was no staying in the house. It is amazing how that many people could fit into one house. Again, when you consider my grandparents, their children (my aunts and uncles or the spouses), and the children, the friends, the neighbors who came over the other relatives it is amazing how that many people could exist and that little old space; and heaven help me to understand how we all went to the bathroom. This house was one of the places I learned to cook. The four places I learned to cook: 1) this house, 2) my own home, with my mother, 3) my grandmother Mary Thompson's, 4) 924 Jackson Street, with my great-aunt, Drucilla Edwards. The first drink of coffee I ever had was in this little house in Birmingham. My grandmother made me a cup of coffee and put in way more sugar and cream than coffee and let me have a cup.

I am closer to my cousins because of the way we all grew up and existed in this house. There were times, occasions, that we would all be there and that was nearly every summer. When you grow up that closely with your cousins they become more like sisters and brothers.

924 JACKSON STREET: ANOTHER HOUSE WHERE I WAS RAISED

It seems the more I think about things after I write things, I edit things try to put them in the proper place in the book. I write one thing, then I think of something else that should be a part of my life story.

A very formative part of my growing up took place at a home on 924 Jackson St. in Nashville Tennessee. I would be an adult when I would come to know that the community surrounding 924 Jackson Street was named Hope Gardens. Hope Gardens existed off Jefferson Street. Ninth and Jackson Street. Hope Gardens and 924 Jackson Street is so close to Bicentennial Mall and Farmers Market, that when I was a kid, we walked to those places and purchased produce that was REALLY grown on farms in the middle Tennessee area. Sulphur Dells baseball park was located practically in the same location as First Horizon Park, along with salt licks and First People of this continent burial mounds.

924 Jackson Street was the home of my great uncle and my great aunt Mr. William Edwards and Mrs. Drusilla, Pair Edwards. They were just like grandparents to me, maybe even closer. We called Mr. Will Edwards "Brother", and we called Drucilla Pair Edwards "Tee" because as Carl was learning to talk "Tee" was all he could muster; not auntie. My mother called "Tee" "Sister", but we all called Will Edwards "Brother."

I spent copious amounts of time at 924 Jackson Street. My great aunt and uncle ran a boarding house at 924 Jackson Street. A boarding house was a home (a step away from a hotel, but very similar to a bed and breakfast) where people coming to Nashville would rent a room. They would stay for however long their business visit required them to be in Nashville. Some were regulars. They came all the time, in an intermittent fashion, while others may have been sort of what I call "one-off" visitors. Meaning that they came, and after they left, you didn't see them anymore. 924 Jackson Street two kitchens. One kitchen was for the guests if they wanted to cook their own meals. The other was the main kitchen. It was fully apportioned. My great-aunt "Tee" was a superior cook, just like my grandmother. If either of my grandmothers were to dig up some dirt and prepare it as a meal, you would eat it because it would taste that damn good. That's not hyperbole. Some boarders might pay a little bit extra and get a meal along with their stay. I remember my aunt and uncle would be up before the crack of dawn. I thought this was early at the time. However, they went to bed at 7:30 or 8 o'clock. 8 o'clock was late for them.

Growing up, anytime I, my brothers, or sister wanted to stay over we could spend the night with them. If they didn't have a boarder for the rooms, they had rooms for us upstairs for us. It was a little room where you could even lock the door. When I was older, I would go spend the night or the week. In college, especially when I was doing a play, I might spend the whole duration of the time of play at 924 Jackson Street. "Tee" and "Brother" would give me a key to the house. I was able to come and go as I pleased. It easily became a second home for me. And it was ju924 Jackson Street that had such a powerful influence on me. Being around these two elders, and the love and the care that they had for me and all the Dobbins children. It's my understanding that "Tee" actually went to my grandparents (her sister) and asked if she and "Brother" could be our grandparents, because they didn't have any children, and they did not have grandchildren. They were right there. The Dobbins children were right there. That's what they wanted. Our grandparents were not offended by them asking that because they were just close, and I understood why "Tee" and "Brother" asked. For all intense and purposes, I have multiple sets of grandparents.

Another interesting thing about being at 924 Jackson Street in Hope Gardens is that eventually all of the people who lived on Jackson Steet, Locklayer, Wren, and all of the streets around Jackson Street would become elderly. The interesting thing is that some of the young people who were about my age turned to hoodlum ways. But it was one thing about them being hoodlums in Hope Gardens: nobody bothered "Tee" and "Brother", or any of the other elders. In fact, they were actually very protective of the elders. No one ever needed to let anything happen to those old people. If anything were to happen there would have been hell to pay.

About the time I got into college there was a club down the street at tenth Jackson in a building that had been a grocery store. At that location of tenth and Jackson, all night long you would hear a lot of screaming and shouting, then sometimes gunfire. You might even find out the next day that someone had been killed down there; and that's what you had heard. But I will say nothing diminishes my love for "Tee" and Brother, and 924 Jackson Street. Absolutely nothing. It is a place where all of the Dobbins children learned a good deal about reading. "Tee" would take us out and sit on the front porch on the swing sofa. (I hate that somebody has stolen that sofa set and chairs because it's probably priceless.) She would have us read the newspapers. I believe she wanted us to read so we would have that practice and gain reading dexterity.

A memory I have is a time I was in college. Brother said he was going to hire somebody to paint the front porch. I asked him "why do you need to hire someone" I'll paint it for you." I painted the porch. All to the satisfaction of Will Edwards. It was a day I would never forget. July 13, 1985 (I had to look this up.) Live Aid was being broadcast that day. The first part of the concert was in England's Wembley Stadium and the second part was in Philadelphia's JFK Stadium. I recall this so much because as I painted, I had the radio on during all of the performances. It was broadcast live. I remember Phil Collins performed in London the first part of the day, then took the SST or Concord to New York to perform in the United States that afternoon. What Phil did was mind boggling at the time, but it was very cool stuff.

Hope Gardens has all changed. When I was a boy into adulthood, there were no white people there. There were no white women, with their ponytails bobbing up and down as they ran along the streets. Hope Gardens has become completely gentrified. Once those little homesteads that I remember are sold to developers or well-to-do white families, it becomes exponentially more difficult for Black families to live there.

THE BOYS CLUB

The Boys Club… where do I start with this one? While at Tusculum Elementary my parents informed the older three boys that Friday we would not walk home as we normally do, but we would board the bus to ride down to the Boys Club. The Boy's Club is now known as the Boys and Girls Club and was located on Thompson Lane. This was another great experience because you met so many different boys and had so many experiences. It was at the Boys Club that we learned how to navigate life, in general. The Boy's Club is where we learned to swim (by that I mean Carl, me, Kenneth, and Joel). My sister never learned to swim. We took basic beginners swimming classes; and to pass beginning swimming you had to be able to swim the length of the pool. You also had to be able to float, and tread water. Once we passed basic beginning swimming and were certified, we were able to swim in the deep end of the pool. There were hours that were open swim periods. Everyone waited for the open swim and naked boys changing into swimsuits was the sight. We all had a great time. The Boys Club also had organized baseball teams, divided into leagues according to age and size. There were multiple baseball fields to the rear of the Boys Club. It was nothing for young men to spend hours in the blazing sun playing baseball, then rushing in afterwards to make sure they did not miss the open swim. Other activities at the Boys Club included arts and crafts. I can't tell you the number of pots and ceramic items that we glazed and put in the kiln for firing. There was string arts and we wove bracelets of all kinds from plastic rope that we were provided. There was drawing, painting and visual arts. This was a great benefit to my parents who came and picked us up when they get off from work. We were worn out, tuckered out and tired, which was also a great benefit to my parents. During the summer we practically lived at the Boys Club during the day, had lunch and snacks there, and quite simply, just enjoyed the hell out of it.

Things for me would come full circle when I became an adult and had children. My two sons would attend during the summer that same place which was now known as the Boys and Girls Club. Their attendance at the Boys and Girls club brought back so many memories because that is where my sons learn to swim, learned about team sports, and how to navigate friendships and relationships. This time around, however, the Boys and Girls Club will also serve as a means for experimenting with relations between the two genders. Ironically his swimming coach and Charlie Finchum steel work at the boys and Girls Club. they were fixtures from my childhood into becoming fixtures for my son's childhoods.

JUNIOR PRO FOOTBALL / DEJUAN'S COMMENTS

Recently my brothers Carl and Joel decided that we would get together and take a brother-bonding bike ride through Shelby Park to Shelby Bottoms. We met that day close to Nissan Stadium and made our bike ride. It was a great ride; we spent an hour and a half and rode fourteen miles. One of the best parts was that as we rode through Shelby Park, we reminisced about our childhood days playing Junior Pro Football on the fields of Shelby Park. We would arrive early in the morning go to the main hut for weigh-ins and proceed to play our football games. Being from

Providence we were always tough and could hold our own, even though we were always the smallest player on any of the teams that we played on. Joel informed us that on one particular field where his son, Jordan, hit his first home run, Joel had run many touchdowns. I personally was reminded of all the big defensive hits I put on players during my time playing Junior Pro. I was a known "headhunter." I loved the contact. I remember playing against my good friend Demetrius Taylor's team from Bordeaux. They were a tough bunch. Many of them went on to play football for coach West Elrod at Maplewood high school, college; and some even professionally. They were a good tough, hard team that issued out beatdowns nearly every Saturday. I'm proud to say I'm one of the players they always remembered because I never gave an inch to any of them, as tough as they were. Many of us became friends stayed friends. We had already known each other, and there was a great deal of respect for each other because we were so competitive, and so capable. As a side note, I will recall that Demetrius' team played another team that was predominantly white, and very formidable. We really wanted the team from North Nashville to give those white boys a shellacking. When my team played the predominantly white team (and I stress that I was the only black player on my team), Mr. Williams, who coached us (along with my dad as an assistant coach) stressed that none of us give that team an inch …and we didn't. I played with guys like Tony Glover, and Ron Aydelotte. Both Tony and Ron had excellent high school and college careers. (***Add in two hits with Tony Glover in practice) They were both tough as nails. What would come to me just a couple of months ago would be a compliment from Dejuan Buford. Dejuan saw the picture on Facebook of me, Carl, and Joel. He stated that we were his heroes. Dejuan was also a product of Providence, another Providence exceptional athlete. Dejuan started his career in Junior Pro just like my brothers and me. In fact, it was Dejuan and his cousin, Gary Hockett, who came alone after the Dobbins boys. Dejuan and Gary's father's will bring them to watch our games, and our parents would take us to watch their games when we were finished. Dejuan said that his father always told him to keep an eye on how we played and that was how he should play. Between Dejuan And Gary's fathers they gave Joel the nickname O.J. Joel wore the number 32, and like O.J. Simpson. Every time he touched the ball there was the potential for him to score a touchdown. Dejuan would go on to play high school football at Antioch High School. So did Gary. Dejuan went on to play at Middle Tennessee State University and was an all-Ohio Valley Conference player. Gary's career was cut short by an injury, but Dejuan would have gone on to have a career in the National Football League.

PROVIDENCE ELEMENTARY SCHOOL

The first school I attended became known as the "Little School on the Hill." Providence elementary school. I went to Providence until I completed the third grade. By that time desegregation had taken hold in Nashville. Providence Elementary School was closed. I will not use the term "phased out" because it was closed. Me, my brothers and sister were sent to Tusculum Elementary School. But, going back to Providence Elementary. It was located atop a super steep hill. You had to climb a mountain's worth of steps to get to the school, no matter if you approached it from Nolensville Pike, or if you approached it from Flora Maxwell Road, it was a hike. I will provide a reference point to where the school stood: Providence Elementary School was located on the same spot as the Southern Hills hospital complex. The school was located on that site because the Maxwell family; stalwarts of the community, donated the property for the school to be built there. The Maxwell family home was located on a farm to the rear of the school location - towards Antioch Pike. Providence Elementary school was the school built by the black persons of the community. It was a great school. The physical building was second to none. The cafeteria staff was par excellent. Their cooking and their abilities rivaled what you would find of the talents of the finest chefs anywhere in the world. I still remember the rice pudding with raisins. I don't know what they did to make that rice pudding with the raisins, but it was super good! All of the lunches were excellent! I'm gonna leave lunches for a while and move on to talk about the teacher I remember the most: Mrs. Jackson. Mrs. Jackson was just an example of all the other teachers. She was a symbol. All the other teachers at Providence were filled with so much compassion, nurturing, along with a healthy amount of tough love. That was expected. I don't think that a child could have had a more charmed beginning to a school life. Beginning with kindergarten (and for me, going through third grade) some of my fellow students included Marcus Tucker, Michael Shelton, Vicki Barber, Zelnata Chapman, Junior Davis... the list is longer, but those are names I would call most immediately. In kindergarten I had what I considered to be a minor traumatic experience. Before you could go to recess you had to write your name on the board. Persons who had names like John, Sam, even Michael, would go to the board and write their name in relatively quick fashion. My first name is Washington. For a kindergartner Washington is not a name that gets put on the board in a couple of seconds, so I was always the last one in kindergarten to go to recess. I will also say that I recall having purchased an Ice Cream Sandwich. Let me explain: an Ice Cream Sandwich, in those days, was square. They were piled thickly with ice cream. Even though we had the longer, slimmer versions of the Ice Cream Sandwich we also had the fat square ones. I remember having sneaked it out of the cafeteria because I did not have time to eat it during lunch. I had taken it to the room. As I was about to sneak to the bathroom to eat my Ice Cream Sandwich someone knocked on the bathroom door, complaining that I was taking too long, and that they had to go. Of course, the teacher came to the door, and knocked. She told me that I needed to hurry. In my haste to follow the commands of the teacher I flushed nearly the entire Ice Cream Sandwich down the commode. You can imagine what happened. A couple of minutes later water began to flood the classroom from the commode. I said I did not know how all this transpired. I did not get into trouble because it was simply assumed that I had flushed an inordinate amount of paper down the toilet. A second event that I remember: A kid in third grade and I got into a verbal altercation. The other student and I then passed disparaging comments about each other. Whereupon I ended up calling the student and MF. Of course, the student immediately told the teacher, who questioned me strongly about my choice of language. I denied that I called the student an MF and that instead I had referred to this student as a "monkey face." I don't think the teacher believed me. The teacher called my mother, who again closely questioned me about my choice of language. I told my mother the same thing: I called the student "Monkey Face", nothing more, nothing less. I don't think my mother actually believed that; and even though I did not get punished for it, I believe my mother understood that my father was a Navy man and country boy. She knew that my father used language that was meant for the Navy. But, of course, I was constantly hearing that language, yet I was not supposed to use it. None of us were supposed to use it. However, how do you hear it all your life and not use it? Again, I did not get into trouble for it, but it was one of those memories that I have.

Another memory that I have related to Providence elementary is that my mother was substituting at the school one day. Let me interject here that the principal of Providence Elementary School was Reverend Sweeney. Reverend Sweeney was another member of the community and was well respected. As I was saying, my mother was substituting this one fateful day. A student: I will just refer to him as "R". "R" kept kneeing me in the butt. I asked him to stop several times. He thought it was very humorous, and he kept right on. We were in line for lunch when this happened. My mother, who says she does not remember this event, was bringing her class to the cafeteria for lunch. I told her "Mama, can you tell "R" to stop kneeing me?" I don't know, except that it was a combination of her being responsible for her class and not wanting to take her focus off of that, not wanting to show favoritism to me, and the fact that the mindset of people growing up in Providence and living in Providence is you better learn how to take up for yourself. Whichever one, or combination of those mindsets, it happened that my mother did not come to my rescue. As a result of taking one need too many knees to the butt, I turned around and I punched "R" in the nose, setting off a gusher... and blood ran from his nose as my teacher came to his rescue. At that point we were asked what happened. It was obvious that I punched "R" in the nose. Now came the time for my first official punishment in school. Reverend Sweeney called me into his office, took my hand, and pulled my fingers back and struck the middle of my hand with a wooden ruler three times. After that I had to apologize to "R" for bloodying his nose. I can tell you, no event like that with "R" ever happened again. I say it again with great pride because at Providence Elementary, and in our village, young boys were either trying to stake their Alpha position, or say, I will not allow you to impose your Alpha will on me. Such were the days where either wrestling, tussling, or grappling showed a young boy that they could hold their own. Sometimes, it was an all-out physical fight, or sometimes tussling evolved into an actual fight. It is rare; from my recollection, that teachers saw what was going on and intervened. The students settled disagreements themselves. Typically, once a disagreement was settled it was settled, and life went on. Generally, you became closer friends. Let me say also about our proud school: There are commemorative plates in the homes of people in the village that clearly show our little "School on the Hill". Someone; I believe one of the descendants of Sadie Overton, found our Providence School alma mater. It was just an incredible moment... an incredible place filled with incredible people that is a part of the charmed life that I was able to have.

TUSCULUM ELEMENTARY SCHOOL

As I entered the 4th grade, I was told that the only school I had ever known would be closed and that I would be transferring from Providence elementary school to Tusculum elementary school. Tusculum elementary school was predominantly white in terms of student population and teachers. I won't say that it was a challenge, because sometimes when you are that young you inevitably go with the flow. I do recall some amounts of prejudice, but my focus was not on the prejudice nature of the school environment but doing the best I could in terms of education and learning. That mindset came from two places: my mother and father, and the fact that at Providence elementary school (due to the rigor or the rigorous nature of the academics at the black school-and let me say also because of the nurturing manner of the teachers who taught me at Providence elementary school) you were always focused on academic success, and not the abundance of prejudice which you encountered and had to overcome. One of the unique things that I must point out is a friendship that I made my first few days at Tusculum Elementary school. The young man's name was Zednik Chaluka. If my memory serves me correctly, he was Czechoslovakian. I remember that he must have felt as differently as I did. I won't say the same, but I will say different. Zednik moved after my 4th grade year. I'm not sure where, but on occasion his name pops up in my mind, and I do wonder what became of him.

The first classroom I had at Tusculum was in the old part of the building, which was amazingly old (probably the original building.) This classroom was located in the basement part of the old section of the school. It must have been made to withstand an attack during the Cold War. This old section was built like a bunker. It was made out of concrete and rock; and I do believe it would withstand a severe bombing. When it rained, sometimes the classroom flooded because of the design, and location of the windows, and the lower level of the classroom. There were drains in the room; but sometimes they did not work properly. I remember being moved to Mr. Williams room. Mr. Andy Williams was the single teacher. Mr. Williams was a very good man. He worked hard as a teacher and never made me feel that I was any different than any of the other students. He challenged me to do my best and work hard. I believe he was a very fair gentleman. My brother and mother still see him on occasion at the grocery store. At the time I write this we are in the middle of the Covid 19 pandemic, and there should be no physical touching in order to not spread the disease, so I suspect when they see Mr. Williams there's just waving now and glad tidings: but no hugging.

It was at Tusculum Elementary school I was introduced to the band. Everyone wants to be a drummer, but it is up to the music teacher to determine what instrument pretty much you start out playing. There is a picture that I believe Bruce Coomer posts to Facebook from time to time; of myself, him and others of us in the band at Tusculum Elementary school. I started out on the trumpet as did my brothers. From that point on all Dobbins children will pretty much be involved in music one way or another.

I recall one day (and it may have been in the 5th grade maybe the 6th grade) that I recited or read Go Down Death: A Funeral Sermon, by James Weldon Johnson in class. I should have known I had a future in the theater because the entire class became very silent. The teacher appeared to become very emotional as I read with great dexterity and emotion. It is one of those moments that you never forget. I believe it had a profound shaping for my personality in my future. I made new friends at Tusculum Elementary school. Damon Sudbury, the McGahan brothers, Don McCloud-who went on to become a Navy SEAL. Bruce Coomer, Stan Watson (a very talented artist) and many, many more. I recall one day that a storm appeared to come out of nowhere. The classroom I was in faced North toward the playground …this was all plate glass window. There were children out on the playground. In the classroom we watched the sky turn black. Out of that black sky dropped a funnel cloud, that funnel cloud made a track across the playground. I remember the children running and screaming. I remember the teacher telling us to get away from the window (another moment that is indelibly etched in my mind. It was also during this period at Tusculum Elementary school that me, my brothers, and many other young men were introduced to, and taken to the Boys Club Friday afternoons after school.

McMURRAY JUNIOR HIGH SCHOOL

There are lots of things I remember about McMurray Junior High School. I remember, it was my first day there. I met my best friend for life Bobby Flowers. I don't know if you call it a chance meeting at this point…I don't even recall how we met, except that we probably ended up in the same homeroom and then taking the same classes throughout junior high. Some of my Providence friends, at first, thought I was crazy for becoming friends with a white guy, but soon many of them, for their own reasons, had their own white acquaintances. Bobby and I would go on to remain best friends - even to this day; and if there is one piece of advice I followed from my parents it was: Pick good friends. People you can trust because that would probably be a great factor in keeping you out of trouble. I can recall my favorite teacher McMurray Junior High was Mrs. Eleanor Graves. Mrs. Graves taught biology and science and was married to one of the prominent upcoming pastors in Nashville. She never acted like that was her situation in life. To this day I still know her, and still respect her. She acts just as regular as the first time I ever met her. She had a great sense of humor, and was super knowledgeable about biology, chemistry, and science. I remember that it was in her class that we began to dissect earthworms, frogs, and embryo pigs. I do not believe they let junior high, or middle school students do that today. We had sharp scapples and followed her instructions implicitly. The other teacher who I have great memories and fondness for in junior high, was Mrs. Velma Otey. Mrs. Otey taught English. She just had a wonderful personality. Long before I met her, I had met her husband; Mr. Reverend Doctor Inman E. Otey. Mrs. Otey would tell us stories of their affection for one another, and how he referred to her as his "Little Chocolate Gumdrop." One could not help but to understand that he must have been a remarkable man because he was married to a remarkable woman. Later, as I attended Pleasant Green Missionary Baptist Church, not only did I get to know Mrs. Otey better in more ways outside of the classroom, but I also got to know Mr. Reverend Doctor Inman Otey. I got to know their daughters; Valerie and Veronda, and their son Inman Otey, Junior. It was during this time that my sister, Angela, was a member of the Alpha Kappa Alpha junior group Lambda Iota Theta. I took Valerie to one of their LIT socials, which brought me even closer to that family. I digressed a little, so let me get back to junior high. It was during my junior high period I had the most fights and physical encounters. There were two young men who people liked to make fun of because they had different perspectives growing up in life. One was autistic and the other suffered from a condition known as mongolism. People in junior high were sometimes mean and would pick on the most helpless of their fellow students, because I guess that somehow made them big in front of everyone else. The worst fights that I ever got into was when I encountered people making fun of either one of these two young men or treating them impolitely. I guess I gave as good as I got, but in true Dobbins Providence style I held up my end of the conflict. I am probably most honored by my defending of the defenseless, even though the encounters were not always pleasant, nor one-sided to my advantage.

Another thing about McMurray Junior High - this is where I got my second, third, fourth and fifth paddling's at school due to my behavior. On one occasion it was just senseless student horsing around. I was called into the principal's office, confronted with my transgression. The consequences were swift and severe. I was told to bend over and grab the front of the principal's desk and take whatever licks were assigned for the infraction. I can say with all truthfulness I took my paddling's like a young man. On one hand it was a badge of honor, and on the other instance a badge of shame, but somehow in the long run I was just one of the guys. I was not a goody- two shoes nor was I a criminal, just one of the guys.

There did come a time however that my parents did something that my parents never did. They went to bat for me because of a time I was corporally punished. The story went like this: There was a new student who came to McMurray from Detroit Michigan. This student was named Maurice, and Maurice was a big stocky fellow. Maurice decided one day he was going to set an example for the rest of the class of his physical prowess. I walked into Mr. Ronnie Smith's classroom after lunch. Mr. Smith had not arrived in the room yet. Maurice saw the perfect opportunity for him to show off to the rest of the class. He grabbed me as I walked into the room and body slammed me onto one of the long tables. Mr. Smith taught science, so every science room lab in every school in America has these long tables. No sooner than Maurice snatched me up and slammed me on the table Mr. Smith walked into the classroom. His immediate response was that we were both horse playing, so he gave us both three strokes with his paddle …And, I can safely say he tried to knock what little ass end I had off. No paddle swinging during my time pledging the Aristocrat of Bands or Alpha Phi Alpha could have had more to be proud of than Mr. Ronnie Smith. Also, let me just say as a side note (and there will be several as I go through here) Mr. Smith was an assistant coach to coach at Temple at Tennessee State University; an assistant with coaching the world-famous Tennessee State University Tigerbelles. Mr. Smith also sent me home with a thousand time right off: "That I would not horseplay in class." I went home and began the arduous task of completing the 1000 time right off of the statement. My mother, who also was a Metro school teacher, came home and saw me executing my write offs. She asked me what I was doing. I told her I was doing write offs for Mr. Smith. I told her truthfully what happened, fully expecting a severe lashing. But my mother, much to my surprise, told me to stop writing off right there and not to write off anything else. When my dad got home, she told me to tell him what happened. I told my dad. There was an explosion of anger that came from him in response to Mr. Ronnie Smith's assignment. The next day there was an occurrence like none that ever occur in the Dobbins household. My dad was famous for speaking his mind and being cruelly honest. I was much surprised with all of this. My parents always took the side of the teacher. If we did things in school which caused us to be punished there was no one's fault but our own. I was shocked to learn that my parents had come to the school to talk to the principal and talked to Mr. Ronnie Smith. I am told; because I was not there, that there was quite the commotion in the principal's office. I don't know what was said, or how anybody saw it… except I have heard from student workers that there was a lot of yelling and screaming that went on in that moment in that office. I am also told that there was a commotion, and a physical altercation between my dad and Mr. Smith. Of course, you must understand about my dad when he felt he was right. He did not apologize, mince his words, nor back down from anyone for any reason. Years later when I would become a Metro school teacher myself, Ronnie Smith and I would become good friends. He became a mentor figure to me as an upcoming teacher. My mother, however, held a grudge against Mr. Smith for many, many years. I don't know what incident changed her perspective of Ronnie Smith, but there did come a time after (again I say many, many years) that she forgave Ronnie Smith, and they would actually become friends. I'm sad to say that Ronnie Smith has since gone on to glory, but one of the things that is most important to me is that after the incident occurred, he and I were good and we remained good friends throughout the years.

The next thing that I remember about McMurray Junior High was G. T. I first came to know G. T. because he appeared at school one day. G. had just been released from Jordania, one of the places of incarceration for minors at that time. G had green hair, and he fancied himself a remake of the incredible Hulk. This cannot be far from the truth because I had never seen a young man of my age who was that physically imposing. I also believe that G. T. was a certified sociopath. He was just pure mean and evil. When you would see G. T. in the hallways you would cut him a wide berth, and hope that you never were in the hallway alone in his presence. His first day at McMurray, G. T. called out C. H. to a fight. At this time C. H., who lived up the street from me, had always been the biggest and the toughest kid at McMurray Junior High. Big C. with go on to play football at Overton, but on this day C. H. and T. met across the street from the school in the church grounds. We all knew big C. was going to give G. T. the beatdown he truly deserved. As the fight started big C. showed his well-established boxing skills. He popped G. T. in the face with two savage, severe, hard punches. Well, we just knew that this was the end of land T., but to our surprise, I think we all learned that G. T.'s stay in reform school was much more than just a passing occasion. After taking the best shots that big C. could offer, G. T. rushed him and tackled him, and had him down on the ground, and preceded to choke him savagely. He asked C. H. if he "gave" (meaning, did he give up the fight and admit defeat). Reluctantly C. H. did give up. I guess his life was more important than trying to win the fight. C. H. defeat at the hands of G. T. not only represented a loss for him personally, but he carried the weight, the hopes, and the dreams of most of us at McMurray Junior High to Davy Jones's locker with that loss. When it was over and C. brushed himself off, G. T. went his way, and C. H. went his way, and it was never spoken of again. We never saw one school official interact with that situation. They had to have known what happened, but I believe that they thought that C. H. would pound blend T. into a pulp and then they would not have to be bothered with him. when that did not happen There was nothing for them to do or say, because they had not done anything at the beginning to get in the way of it or stop it. One other happened with G. T. This event would spell the end of G. T. and McMurray Junior High. We were sitting in class one day. Our class was next to the boy's bathroom. As we sat in class, we heard a powerful explosion. Once we really get our bearings back after hearing that and wondering what happened, water began flooding up under the door to our classroom. G. T., it seems, had dropped an M80 cherry bomb firework into one of the toilets and then flushed it. The damage was severe. Not only was G. T. expelled, but that was the last any of us saw of him. Every time I see a young man (or even a young lady) with green hair I wonder what happened to G. T.

I also remember it was at McMurray Junior High that my oldest brother Carl really emerged as an outstanding musician. Carl also excelled in the sports of baseball, wrestling, and he developed into being a very good high hurdler in track and field. It is little things like that that pop into my mind. I should have also known that I would have a career in the theater. My first inkling of this knowledge really came as early as Providence Elementary School, when I would expressively read things in class; and it just seemed that I had a natural knack for the theatrical. The next showing moment came when I participated in the musical "Signor Pimpernel." I played the part of the hard driving Sergeant …if you can imagine any junior high school student being able to perform that role. We gave a brief presentation to the school during an assembly. I was never afraid, although there was the natural amount of stage fright that occurred. I went on to successfully execute the role much to the applause of friends who on other occasions might have made fun of you or would have been critical. They were neither … they were congratulatory and supportive. I should have known then I had a gift for the stage. When I matriculated on to Overton High School, I did a reading in Ms. Daws English class. I'm not sure where she attended college, but after reading a series of poems and other materials in her English class Ms. Daws came to me and told me she could get me a scholarship to either University of Southern California, or U.C.L.A. I did not take anything seriously when I was in high school, so I flippantly dismissed the idea. I had relatives in Los Angeles, so I really should have made use of her generous offer.

JOHN OVERTON DAYS

Amongst those days at John Overton high school, I remember my first or second day as a sophomore age at Overton I was standing outside of my homeroom classroom. Two young ladies got into a fight right there in front of me. They were big athletic girls, so they were not shrimps by any stretch of the imagination. These two "Amazon" young ladies fought with the ferocity of any man or boy that I had seen. That was kind of scary, and I learned, after seeing the amount of blood and the cuts on each of the young ladies, that there was a way that young ladies (and, I guess, young man) could hide razors in their mouth. At the time of an altercation, they could get these razors out without cutting their own mouths. They would use these razors to cut the other person. That was interesting and scary to find out about.

It was also during this time at John Overton high school that I met my first real girlfriend. We would break up. After that breakup, about 30 years later, we would reunite and she would become my wife. The way that we first came together happened when a young lady name "C" came to my homeroom and said, "I know a young lady who would be just perfect for you to meet." Before I could even open my mouth and have any type of response, she had me by the hand, and was dragging me off down the hallway. When she got to a particular young lady, she took my hand and she put my hand in the young lady's hand. "C" said "there, y'all need to get to know each other." Little did she know how correct she was, because we did proceed to get to know each other. We did proceed to hit it off well. We didn't argue, we didn't fuss, we didn't fight. We just got along; and we got along for a year before Washington turns sixteen and did the stupid thing that a sixteen-year-old typically does…chases after the greener pastures, or what he thinks are the greener pastures of another girl, not only to be disappointed in that, and by the new relationship. To walk away from a relationship that was working so well when there was not a need to walk away, but again I say when you're sixteen you do things that only a sixteen-year-old can and will do.

At Overton high school I was a part of the marching band for the three years. While I was at Overton, I do mention my little departure from the band to try out for the football team. This did not end as well as I would have liked. For the most part I was a member of the band. I participated in music whether it was choral music or instrumental music.

Another thing about the Overton high school years is that L.D. and I were cousins and didn't know it. Our grandparents married opposite sisters and brothers. L.D. and I did not know all through high school that we had this close relationship. We did not know we were products of identical gene pools. God knows what he's doing. It was a good thing that we did not know because had I known that this person was my cousin I might have ended up in jail, prison, or maybe dead. That is because L.D. was a stone-cold criminal. To this day we laugh about that and he knows that he was a criminal. It was not even mentioned at our graduation (where I know his grandparents, my grandmother, his parents and my parents attended) when we both graduated that we were related. But cousin L.D. told me one time "Washington, you know our race needs all kinds. We need smart people like you, but we also need the tough people like me and we all have to work together to make the race go forward." L.D. was very astute and those were good words. I've heard those words spoken in many different terms later by many prominent people.

At Overton high school I made many good friends including many of the children of well-known country music artists. This includes the Tubb brothers (the sons of Ernest Tubb), Sedina Hubbard, whose father was Jerry Reed, and the Tillis'. I was classmates with Pam Tillis, whose dad was the great country music artist Mel Tillis. I became friends with Fred Rose, whose grandfather owned one of the largest country music publishing companies, and was partner to Roy Acuff (who was always considered to be the "King of Country Music.) These children of celebrities were as regular as regular could be. They were as nice as nice could be. Later in life when I had the opportunity to reconnect with Dean Tubb and Pam Tillis they both remembered me before I recognized who they were. This is just how down to earth they were, and the type of friends that we all had become.

MR. DeFORD BAILEY

I really don't know how I could end this segment on the children of noted country music high artists without talking about DeFord Bailey. I talked about the children of country music artists such as Jerry Reed, the Tubb brothers, Fred Rose and others. I would be totally remiss if I did not mention that I also attended high school (and through college) with the grandson of the great country music artist DeFord Bailey. DeFord Bailey is a name that is not as well-known as Tubb or Tillis, or Reed. It is a fact that the name DeFord Bailey, an African American man who was a great harmonica player, violinist, guitarist, and just all-around super musician, was never talked about in the halls of country music. Bailey, until very recent history, was never a member of the Grand Ole Opry or inducted into the Country Music Hall of Fame. When I refer to "recent history" I really mean in the last twenty years. The truth is that had there not been a DeFord Bailey, there would not have been a Roy Acuff. Roy Acuff, known as the "King of Country Music" got his initial introduction to the world of the touring musician being mentored by African American touring veteran DeFord Bailey. Bailey Roy Acuff around on the tour and showing him how you go about being on the tour and yet for him not to be inducted into the country Music Hall of fame and into the Grand Ole Opry immediately it's sort of a travesty. I first heard the name DeFord Bailey in high school from classmate Joe Thomas. Joe Thomas always talked about his grandfather. Much in the same way I, like many young people, just kind of give that a periphery kind of attention or awareness. I did not pay much attention to the important information that Joe Thomas was sharing with me because at that time I did not have the reference point of history that would have given emphasis to the importance. Joe Thomas may or may not have understood the significance of the import of the information that he knew about his grandfather. In college, I would go to study the history of the theater and just become a person interested in history. I would become interested in African American history, and of African American history in Nashville. That is when I realized that African Americans were there at the very beginning of what would become known as the Grand Ole Opry. I know that people recognize what I call a resurgence of the African American presence and interest in country music however African Americans were there at the very beginning. and when I say the beginning, I mean that on the banks of the Cumberland River that the blacks the whites the Irish the Native Americans the whoever ever Evers that were there all work together. And at the end of the workday, they all sat down and made music together. religious music sort of served as their centerpiece or the common focal point for all of them and it is the reason that captain Tom Ryan had a gospel Tabernacle built for these musicians to perform their music in remember that they the musicians were black as well as white if I can put it that clearly and they all made music at what would become Ryan's gospel Tabernacle which would later become the Ryman Auditorium which would later become known as the mother church of country music and I say all of that to say that black folk or African Americans are only rediscovering their connection to country music I believe it is a birthright that we walked away from gave up ignored forgot about however it happened and now we are coming back to it but also at the beginning I will say that D4 Bailey played a huge part and DeFord Bailey was the first person not just the first African American he was the first person period to perform on the 1st show that would become known as the Grand Ole Opry and it is a country music fact that was never talked about and it should be talked about is not talked about enough it should be talked about more and and a similar type of influencing went on in Montgomery AL where a man named T tot guided the first or the initial career of a man named hey Williams senior meeting people who are historians at country music especially Marty--------------- will kill you and of the African American influence on what we know as country music it's so I could not leave this section without mentioning D4 daily whose grandson was Joe Thomas if we were there at Overton high school together and also in the band at Tennessee State University together and have remained good friends to this very day.

GOING OVER TO BOBBY'S

As I have said before, Bobby Flowers and I got to be fast friends...brothers, very quickly and very easily. Who can ever say why people are drawn to each other, but we were, and always stayed brothers. I can remember going to his house and he coming to my house. There were a couple of ways that we could manage that: either ride our bikes the back way using Edmondson Pike to Blackman Road, or we could go Nolensville Pike and ride up the big hill at Harding Place to get to his neighborhood, or for him to get to my neighborhood. However, we both went or came to each other's homes. We both had meals in each other's homes. We both got to know each other's families in each other's homes. Bobby's mother, Rose, was a true artist in every sense of the word. She was (and, is) highly creative. She would paint their mailbox. She also just painted paintings because she was artistically talented like that. The thing I remember and think most about Mrs. Flowers... Mrs. Claypool, is that she could cook like a magician. I grew up around great cooks. My mother was a great cook, and she had been trained but my great aunt, my grandmother in Birmingham, and my father's mother, who were expert cooks. They did not have to measure things out, or if they did it was so second nature that they did it so effortlessly they made it look as if they were not trying very hard. The food they cooked was outstanding. If they cooked a lump of crap it was so good you would eat it without hesitancy. Such was the skill of Bobby's mother as a cook. I grew up around well-prepare food. Well-seasoned food. I was not a casual partaker of food; I was a trained partaker. I was a skilled partaker. In fact, I was a fledgling cook myself. I knew good food when I was around it, and

Mrs. Claypool/Mrs. Flowers was on top of her game. One day Bobby called me and he was pretty upset because his parents were splitting up. and in the middle of all of that conversation a bubble just rose to the top of the water in my brain, and I said, "Your dad has to be an idiot." Bobby asked, "Why do you say that?" I said, "Who could get divorced from such an outstanding cook and homemaker as your mother?" "Only an idiot would do such a thing." I'm not sure that that arrested Bobby's nerves right then, but in my opinion, it sure was the truth.

MRS. FLOWERS/CLAYPOOL

There was a time when Bobby's folk were out of town. I went to sleep over at his house to give him company. Bobby's mother had filled the refrigerator because she knew that I was coming over (she must have heard I liked her cooking). Bobby and I had dinner and we settled in to watch a movie. The next thing I knew it was daylight and Bobby was looking at me rather strangely. Bobby said, "I was talking to you and the next thing I knew you were sound asleep.". Well, what can you do but apologize? I guess I could have been better company.

THE BOBBY ESCAPADES

The next part of this story is what I call the Bobby escapades. As innocent as Bobby and I acted (and often professed to be), we were both quite mischievous. There were times when Bobby and I would get together (most of the time this was when we were in high school) Bobby would borrow his parents Oldsmobile Cutlass 442. We would ride the streets looking for innocent mischief. There was a time where we rolled down to Radnor yard, close to Harding Place. We got out onto the train tracks. Your nerves must be good when you are young because sometimes, we could hear trains moving. Sometimes trains next to us would start moving. It is a true miracle that we never had an accident or got killed running around in that train yard. Other times we might spend time painting some message or the other in the train bridge underpass that led from Travelers Rest to John Overton High school. I do not remember the details of any of the messages, except that most of the time they pertained to a graduation message of some sort. It is quite exhilarating to be riding the bus to school in the morning and knowing that everyone sees your message spray painted on the tunnel…to hear people make comments and secretly knowing that they were responding to your handiwork. Another prank that Bobby and I got together and pulled was when we took a deer that someone had left on top of the entrance to the band room and took it upon ourselves to hoist it up to the top level, main entry to John Overton high school. We placed it strategically at over the front entrance of the school where it could be seen when the buses pulled in. As we moved this ceramic deer into place, we realized that the roof of these high schools, (or at least Overton High School) was lined with tripwires, sensors, or alert wires. As we moved the deer into place, we could see several security cars or vehicles pull into the parking lot, and the gentleman got out to see what/where the disturbance was at the school. We held our positions, and eventually the security cars left and we were able to come down off the building. I can't tell you how my heart raced that night, and maybe it raced even more when; again, riding the bus to school the next morning the whole school could see, and talk about the new entry ornament (the new statue) that now adorned the front of Overton High School. Mr. Stanfield made an announcement that morning about the new artwork.

MOTORCYCLE DAYS

My dad was one of those kinds of guys who said if it's in the driveway you need to be able to operate it. I took every opportunity to hold up my end of that bargain for him.

In junior high became friends with Jimmy Staggs through Bobby Flowers. Jimmy had been an avid motorcycle rider. I think he started out with a Honda CB100. The next motorcycle that he purchased was a Honda CB 450. For years the CB 450 was Honda's largest production bike. My uncle, Scott Saunders, owned one of the very first ones. Jimmy would come over to my house on Winston Avenue and bring Bobby Flowers along. I had been used to riding minibikes and the Honda CB100. One of my Boy Scout troop members, Damon Sudberry, owned a Honda CB100. Sometimes we would leave McMurray Junior High and go to his house. He would bring me home on Nolensville Pike on his CB100. So, I got used to riding other people's bikes. I never owned a bike myself because my mother just was not feeling the bike thing. When you don't have a job to buy a bike, and if you don't have relatives that can buy you a bike, along with a parent that will consent to you having a bike, you can never own a bike. But I was always riding someone else's motorcycle. Jimmy was very gracious. Jimmy would ask if I'd like to take it for a ride. Of course, I couldn't turn that offer down. I got used to riding that Honda 450 up and down Winston Avenue. I got pretty good at riding it. We all got used to seeing Jimmy at school with his Honda 450. One day, someone pulled into the parking lot on a much bigger bike. This bike had a much bigger, throatier sound.

We all looked out of the window at school to see what this new sound was. When the rider took their helmet off we saw that it was Jimmy Staggs. Jimmy had brought a new motorcycle, and to top everything off it was a Honda 750-4. This new motorcycle was just the talk of the school that day.

Even my cousin, Dwayne Kinnard, was impressed. Dwayne Kinnard owned a Suzuki 380 Sebring. The Sebring was a two stroke, air-cooled motorcycle. This was a pretty revolutionary innovation back then. Dwayne's Suzuki 380 Sebring would run like a scalded dog. It was right in there with the Kawasaki 750's, 500's, and 350's. These were all two stroke bikes. Two strokes are high revving bikes that can really get up and move. The Suzuki 380 Sebring was one of those premier bikes. When Dwayne would pull out of the parking lot there was just a wave of blue smoke. We called all these two stroke Japanese bikes "rice-burners." The blue plume of smoke was created when the two-stroke engines burned the oil with the gasoline. The 380 (as it was with all two-strokes) would basically outrun a bunch of other motorcycles on take-off. Other bikes may catch up with it a little later, but if you wanted to sprint race, nothing beat a two stroke, whether it was Suzuki, Kawasaki or Yamaha - nothing beats a two stroke on the take-off.

Getting back to Jimmy Staggs. Everyone, including my cousin Dwayne, was just floored by this new bike. This 750-4 was a bad bike! As usual, Jimmy and Bobby would come over to my house, and he would bring the 750-4. I got a couple of swats at riding this nice bike. A very sobering event would soon take place. Jimmy and Kevin Maxwell, who played basketball, ran track, and football at Overton were out riding on the 750-4. Jimmy was speeding, and a police officer pulled in behind him to stop them and give them a ticket. Jimmy evaded pursuit. As Jimmy and Kevin were turning off Blackman Road onto Danby Drive, a lady opened her car door. Jimmy clipped the car door going at a high rate of speed. Jimmy and Kevin were hurt pretty badly. For a long time following that incident Kevin had to walk with a cane. I don't think that he was ever the athlete that he had been, at least not at Overton.

The last motorcycle that I rode (and again I stress I never owned a motorcycle; I just had the good fortune of having friends who did) was the big bike for Kawasaki. Officially, this Kawasaki was designated the K1 900. I used to call it KZ900. Whatever the name designation, at one time it was the world's fastest production bike. At Tennessee State University I had a friend who owned a KZ900 or the K-1 900. He would let me ride it in the parking lot a few times. It was a very, very nice bike.

Ms. SYLVIA KARNOWSKY

Amid talking about all my high school escapades, I really can't leave this section without talking about one of my favorite teachers. This teacher happens to be one of my favorite high school teachers because she taught history. Ms. Karnowsky was also the senior advisor. I have always been enthralled by history. It may be because I was always exposed to my grandparents and great-aunts. Whatever the reason, I've always loved history and Ms. Karnowsky, in my opinion, was the history teacher to end all history teachers.

I believe Ms. Karnowsky was of Russian descent. She had red hair and she smoked like a coal burning freight train. There were times right after class that Ms. Karnowsky would literally run out of the room, fly into the teacher's lounge that was very close to her room (Heaven help anyone that got in her way). You could see the smoke rolling from under the door. From time-to-time Mr. Stanfield, the principal, would admonish Ms. Karnowsky for smoking in the building, but that didn't stop her. It never got her fired. The thing I like most about Ms. Karnowsky and history is that she was blatantly honest about the events of history. She was smart and she knew history. Ms. Karnowsky was the first person that I had ever heard say that Lincoln's Emancipation Proclamations did not free the slaves. She let it be known that it was Sherman's March to the Sea, burning down the major cities in the South along the way, that broke the back of the Confederacy and brought an end to the Civil War. I will never forget that. I always told people (and still tell them) that. I really loved her history class, and I learned things that other teachers were probably afraid to teach students. It also taught me that as a teacher, that I had to walk a little on the edge when it came to telling the truth about certain issues. I knew that certain things were true and right when it came to the Civil Rights movement because I lived through the "sweet part" to the ending part of Jim Crow. I engaged in conversations with my elders (grandparents, and great aunts and uncles) who let me know what slavery was really like. When I read things in books, or hear people make certain statements, I don't just go with the flow, because of those conversations combined with Ms. Sylvia Karnowsky's example. I learned that there will be times that it will feel dangerous to speak the absolute truth about situations in history. It's important for us to never forget the truth, and never to change history. The other disappointing thing is that history is being rewritten. It is ironic, to me, that the people who talk about the rewriting of history are the ones who want to change the facts and the reality of histories that they don't like into things that they like. The harm and the damage is this. It's like what the pigs did in the George Orwell book, Animal Farm. Once the pigs took control of the farm, they began to systematically change the history of the occurrences of the farm. They continued to do this as the other animals were either too old to remember the exact history or had been born long after the events had taken place. The real harm to all is that you only know what I want you to know, and HOW I want you to know it.

My dad was a history buff, as well. While in the Navy my dad got the opportunity to travel all over this planet. He saw a lot of places, a lot of things, a lot of different cultures, and a lot of different topography. After the Navy my dad enrolled in Tennessee State University. He was taking a history class from the great history professor Mingo Scott. One day in class professor Scott said something about somewhere in the world. My dad, being a Navy veteran and an "A" personality, spoke out in class in direct opposition to the expert professor. No one contradicted what professor Mingo Scott said. But, there was my dad with the nerve to do this in front of the entire class. Whatever the place or event was my dad said "no, that's wrong." Professor Scott said "well, I'm the professor, I know......... and blah blah blah blah, and how dare you contradict me." My dad said "well, have you ever been there?" Professor Scott said "no, I have not." My dad said "well, I've been there. I've stood on that spot. I know what happened. The information you provided was wrong. I'm sure I know how that stood with Professor Scott. He couldn't have liked it very much. I'm sure he had a huge ego and everything else, but my dad was one of those kinds of persons who just spoke it up and that was it

FAMILY STORIES YOU HEAR IN YOUR YOUTH

There are histories and remembrances that family have and talk about. You know they're true because there's no way I would not believe what my grandmother and my great-aunts told me about, in terns of family history. A major subject that my grandmother and great-aunts talked about a lot was that my great- great- uncles (on my father's side) were heavily involved in the horse racing industry. People don't realize it, but Nashville at one time, had a horse race industry that rivaled, or may have been more prestigious than the horse racing industry of Kentucky.

The story is that my dad's great uncles were well known in the horse racing industry. They bred, trained and raced thoroughbred horses. They were well-known, prominent, and had connections with people in Kentucky who were in the horse racing industry.

I never doubted that what my grandmother told me was true. Many persons of the Dobbins part of my family looked white. I suspect they were white. My great-grandmother, Ranie and her second husband Jack, both looked white. Fayetteville was a family location my grandmother said the Dobbins originated. My grandfather looked white enough that he passed for white when it suited him. My dad was very fair skinned with wavy hair.

I heard names like "Racehorse Charlie". William and Benjamin Dobbins. I heard that they all were notorious drinkers. They were bad alcoholics; so, alcoholism seemed be a generational thing. I had been told that" Racehorse Charlie" developed a device that fit between the legs of training racehorses that kept their knees from knocking together. My grandmother and great-aunts said that "Racehorse Charlie" was the genius in terms of understanding horses, training, racing and everything. Majors was another family name I came to know through conversations with Aunt Fannie. "Racehorse" Charlie was a Majors. There was also George Majors. Occasionally, my dad would bring his uncle to the house. I always thought it was George Majors he had brought with him, but my mother and my youngest brother Joel tell me that it was Charles or "Racehorse" Charlie that my dad had brought to the house. I remember he was very quiet and had very piercing eyes. He was very red of complexion, and very Native American in appearance. I regret that I never engaged him in conversation or went with my father to bring him from his home in Lebanon Tennessee (Wilson County).

One day I was on Eighth Avenue in a shop buying some personal protection material. I actually went into the shop on a lark. It was not intentional on my part, but I always believe that God leads you to places for a very specific reason. I wrote the owner of the shop a check (what's that???). The owner, who was white, looked at the check and said, "Your last name is Dobbins?" I said "yes" Then he said "I knew some Dobbins growing up. Of course, when someone makes this kind of statement, my first thought is, I want to hear you talk about the racehorse industry connection; because if you don't talk about racehorses and the industry, we're not talking about the same Dobbins. The first thing out of this gentleman 's mouth was "The Dobbins I knew trained thoroughbred racehorses." I almost fell through the floor. The gentleman went on to tell me their names were Benjamin and William Dobbins. Again, I could've fallen through the floor, because these were names that my grandmother and aunts had told me about. The shop owner and I had a long conversation. He went on to tell me about the one I had always heard was "Racehorse" Charlie. He referred to that person as "Long" Charlie, but the description he gave was that Charlie was darker than his uncles (which stands to reason because Charlie was a Majors (my great-grandmother's first husband and family). The Dobbins and Majors would stay close. I thought "my God!" The gentleman went on to say that Charlie was taller that Bill and Benjamin Dobbins, and therefore he was called "Long" Charlie. The man said Charlie was a genius when it came to horse racing. The gentleman went on to tell me that Benjamin and Bill Dobbins, or William Dobbins put him on his first thoroughbred racehorse. They taught him how to jockey. He said, "From that training I went all over the world jockeying thoroughbred racehorses." Well, you know I almost died just hearing these words from this white man. Here HE was telling me stories that had always been told to me. Virtually the same story. I pulled myself together enough to ask him "what did William and Benjamin Dobbins look like?" He said "Well, they were what we called "Red Irish". I asked, "did they look white?" He said "Yes, they looked white; but we called them Red Irish." He went on to say, "My father told me that I better respect them; and listen to them better than I did my own father." I said, "if you don't mind, I would like to come back and interview you, and record your words." I said, "These are my ancestors, and you are the first person outside of my family to corroborate the words I've always heard. I also told him it was important because it documented a huge part of my family's history." He said "I don't have a problem with that. Just let me know and we'll set it up." We did set an appointment for one week later. I contacted my brother, Joel, and I told him what had transpired. I knew that Joel was also very interested in family history and would enjoy doing the interview. Joel also had a really good video camera.

So on the appointment day, Joel and I returned to the gentleman's' shop with video camera in hand. I had a list of questions that I wanted to ask him. When we got set up and started, the gentleman said he wanted to explain how he came to know the Dobbins. He went on to say that his family came up to Nashville on a train from somewhere in the country. I cannot remember what part of the country he said, but the reason they came to Nashville is because his brother had become very ill as a young boy, and they needed to get him the medical treatment that was here in Nashville at the time. He said the train stopped at a station located near Eighth Avenue South and Wedgewood to let them off. Somehow, He said that he had been introduced to Bill and Benjamin Dobbins by someone in his family. I'm pretty sure the white part of my family is from Fayetteville in Maury County. I say Fayetteville Tennessee because my dad's aunt Cora Scales was the daughter of a prominent doctor in Fayetteville.

The gentlemen went onto say that these men put him on his first thoroughbred racehorses, taught him how to jockey and, again, he went all around the world jockeying thoroughbred racehorses. And he did go to say also that horse racing in Nashville was bigger than it was in Louisville, Kentucky at Churchill Downs at that time. The horses were stable where the Kefauver Courthouse is now. This corroborated what my family said. Also, he said the horses lived better than people in those stables. They would warm up the horses up by walking them down Eighth Avenue to Wedgewood. At Wedgewood they would make the left-hand turn and go into the Fairgrounds to the racetrack. I do know that there are pictures of the racetrack and the pavilion in the Metro archives. He said you can still see part of the race track from certain parts of the fairground area.

I'm sure that there's more to the story that I can't think of right now. But the information he gave us that day was astounding. He did go to say that his brother, whose desk was across from his, passed away the day after I had come in last week. That made getting this interview even more important. There is a recording that exists. Perhaps at Joel's house, somewhere. I think that Joel thought that I kept the tape, but I assured him he had the tape. He said he would just need to find it.

In addition, my grandfather cut the stones for the base of the original Battle of Nashville monument. My dad's father died of emphysema at age forty. My father was nine at the time. Stonecutters apparently did not wear particle masks in those day. It was because my grandfather had inhaled all those particles of stone that led to his death. I realize many people will denounce this story. It is another thing that my elders told me in a very pointed way. I believe it is important to know these things, because there was (an still exists) a mind-set that the stories told in white (and other families) are documented, and therefore true, but the stories that are passed down orally in Black families have no validity. It is the same way that Blacks did not receive the same commendations for actions in wars because they were Black. NOW, in this season of rewriting history, I am constantly annoyed that the history and contributions of African-Americans is constantly marginalized. That statue, that has now been moved to Battlefield Park on Battlefield Drive, is NOT a Confederate monument. It is a Peace monument that honors the lives of the young men on both sides who gave their lives in the Civil War. On the original side of the monument stood a tree. That tree is known as a "Witness" tree, meaning it witnessed the horrors that took place there during the Civil War. That tree is still there. A plaque, or monument should be placed in that location since the monument is now gone.

TOM COLLINS

As I move forward this part of the book is a tribute to my good friend, Tom Collins. Tom Collins would become one of the biggest, and most decorated and awarded producers in country music. People may not really believe it, but the Dobbins were actually good family friends with one of the top producers in all of country music...Mr. Tom Collins. Our relationship began because my mother was teaching at Bellshire elementary. and his soon-to-be wife were teaching there. The wedding of Tom and Jennie took place. The Dobbins were invited, and my mother prepped up five young children. We dressed up in our finest shirt and ties and attended the wedding. I am, to this day a huge Ronnie Milsap fan. My first encounter with Ronnie Milsap was at the wedding of Tom and Jeannie. (I shall come back to Ronnie a little bit later.) Ronnie Milsap sang Let's Take the Long Way Around the World at the wedding. I didn't know Ronnie Milsap from Buddha Class, but I knew that he had done a tremendous job. When my mom and the five of us went to Tom and Jenny's wedding everyone thought we were related to Charley Pride because we were the only black people there. Tom had been partners with Charley Pride in a publishing company Pi Gem and Chessmen Music. Of course, we were not related to Charley Pride. Charley was not able to attend the wedding. Tom Collins was also good friends and tennis partner with Thomas Cain. Thomas Cain was an executive with BMI (Broadcast Music Incorporated).

Tom Collins allowed the Dobbin's children to stay in contact with him. Tom was producing Ronnie Milsap, he was producing Sylvia, he was producing Barbara Mandrell, he was producing Johnny Rodriguez. When he was not in the studio, when he was not doing other important business for his production company, if any one of the Dobbins children called him, he made time to talk with us on the phone, and he would make time to see us in his office. I don't know how my brothers feel about the graciousness of Tom Collins, or even if they think about it at all, but I was always supremely grateful that a man of his import would take the time to talk to us as we came along. It meant a lot to me (it still means a lot to me). I probably had the most contacts with him. The most sustained contact.

There came a time when Tom Collins told Joel and I that he was looking for a black female artist to produce to record. Tom Collins told Joel and I that he was on the hunt for the next Black country superstar. He was going to get that person a recording contract with a major recording company. He already had the contract; he just needed the artist to plug in. Joel and I looked for a couple of years for such an artist, and then we ran across or came into knowledge and relationship with Roberta Madison. I was really blown away by Roberta Madison because she and the late Scat Springs sang at Joel and his wife Renay's wedding the theme song (the love song) from Aladin "A Whole New World." Roberta and Scat were better than the Disney recording. Joel and I were able to obtain a recording of Roberta Madison. We took that recording to Tom Collins. Tom is really a genius. Some of the things that I've read since he and I used to maintain close communication enriched my appreciation of him. When he heard Roberta Madison and talked to her in his office with Joel and I. When Joel, Roberta and I left Tom Collin's office we went and talked amongst ourselves. Joel and I concluded he was going offer Roberta Madison a recording contract. He did that. Tom Collins called me to let me know that Joel and I should begin creating a marketing strategy look to help promote Roberta Madison. You could not have asked for a better opportunity. A couple of days later Tom Collins called me back. Tom says Roberta doesn't want to do it. Roberta Madison told him she could not record country music. What Tom Collins had in his mind was a black Reba McIntyre… a black Barbara Mandrell, a black female counterpart to Charley Pride. So, it was quite disappointing when Joel and I learned Roberta Madison turned down this offer; but you know God knows everything. The career would not have been long because not much later Roberta Madison was diagnosed with an aggressive form of cancer that took her life within a couple of years of the offer. Also, let me pause here to say there were other black country music recording artists: O.B. McClinton, Ruby Falls who were making significant strides in the world of country music long before Darius Rucker and some of the other black artists who now have significant country music recordings and performing careers. I always thought it was so strange that these black country music artists who were on the rise would all die of cancer. It had been many years since I talked with my friend Tom Collins. The last thing that I had heard was that his father was ill, and he was doing quite a bit to take care of his ailing father. Tom's son Bradley is also a music executive. I reached out to my friend Tom Collins through his son, Bradley. Bradley and I successfully connected through Messenger. I wanted to let him and his father know how much I appreciated and valued the friendship his father had extended to me. I wanted to let him know the visionary his father was. Bradley told me his father had no problem with him providing his cell phone number to me. I did call Tom Collins. We talked for a while, and we even made loose plans to see each other face to face in the near future. I also wanted to congratulate him on his accomplishment of purchasing a rather large music publishing portfolio which became Tom Collins Music.

RONNIE MILSAP: WHAT HAPPENS WHEN YOUR MOUTH DOESN'T WORK

Without a doubt I am one of the world's hugest Ronnie Milsap fans going. It is probably the worst kept secret in the world; but I am.

I was aware of Ronnie Milsap from attending Tom Collins 's wedding to Jeannie. Ronnie sang "The Long Way Around the World." During the mid-1990s I had the opportunity to do multiple concerts with Ronnie Milsap at the Geo Celebrity Theater at Opryland U.S.A. theme park. It's hard to imagine you're a fan as big as you are of a particular artist; and having the opportunity to work with that artist. I have always appreciated his work, and here I was working with Ronnie Milsap. The part of the story that I really want to just share is, I've been in the presence of a lot of celebrities, but never, ever, ever once in my life have I not been able to just have a simple conversation with someone, but as things would go I found myself standing right next to Ronnie Milsap before the start of one of his concert's, and words would not come out of my mouth. I knew that Ronnie Milsap knew that I was standing there; and he probably knew I wanted to say something. I mean my mouth would not open. It would not work. It would not move.

I told two people about this occurrence. The person we called "Dude", who was Ronnie Milsap's personal keyboard tech. "Dude" said "he's like the nicest guy in the world. Just speak to him." I could not do it!!! I called Tom Collins, my friend, and I told him what was going on. I said "Tom, I'm doing shows with Ronnie. I just want to say something to him. Do you think it would be okay?" Tom said "Yeah, just say 'hello' to Ronnie. He's the nicest guy in the world." Okay, here I was after having these two conversations, standing right next to Ronnie Milsap and STILL not being able to open my mouth to say a word. Again, I have to say I'm one of the biggest fans of Ronnie Milsap going, and it's just one of those incredible moments. I've heard other people talk about moments like that, where you're with someone that is so awe-inspiring and so awesome. Then you have that one time that you cannot get anything to come out of your mouth. That was the real encounter that I had with Ronnie Milsap.

WEED SMOKING

I did smoke marijuana; and the answer is, yes, I did inhale! I mean, what would be the point of smoking the demon weed if you weren't prepared to inhale - and inhale deeply, and fill up your lungs? So, I did!

I think the first bit of marijuana that I smoked was in middle school (junior high). There were some young man in the neighborhood who had procured either marijuana, or marijuana cigarettes. Most mornings they had procured the marijuana. We would roll a joint while waiting on the bus to arrive. We would all smoke some of the marijuana. I'm not gonna say all of us, but I'm gonna speak for me. There were those that brought the weed. I didn't buy it because I didn't have the money to buy it. I didn't know where to buy it, so I didn't buy it. It's a funny thing about marijuana smokers and drinkers. They freely share among friends, and so that's how it all got started…friends sharing with friends.

I do remember getting relaxed in the mornings before we would enter high school. I'm not sure whether the principal or principals knew or not that we were smoking; but that's what we did, and it was some who even smoked at school. Some people smoked at school because they could go out behind the hill between the tennis court and the football stadium, and fire them up quickly, and then get him back into the school. Typically, before they were even missing. That's kind of how it went at high school. On most occasions we smoked before the bus came to take us to school. That was a became a routine thing.

I remember perhaps the worst thing I ever did while high on marijuana, or weed, happened in the morning class where Ms. Rhame was the music teacher. Ms. Rhame was the kindest, most gentle, compassionate soul in the world. Each morning Ms. Rhame read to the class a passage from the book, The Prophet, by Kahlil Gibran. I recall one morning, when I walked into the classroom. I was sitting; probably on the top riser (because I was either singing bass or tenor), and M. Rhame was trying to get us prepared for our morning singing adventure in class. Social emotional learning had nothing on Ms. Rhame, those teachers at Overton High School. They were practicing it and were so well-versed in it without it being called Social Emotional Learning. These master teachers instinctively incorporated it as a matter of habit. They were just great teachers!!!

Well, this one morning I don't know what took hold of me, but I yelled out inappropriate curse words while Ms. Rhame was trying to get her morning ritual together. I was just totally rude and disrespectful to Ms. Rhame. I'm sure it broke her heart because I could see that look on her face. I believe it was extra painful, especially since I really wasn't the kind of student I allowed myself to be that morning. To be honest I don't remember if I ever apologized to Ms. Rhame, or not. If I didn't, I should have. I should have let Ms. Rhames really know how much I regretted that disrespectful outburst. I believe I'd visited Ms. Rhames several times after. I visited her at school, but I am not sure if I really ever apologized profusely enough for my actions on that one particular day when I was intoxicated by weed (marijuana, THC, or whatever you want to call it).

The weed smoking carried on into college. When you have that kind of time freedom between classes there's just all kinds of opportunities to smoke weed. Weed was readily available on the campus. There were so many dealers that you knew where to go to find weed (or, who had the weed). Tennessee village was not far away. Again, I didn't buy much weed because there was so much weed available. Friends were always rolling a joint or two, and amongst friends a shared joint or two was always available. There were also what we called "Oil heads" mixed in, so there was always some drinking to mellow out the weed, and some weed to mellow out the alcohol. I smoked the best of the best of weeds, starting with Acapulco gold. Gold had a strange effect on me. I don't know how it affected anyone else. I will get high, then you felt like you were coming down. And then, suddenly it was like the mad crazy roller coaster loop. I would go flying back up, and I just thought I would lose my mind when that happened. So, it was like, okay, I can't smoke too much of this Acapulco Gold. As good as it was, it did have that effect on me.

I also smoked Maui. Yeah, the good stuff, the Maui straight from Hawaii. That Kona, that rich, volcanic soil. The first time I smoked Maui friends brought over a joint. This joint was not like the big fat "doobie" joints that we were used to smoking. It looked like a little matchstick. I looked at that thing they called a joint. I said, "you must be mistaken. There were seven or eight grown-ass adults here. There is no way that matchstick is gonna get anybody high." We proceeded to take a big (and that's exaggerating) "hit." I'm still thinking there's no way that's gonna get anybody high." I didn't even feel like anything went into my lungs. I'm laughing. I'm telling them "you know what, you guys, this Maui is greatly overrated." Then about, I would say 15 minutes later, something came over me and I had to go sit in the corner, because man, that was everything they promised and then some! I just had to just sit back and take in that moment. The "Maui Pauwi"!!! I guess that's what we should call it: Maui Pauwi!!! Along the way I've also smoked Panama Red (or red bud), Colombian, Mexican, Thai Stick, Jamaican - you name it I smoke it. I smoke the best of the best! After a while I didn't like the loss of control that occurred when you were high, and I put the marijuana away.

I will also mention that I had a friend who had been a member of the women's track team, and later became a majorette for the Aristocrat of Bands. I think she became a member of the chapter of one of our many great sororities. This young lady and I were just friends...just friends...let me reiterate...FRIENDS only. There was no hanky-panky, or anything like that. We were kindred spirits; that's all. This friend was attending summer school. She lived in a state that was far away, and it was not financially practical for her to try to go home. She and I were driving into Opryland theme park one day. I was working in the theme park in Live running a follow spot for the show For Me and My Gal. On one of my days off I went out to the campus and picked her up. We headed into the park. While in the long line waiting to get into the parking lot, she asked me, in that "baby-doll" voice of hers, if I smoked. I thought "smoke???" She was an athlete. I thought she meant smoking cigarettes. I said, "no." I asked, "what do you mean smoke?" She said, "do you smoke?" I told her "I used to puff on a cigarette every now and then." She provided clarity. "No, do you smoke marijuana?" Is it okay if we smoke a joint before we get into the park?" I thought "what?" I said, "it's all good." She took out a joint and fired it up. We smoked the joint on the way into the theme park, and by the time we got to the parking area, parked, and walked into the park, we were pretty much all mellowed out.

I want to say I had never seen Opryland look like that before. The colors were so lush; so green. The music was so vibrant. We walked over to the area of the park where my brother Carl was one of the games leads. We talked to Carl for a minute, then walked around the park. I showed her the park. Later, I said to Carl "You know, we had smoked a joint before we came in. Could you tell we had a good "buzz"? Carl said, "that's all I could tell." Yeah, I knew you guys were high the second I saw y'all." Well, couldn't hide it either. Again, I say I knew she was she came from Alaska. I just wanted to make sure she had a good time since she was here. She and I had become friends and I want to say she was a beautiful person. She had a beautiful soul. She was a sister, a friend, and that is all there was. I'm very serious about that. If it was one of the other kinds of deals, I would've told you.

Back to my main point: I smoked weed. I smoked the best. I knew the names. I knew the smells of the different types of weed. I don't look like "Mr. Innocent Goody Two-shoes or anything like that. The point I am making about the drinking, the smoking that they weren't the thing for me. When you read some of the other chapters, you'll find that I eventually settle on sex with young ladies. Once I discovered the ladies it was on, dude! It was REALLY on!

I DON'T DRINK

Deyanne and I have an extra refrigerator that we keep in the garage; mostly for run overs of extra food and things that we have cooked – especially on Sundays. Things that have been cooked and won't fit into the refrigerator in the house. But, as I looked at the types of drinks that were in the refrigerator, which included Ice Water and Gatorade, but also beer and some Hard Mike's coolers.

The fact is I tend not to drink hard liquor at all, and don't keep it around. Even if I kept it around, I would not drink it. Now, I have a bottle of Uncle Nearests whiskey in my safe in the closet, and I keep that because of the history of Uncle Nearest; and the fact that that was an expensive bottle of whiskey. I just want to hold onto it for a few years and see if the value goes up. I've been told that Uncle

Nearest is no longer distilling. That could be wrong, but that's what I've heard.

However, it brings me to the point of why I don't drink hard liquor or spirits at all. Well, I think the first reason is my dad drank enough for everybody in the family, and then some. I believe it was a part of his Navy experience. I believe his heavy drinking (in some ways) did contribute to his early death at age 54. My dad would come home from work, and immediately on the living room coffee table would put down his bottle of whiskey or Bourbon Deluxe, scotch, or whatever brown liquor he had purchased. Then he would pull out a six pack of beer and proceed to drink what is known as "boilermakers". Boilermakers is shots of bourbon being chased by shots of beer. That must be a navy drink. It could be a military drink, but it is enough to get you going. It was my dad's drink of habit, and consequently it would change my dad's personality dramatically. My dad was almost like two different people. He was the person who, when he was seriously sober, was the greatest dad in the world. But, after my dad had a few of those "Boilermakers" go down he was a very difficult person to contend with. That, in my opinion and my perspective, didn't make him any less of a father. It made him more difficult to deal with. Most times he had no recollection of the things that went on in the morning after that he had been drinking.

And I must say my dad had one heck of a constitution. The day and time my dad stopped drinking and stopped smoking is clearly etched in my mind. My dad was a notorious chain smoker. He smoked Pall Mall filter less cigarettes that came in the red package. My dad was a chain smoker. In other words, he lit the next cigarette from the one that he was finishing. I tell you; you must have a strong constitution to pull that stunt. Just try to smoke one Pall Mall filter less cigarette. It would probably kill you. Believe me, I tried to smoke just one Pall Mall cigarette. That almost killed me. I then tried a Camel filter less cigarette because it was said Camel cigarettes were made from the finest Turkish tobacco. WHAT THE HELL??? My dad could go through a pack of cigarettes in no time. I would say that between the smoking and the drinking, both led to an earlier, untimely death of my father. But, let me hasten to say my dad went to the doctor. The doctor told my dad that if he did not stop drinking and smoking there was nothing he could do for him; and that there would be no reason to come back. Literally, that day my dad never took another drink and he never smoked another cigarette. If you can imagine knowing a person your entire life; into your mid 20's, and you know them to drink and to smoke heavily. Then you see that person stop doing both "cold turkey". I mean just "cold turkey." It's a pretty amazing feat. My dad did just that. But again, because of his early demise (age 54) I saw which I think either hurt me or affected me growing up I really never took the drinking.

THE ROOM TURNED UPSIDE DOWN

Now, let me say for my college years -yes there was drinking that went on being a member of the Aristocrat of Bands. Yes, we had "weed, wine, and oil heads." Being in the theater; yes there were plenty of "oil heads" (I think this was just a college rite of passage), but I think that the thing that really made me stop drinking, and not drink is one night we were doing a play in Memphis Tennessee. There was Lee Summers, Barry Scott, Johnny Hollingshed, and me. We were all in the hotel room. We went out to the liquor store and purchased things like: Malcolm Healffer Chocolate Cow, Mogen David Wine, M.D. 20 20, vodka, gin, and all manner of spirits and alcohol. We went back to the room and started drinking. The more you drink the less you can taste the alcohol (at least for me), and the more open and uninhibited you become in your drinking. I began to guzzle, not just sip, and we were mixing drinks of all kinds. Well, somewhere around two or 2:30 in the morning I was sitting on the bed. The room, it seems, turned upside down. I mean, literally turned upside down. I suspect that is my eustachian tubes became effected, because my equilibrium was really messed up. I knew then I was going to be massively sick. I could not even stand up. I got down on my knees and started crawling. It seemed like the floor was the ceiling, and I was crawling on the ceiling. I barely made it to the bathroom, where I had an extended intimate meeting with the "porcelain goddess". No one came in the bathroom to check on me. I started thinking "wow, I could've died throwing up my guts the way I did, and no one would have even known or cared." I know that if I'm going to put a day and time on where I really, really, stopped drinking there it was. I admit to having my share of encounters with alcohol in college, even a little bit after college, but alcohol was not my thing. I did not like the way I felt being drunk. Now, I might have a little beer or a little cooler every now and then, but it's not really enough to give you even much more than a pleasant buzz. But, those are the reasons why I don't drink.

THE IRONIC TWIST/ THE UNFORGETTABLE OFFICER

I've chosen to label this particular remembrance, THE UNFORGETTABLE OFFICER, because that's just the way I feel about it.

I had turned eighteen four days before this event occurred. A friend and I went to Harding Mall, a mall close to my home one July day in 1976. We walked through several stores, then proceeded to go into Castner-Knotts; not for anything in particular, we were just walking around, looking around.

We were about to leave Castner-Knotts and come home, when all of a sudden, we were approached by two large white men. Of course, I had no idea why they were stopping us. One of them said "Take everything out of your pockets". The only things I had in my pockets were my personal items, including my drivers license identification. My friend removed the contents of his pockets. Then they said, "That's what we were looking for." It appeared that my buddy had picked up a little charm bracelet or necklace; or something along those lines, and apparently, they caught him shoplifting.

As things would go, as these two security guards questioned us, they learned that my friend was still the age of seventeen, but as I said, at the beginning of all of this, I showed them my driver's license, so they knew that I had turned eighteen four days earlier. It really sucked because I had already been accepted at Tennessee State University, and I was planning on being a college freshman in August. The decision on their part was to allow my friend to go, but they kept me, even though I had done nothing, had nothing in my pocket, nothing. They decided to hold me and charge me with delinquency of a minor on a shoplifting charge.

Now, let me interject a personal note here. even though I think that we still need to do some work within our own communities; in terms of guidance for some of our young African-Americans. We do have members of our African-American communities who engage in irresponsible activities, such as the large-group rave shoplifting craze. I'm just going to say it. Some African-Americans; and I may not care about what the other cultures, ethnicities, or nationalities do, but I am always going to be concerned about the sometimes-lawless conduct of African-Americans in this country. The African-American culture has come way too far. We had to overcome way too much to allow ourselves be seen in these types of negative lights. I really don't care how you try to justify these types of activities based on our continuing marginalized position in the United States. Also, when I law enforcement officers whose actions are clearly in the wrong, I call them out as well. The unjust actions of officers and security takes me back to this day in Castner Knotts.

The Castner-Knotts security called a Metro police officer. He appeared to be a giant. Because I was so tiny, I guess they all looked giant to me. This officer look giant also, especially in terms of my situation at the moment. He talked to the security people at Castner-Knotts about what happened and how they wanted to proceed. They wanted to move forward with charges against me, and all he could do was respond to what they said in terms of the incident. I don't remember him asking me very many questions. But he did tell me we would have to go to the car, and we had to go downtown to be booked. The remarkable thing that happened and leads to the reasons I'm supportive of police officers. One, we can't have people running around in society who want to take advantage of the rest of us. It's not fit for them to be around us law-abiding citizens who mind our own business – and don't think I have a right to take your property as mine, or even take your life with no regard for you or your family; especially when we are obeying law. Second, I've had many friends, black and white, to become police officers. I know officers on a personal level. I'm big on law enforcement, but when officers do wrong, I will call them out, and say their actions are not right.

But this officer, whose name I cannot remember, as he was about to put me into the back car seat of the patrol car said "What I'm about to do goes against all department policy. I'm really supposed to handcuff you when I place you in the car, but I'm not going to handcuff you. Number one, I don't believe that you did what they said. Secondly, because the charge is so ridiculous. This is over nothing. You're not going to do anything silly, are you?" I told him I would not, and that was the end of that.

We got downtown to the police station, and we got out. The officer (again, whose name I do not recall…probably because I was so traumatized) took me aside. He explained, "I'm gonna have you sit on this bench, and I have to go back there and get the people and let them know that we're going to have to fingerprint you." I said "okay, I will be here.

In the meantime, Bill Henderson, a church member at Pleasant Green, also a clerk of the court, was walking through the holding area. I was sitting I looked up and I said, "hey Bill, how are you?" I think it stunned him at first. I think people who work with the public under these conditions perhaps have this sort of mind set. You don't look at people, make eye contact or identify with them. Bill had been moving on, but once I spoke to him, he stopped; and then he looked at me. Again, I think it's sort of a shock to the brain to see someone that you know is in a situation in this place. Mr. Bill Henderson said "what are you doing here? What's going on?" I explained to him what happened, and Bill said, "oh no, that's not going to happen." Bill found the officer. I think he went to the night court judge. Bill eventually came back and said "it's over, it's done. I'm going to call your parents and let them know that they need to come down here and pick you up." That is the way that part of the story ended.

I am putting this part of the story in the narrative at this spot because of its irony. It's total irony.

I went home without having been fingerprinted; not having to stand before the judge, or none of that. But, about two weeks later I'm playing softball with the church softball team. Mr. Henderson comes to the game. He said "Come over here. I need to talk to you about something." I said, "Okay." Bill Henderson said "The Castner-Knotts people have decided that they want to go forward with those charges against you." I thought "What?" Bill said "yeah." "But I've already talked to the judge, and the judge has determined that he is going to throw the charges out." Mr. Henderson went on to say "But, you will still have to appear in court." I don't remember the date. "Whatever you do," he said, "make sure you appear in court." I have said "Yes, I will be there."

The court date and time came. They called my case: Castner-Knot versus Washington Dobbins. This case deals with the delinquency of a minor on shoplifting charge. I stand up tall and proud before the bar. (I like that phrasing.) I went to the front of the courtroom. Bill was already standing there. He gave me that reassuring look. Let me say this. You can say "How dare you have somebody standing in, in your behalf influencing the court to do what it did on your behalf. Sometimes, that needs to happen. But, perhaps if it is a murder case, or something like that, or there's clear evidence that someone has committed a crime against someone. Clearly on camera, or with DNA evidence, or both, rob someone. They may not have this type of connection. But I would say that it was God acting on my behalf. Only God, Himself, could have resolved this issue the way it was resolved. I am going to let that speak for me. I'm done with standing on that "soapbox."

The judge, when the case was called, said "You're charging this young man with this?" He was only four days past the age of eighteen at the time this happened. He didn't take anything. The person he was with took something, and you let them go and came up with this." The judge read them the "riot act." Then he told the Castner-Knotts people not to ever waste the court's time by bringing anything of this nature to this court again. I was always taught to accept the consequences for what my actions were. I did just that in the moment; even though I knew I was innocent. My parents always taught me to choose my friends carefully, and to be aware of what my friends were doing, because their actions could have an adverse effect on you. I accepted responsibility for being with my friend. I was ready to accept whatever would have come next. I also remind you; I grew up in the Jim Crow south. We had not been out of Jim Crow very long when this happened. There was a huge Jim Crow mentality among a lot of white males. (Look at what happened very recently with Justin Pearson and Justin Jones.) I don't say that about all white me, because I will tell you, Mr. Tom Flowers accepted me into his home, into his life as if I was his own son. Mr. Flowers was just one example of white men that I came into contact with who were of exemplary conscious. So, all white men were not prejudice demons (read up on Malcolm X). They weren't all that way, but there were still enough, and many of them in the south had positions of authority. They had the ability to send a young black man away to prison or jail over a $10.00 item. No matter what period of time we live in $10.00 is not something, that reason why you do something like that to anybody. It was racism without regard to how you could ruin someone else's life. How you would not want your life, or you children's life ruined in that fashion. How, as a parent, you would do any and everything to keep your own children safe from that kind of harm, but you would do it to someone else's child, based on your racist attitude. How do you look at yourself in the mirror each morning, how do you go to church every Sunday, calling yourself a Christian, and then go out of your way to ruin an innocent person's life like that?

The irony that comes out of all of this is, that four years, later Carlana Moscheo and LaRaun Scaife hired me as a male model for Caster-Knotts. I was the African-American male model face of Castner-Knotts for a number of years. The irony is that four years earlier, my life could've been different because the actions of some petty racist Castner-Knotts security people could have caused my life to be way different. So, again I am grateful to Carlana and LaRaun because what they did changed my life dramatically, in terms of a modeling career, where if I had traveled on to New York, there is no doubt about the successful career I could have had. I made a lot of money as a model because of Castner-Knotts. There is no doubt that the sky would have been the limit.

THE ARISTOCRAT OF BANDS YEARS

It's this point I want to talk about my years with the "Aristocrat of Bands." I provide this insight with my experience with The Aristocrat of Bands. In one way I can't/don't talk about other HBCU marching bands because I was not a member of those bands. Yet, all of us who had the HBCU band experience can share similar stories and recognize the experiences of all others. The fellowship and kindred spirit that connects us all is unmistakable. We were hard competitors. Just as hard as any athlete who took to the field or court of competition. That is why I have respect for every individual who suited up in any of the band uniforms of any Historically Black College or University. I salute you all! I'm still an Aristocrat!

I'll take a moment to explain how I got into the band and the events that would be memorable for any 18-year-old who has the same type of experience. In my family, my brother Carl was the first person in the "Aristocrat of Bands" in our family. I was the second, and my daughter Kaellyn is the third.

The aristocrat of bands begins because Carl who is an outstanding musician had go to a football game and I think we all went to the same football game where Tennessee State University played Florida A&M university Florida A&M University brought their band the marching 100 or the rattlers of Florida A&M the rattler band marching 100 however they describe themselves Carl saw this band and said I think he told my mother I told my parents this is the band that I want to be him and Florida A&M is where I want to go when I graduate from high school I'm not sure exactly what happened but Carl did not go to Florida A&M and he ended up at Tennessee State University where he entered into the process of becoming a member of Tennessee State University's "Aristocrat of Bands." All Dobbins children had been in bands from elementary school up to college. But, getting into an HBCU band was like getting into a band, only with steroids. I must hasten to say that the process included a great deal of hazing. The year was 1974; and even then, hazing was illegal. Hazing had been outlawed. But back then but it was still done. It was still a very, very common practice, especially at black colleges and universities. So, Carl entered the process of gaining membership into the "Aristocrat of Bands." There's a process of becoming a full-fledged member of the band. The day included long, long... long rehearsal hours. Much attention was given to focus disciplining. Much dedication was required in terms of musicianship. This meant not only being able to handle your instrument musically, but also mastering the showmanship that went along with being a member of a legendary show band. Of course, musicianship was a premium. Showmanship was a premium and being able to execute the dance routines. The marching part would've been easy (even hitting the 90's) because it would have been familiar to what we did in high school. Top-flight high school bands required discipline, but not nearly the amount of discipline that it took for the black college marching/performance band.

Carl embarked up on his journey along with people like Thomas "TC" Campbell. Thomas Campbell went on to play for people like Jeffrey Osborne, Peabo Bryson, Roberta Flack, Natalie Cole, Evelyn King, the R&B group, Cameo, and others. Thomas currently is the music director for the touring Temptations. Thomas was a super saxophonist, stellar keyboard artist and songwriter. Another notable was Robert Ransom. The late Robert Ransom went on to have a career with James Brown as a saxophone player. Kenny Bledsoe was a drummer who played with people like country music performer Teri Gibbs. "Bled" was a snare drummer in the "Rat Patrol". Kenny Bledsoe toured with Cyndi Lauper, the artist who sings Time after Time. Cyndi Lauper and some others and they were many, many other members of the "Aristocrat of Bands" who would go on to music notoriety.

In fact, let me digress a little. Maceo Parker and Fred Wesley were prominent members of James Brown's band. They were also members of Parliament and Funkadelic. They were known as "The Horny Horns." Eventually, Maceo even had his own group, Maceo and All the Kings Men. Maceo Parker ended up writing the theme song for the "Aristocrat of Bands." The "Aristocrat of Bands" is the only band in the world to have its own theme song written by a legitimately commercially established artist. The song is actually called "Aristocrats of Bands." When I was in the band, we played this song religiously following every halftime. There was a link to the song which could have been found on YouTube. I notice that link has been taken down. Bummer!

I did digress a little bit, however becoming a member of the "Aristocrat of Bands" and going through the hazing was really a tough deal. The severity of the hazing, especially in 1974, caused several prospective members to have to be taken to the hospital for care. Let me hasten to say that incidents of this type were not uncommon regarding persons seeking to gain membership to HBCU bands. It was said that you just did not walk into becoming a member of the "Aristocrat of Bands." It did not work that way. They were so impressive. Even though I had gone to rehearsals and practices to watch them I had no idea of just the severity of the hazing which occurred for them to become what is known as "Aristocrats." I had no idea what eventually would be in store for me.

The year was 1976. I graduated from John Overton high school early June. I would also attend Tennessee State University. With attending Tennessee State University, I just naturally become associated with the" Aristocrat of Bands."

The first recollection I had is that one of the first things we had to do was to find paper bags that fit over our head, because we were required to wear paper bags; not regular hats. We could not be "CRATS" so we were "CRABS."

The life of the "crab" was brutal. It was hard. Somewhere around the training and the stoicism of the 300 mixed with Navy SEALS. The discipline was acute. By discipline, I meant that we would stand in the hot sun in the middle of July and August for hours on end. Practice would go all day long, late into the night, and early into the morning. One - the conditioning. People don't realize how much energy it takes to even do a 10-minute halftime show properly, especially with all of the things that we include. It is more than a notion. Conditioning and discipline were at a premium. Any of us who made the "Aristocrat of Bands" mentally and physically easily could make any military unit. The Green Berets maybe; but not the SEALS because the SEALS do so much in the water. But "crabs" would have been capable of doing all of the physical land-based things. If you thought if you were tough enough to become a member of the "Aristocrat of Bands; or any other HBCU band, you did have the right stuff for any of those elite military units. If you were very good swimmer, with excellent skills in the water, you had the right stuff to become a Navy SEAL. Regarding discipline, you could be stung by a bee or a wasp; ants could eat you up, sweat could be dripping into your eyes and down your face. But if you were at attention or in the middle of a routine, you'd better not wipe that away; or slap at something that stung you. If you made a motion that was not requested by leaders, several upperclassman standing close to you would swat you over the head with their towels as a reminder, that you need to be still and what you were told. They had all been through the same process; and it was not an easy process.

There were several steps in the initiation process; which again I say included hazing. Upon the arrival of the freshman or new initiate, the first entry into the "Aristocrat of Bands" was that as "crabs" we could only count off with "uh, uh, uh." Later on after we had been initiated through the "uh, uh, uh" process we then were able to count 1,2,3. 1,2,3 would continue on until right before the first game. Of course, we could not go out onto the performance field and just say 1,2,3. When we were called to attention, at that point, we would have to say "T.S.U.!" Then come to attention. There was an initiation for that to happen. That stage of the process, as well after that you had to make "Baby Tiger", then your section. The final initiation into the band was "Aristocrat". All these initiations included hazing. You could be hit with belts, shoes. Just about anything you got struck with was fair game. In the band there were members of various fraternities and sororities. All the girls, be they majorette or flag girls (just to insert a note- Florida A & M did not have flag girls. They had flag men. The initiation process…I heard…to get into the Rattler Band was so difficult that physically it had been impossible for females to become members of the organization. I'm not even sure if The Marching 100 had majorettes), were initiated by the females. No males participated in the initiation of the females. There were no females marching in the ranks of "Aristocrats in 1976. 1977 may have been the first year that females marched within the ranks of instrument carriers. We were bought into the process by men, boys, and men who may have been in the military. Some were criminals (excellent musicians, but criminals) who grew up in rough areas. Many were members of various fraternities on the campus. Everything that everyone knew about hazing, harassment, initiation, and making it tough was brought to the table. That's what we all went through. The final initiations included having to make your section; whichever section you were in.

Let me say that making the drum section was exceptionally difficult. The drum section was known as the "Rat Patrol." The "rat Patrol" was the centerpiece of the band. Along with the tuba section, these two sections were the centerpieces of the "Aristocrat of Bands." These two sections were the centerpieces of practically every HBCU band. Making the drum section was extremely difficult. One of the flashiest components of the drum section were the cymbals. The Tennessee States University "Aristocrat of Bands" had the two most outstanding cymbal players there were. Those two would be Dozier and Gerald Curry. There were three Curry's. There was "Rock", "Kool-Aid" and Gerald. Gerald was the youngest of the three. I don't remember Dozier's first name but Dozier actually trained Curry to play cymbals. Curry could not have had a better teacher. Dozier was phenomenal! When I talk about these two cymbal players, I must tell you that they were not using the hand-held grips. twirlers or handles. So many other cymbal players were using twirlers. Curry and Dozier were using rawhide strips wrapped around their hands. They were not allowed to wear gloves. It took true commitment because each night after rehearsing - and especially when Curry first started his hands would literally be bleeding. They would be cut up by the rawhide as it wrapped around his hands. The rawhide cut into his hands. It also cut off circulation. That's just the way it was but once Gerald caught up with Dozier, and learned what to do, he and Dozier could do phenomenal things with cymbals. That, I did not see members of any other bands being able to do.

DANCE ROUTINES AND PEOPLE KNEW MY NAME

The band practiced in a location affectionally known as "The Hole". We would instrument up, and then march from the band room to the practice field. This had become such a tradition that multitudes of people from the community were aware of our schedule. "The Hole" was located to the rear of Wilson Hall and Hankel Hall. Crowds had already gathered by the time we started the march to "The Hole." The crowds literally parked cars, walked over and watched patiently as we went through the long hours of rehearsals. Many of our audience members knew our patterns in motion and dance routines as well as we did. When they came the games, they knew all the mistakes and who made them. I became a bit of a celebrity for all the wrong reason. I did relatively well with the patterns in motion. I had enough experience with march band in high school to handle the patterns in motion well. My weak spot was the dance routine. Unfortunately, my rhythm comes from Irish white people. River Dancing is where I get my rhythm. River Dance does not work well for Black College Bands. During practice in "The Hole" my name was yelled out every time we had to stop the dance routine. So, every time the dance routine was halted, the vultures up above started yelling out my name. Things got so bad that while we were practicing in the band room prior to going outside, the drum majors paired me up with the majorettes to practice the dance routines. As I think about it now, it was sort of a double-edged thing. In one sense, they put the "rabbit in the briar patch." In the other sense, I was so pitiful I had to dance with the girls. In any event, I made it, and I always learned the dance routine and did the right thing on the performance filed.

THE MEMORIES / THE TRIPS

The thing about being in an HBCU band is that football games always five out of four quarters. The band was always expected to win the fifth quarter, which was halftime. Whichever quarter your call it we were expected to win our quarter. End of report. When you go to black college football games no one goes to the concession stand or restroom at halftime. You may go to the concession stand during predominantly white football games, but no one goes to the concession stand during halftime of HBCU games. That is sacrilegious. And the band is expected to win halftime. I don't care what else is going on.

Then after "The Aristocrat of Bands" wins halftime the drum section of the other HBCU would meet somewhere in the stadium. They would face up, and just as the movie "Drumline" portrayed, there is a battle of the drum sections. Now you start to understand the reason the drum section practice is so long and so demanding. The drum routines that they contest each other with are terribly intricate. There is no room for a mistake. Absolutely no room. The drum cadences that are used have crazy, sophisticated names like "Stick Control", like "Air Puzzle" and other names. I'm proud to say (and yes, I'm going to be biased when I say this) that the "Rat Patrol" won all the face-offs between the drum sections. Without a doubt. Without a doubt.

JACKSON STATE

Being eighteen years of age and being introduced into the world of the "Aristocrat of Bands", and the black college football experience at HBCU's is quite an experience. I remember taking the trip to Jackson State University in Jackson Mississippi. When we arrived on the campus early in the morning we literally went to the center of their campus and held our own band pep rally. We took over their campus, and their square. Before any component of the school could respond we had done our damage and marched our way out.

TEXAS SOUTHERN

The next memorable trip I believe was the band took to Houston Texas to play Texas Southern University. The game was set for to be played in the Astrodome. The Houston Astrodome is the "Eighth Wonder of the World." When you march inside, and you look up you understood why it is the "Eighth Wonder of the World." I believe the capacity was 68,000 persons under a covered dome stadium. It was just incredible to be in that facility, and to march against the Texas Southern "Ocean of Soul." For an eighteen-year-old young man this was quite heavy stuff. I believe the trip to Houston was the longest trip I made with the band, especially on a bus. I will also hasten to say we passed the time on these long trips by doing our fair amount of drinking alcohol spirits and smoking reefer. Once we were off the bus at the hotel room there was much reefer smoking that went on. Someone wanted to pass around a pipe that was molded as a penis. The bowl of the pipe was shaped like a scrotum. I was already a little high, but I clearly remember saying (I guess seeing that "dick" sobered me up) "Hell no! Ain't no damn way I'm going to put any dick in my mouth!" I remember having smoked some marijuana. We were in the hotel room and Laredo was on television. I don't think any of us realized until a long time into the show that there was no sound on the television. It didn't matter because it seemed that we understood everything that was being said by the characters on the television show. The "Ocean of Soul" held a party for us after the game. It was a very cool moment to be able to socialize like that with a rival band. It just showed, that at the end of the day, we had, as HBCU marching bands, a strong connection, understanding and appreciation for what we did. It was a remarkable trip, and again, one that an 18-year-old can hardly believe that they have the good fortune to be making.

FLORIDA A and M

The third trip that I'll talk about (and seriously) one of the more memorable trips is the trip to play Florida A&M. That game was played in Tallahassee Florida, in the Florida State University stadium. What was so interesting about this game is that Tennessee State and Florida A&M bands had not been to each other stadiums or provided the full halftime show for about ten years. It all started because one band did not have the funds to travel to the other school. The next year the other school retaliated by not sending their band. This went on for about ten years. So, as fate would have it, in my first year in the band at Tennessee State University the administration determined that they were going to make this game a spectacle. So, at the last minute we were told that the university had gotten the money to send the band. Because this decision was made so late there were no hotel rooms available for the band to stay anyplace close to Tallahassee. The band had to stay in Georgia for the night, and then drive the rest of the way to Tallahassee for the game. We left our hotel the day of the game Saturday morning and began to drive toward Tallahassee. We stopped and got something to eat. This made us really, late arriving at the stadium. Along the way we kept hearing the commercials on the radio calling this game a classic. They talked about Tennessee State Joe "747" Adams. They had the sound of a jet in the background. Joe Adams was a high school All-American, not only in football, but also basketball. Along with Joe "747" Adams the football team also featured Michael "Instant Offense" Jolley, a transfer from Georgia Tech University. Running back, Ralph Carnahan, was also a high school All-American. There were also many other excellent, excellent players. They also talked about the TSU "Aristocrat of Bands" battling the "Marching Rattlers."

We got to the stadium late. We had to dress and get into our uniforms on the bus.

When we got off the bus, we stood outside the Florida State stadium and played Toccata and Fugue in D Minor. We could see the crowd on the other side of the stadium rise and try to look over the top of the stadium. We caused a great commotion. They probably should have stopped the game because there was so much bedlam. After Toccata and Fugue, the drummers were given the signal to roll off the cadence. We filed into the stadium in "super-long" formation. It was about as impressive and electric a moment that you could ever experience in your life. It is always referred to as the "peak experience." We fell in there and we rocked that place! They really should've stopped the game because we were so awesome. That's not even mentioning halftime. Talking about halftime! We were so geeked and full of energy. To me, it felt like I was marching on air. It didn't even feel like my feet touched the playing field. It was one of those moments that when you experience is hard to describe it to any other person because it was just so magical.

And, to top everything off, this was one of the first times that I had ever seen young Black people (and I mean maybe eight or nine-year-old doing complex tumbling runs, and complex gymnastic routines. I was shocked until someone told me Tallahassee is the home of Ringling Brothers, Barnum & Bailey Circus. These young people obviously have been trained to do these feats. It was so impressive to see these children doing what they were doing. I mean, nothing that you saw in the Olympics overshadows what these young people were capable of. It was no surprise to me to see African American gymnasts in the Olympics because I saw what these young people were doing it in Tallahassee Florida.

Another thing that made that aspect of the Florida trip so meaningful is that I had been working at Opryland USA as a technician in Live Entertainment for; maybe two years at this point, and having done technical theater at Tennessee State University (learning from the legendary W. Dury Cox) I was very technically aware. When I went to see Ringling Brothers circus, riggers who handled set up the trapeze and other high-wire equipment were all black. I was tremendously impressed. Again, by working at Opryland I knew how complex and difficult this work happens to be. I know the amount of expertise required to execute these knots so that the performers could safely use the equipment. Again, it blew my mind, and I knew that Ringling Brothers, being based out of Tallahassee, the number of Black riggers who had received this training and had these skills just blew my mind. People would not believe that African Americans could be riggers at this level, but they were.

The last game that was impressive to me was the last year that I was in the band. The year is 1979. This was the trip that we took to Southern University, in Baton Rouge Louisiana. We had been told about Southern's band, the "Human Jukebox". Professor Tommy Davis's father was the brass instructor at Southern. We were told that we had seen marching bands, but we had not seen a bed like this one that we would encounter at Southern in Baton Rouge, Louisiana. I will have to say that this band was, member for member, the best band that the" Aristocrat of Bands" would encounter. They were impressive. They were a brass heavy band. I remember this was the year the movie Star Wars came out. Our band put together a symphonic version of the theme to Star Wars. When we got into the stadium, we wanted to be the first band to play the symphonic version of the Star Wars theme. We did, but after we finished Southern 's band "saddled up" and played their symphonic version of the theme from Star Wars. The sound came across the field. It was like being hit with bricks! In that moment I knew that we were in for a "dog fight". We had been told, but you don't know until you have the experience what someone is really talking about. Now, we had been experienced. I think all members of the "Aristocrat of Bands" got an attitude check. We knew that we had better be on our "A-plus-plus-plus" game. We again entered one of those magical moments at half time. We performed, then they performed. It was a stalemate. Afterwards we understood what prof had been talking about. We were highly complementary of their band. Their band members and directors were highly complementary of our band, and the performance that we came and gave. Given the excellence of Southern's band, I think that was one of the biggest compliments the "Aristocrat of Bands" has ever received. What made their complement even more awesome is because we had gone against bands like Jackson State, Alabama A&M, Texas Southern, Florida A&M, North Carolina A & T, and other HBCU bands. But Southern the band from Baton Rouge Louisiana; "The Human Juke Box", was in my opinion, by far the finest band that the Tennessee State University band had ever encountered.

Another memorable is the time that the "Aristocrat of Bands" had the opportunity to play behind Al Green during one of our halftime performances. Before becoming a reverend, Al Green had an angry encounter with one of his wives. It was said that he had had some hot grits thrown on him by this wife. When we were told that Al Green was coming, and he would be singing one of his great songs at halftime. We were admonished that no one had better mention that incident. No one mentioned the occurrence. We did a great job at half time. Again, it's one of those moments where you get to perform with such a huge star like Al Green. The level of appreciation that you have, not only for Mr. Green, but also the level of appreciation that you have for being in the band goes through the roof.

IT NEVER RAINS ON THE BAND

Another memorable moment being a member of the "Aristocrat of Bands" (and, I hasten to mention these were pretty extraordinary experiences to have when you are eighteen to twenty-one years of age) is one of the times we were playing Southern Illinois University, the Saluki's. The game was already pretty horrible because both teams hated each other. There was just one big fight after the other. They couldn't even get off a play without there being a fight; without there being penalties; without players getting ejected. In fact, when they tried to resume the game after halftime it was so bad that the referees ended the game. Both teams were made to forfeit. Before this happened, the band saddled up to take to the field at halftime. As I looked up from our seats in the stadium I looked back across the Cumberland River into Bordeaux. I could see the rain coming. There was just no doubt that it was on the move, and several of us tried to point this out to the drum majors and our band directors. They all said "No. It does not rain on the band. Okay. So, with that, we took to our position in the endzone prior to halftime. I was still looking over my shoulder toward the river. I can see this cloud, and curtains of rain coming our way with pace. As the clock ran down toward halftime we lined up. The drum majors called us to attention. When we responded to the whistle with our infamous T.S.U.!!! we get pelted by raindrops the size of quarters. It wasn't warm rain. It was a cold rain. I think that is one of the only times I can remember that we were expressly told to disband and get off the football field, and out of those uniforms. It was one of those crazy, crazy moments. But there were a lot of crazy moments with the "Aristocrat of Bands." but there were so many more great moments with the "Aristocrat of Bands."

THE BENGAL'S GAME

With the band I had the pleasure of being able to travel to Cincinnati Ohio. The band was invited by the NFL and the Cincinnati Bengals to perform at halftime. When we got to the stadium in Cincinnati you see that part of the stadium is open to the Ohio river. There was a breeze that came off the river. I think it was already a zero-degree air temperature. With the breeze coming off the river it was way below zero. That was the coldest I believe I have ever been. It was so cold I could barely get my lips to vibrate and properly engage my mouthpiece. There seemed to be about two inches of solid ice on the field. They had a contraption that look like a Zamboni on one end and a flamethrower on the other end. Prior to the game this machine would go up and down the field. it would melt the ice and then the rear end would vacuum up the water that was left behind. The Zamboni ran non-stop until the start of the game until it cleared the field of ice. Can you imagine a receiver falling on carpet stretched out over concrete? I'm talking about thin carpet, not shag, plush carpet, but thin carpet stretched out over concrete. They called it Astroturf. It was said that Astroturf helped to increase the speed of the game of the fastest players and made offensive play more exciting. Many players were probably injured because of playing on that type of surface.

Performing for the Bengals and the N.F.L. gave me the opportunity to see star players (now legends) up close and personal. Pre-game, the band stood on the field to play the National Anthem. As the team players were introduced and they ran down between the lines that the band had formed. I got to see players like Darryl Stingley and Steve Grogan for the Boston Patriots. Darryl Stingley, about two weeks later, on Monday Night Football would be injured. Stingley would be paralyzed while playing in a game against the Oakland Raiders. I got to see Darrell Stingley up close and personal. I also saw the only two-time Heisman Trophy winner, Archie Griffith. It was quite an experience. Again, an experience that very, very few young people could say that they had. There is a video of the "Aristocrat of Bands" at halftime of this performance that circulates around YouTube. What great memories, and to be one of the few- very few, college bands to be asked to perform at the halftime of an NFL game – and the "Aristocrat of Bands" has performed at several! We were Tennessee's official band to meet Jimmy Carter at the Nashville airport in 1976 during his campaign for the presidency of the United States. Jimmy Carter did win that year. Very, very, very, very few bands and very few young people can ever claim to have these types of experiences. I was able because I was a member of the celebrated Tennessee State University "Aristocrat of Bands."

THE NIGHT OF THE CORONATION

I had a lot of experiences as an undergraduate at Tennessee State University. I took trips to many HBCU campuses (often taking over their campuses with the other band members. I had the opportunity to travel to numerous theatre competitions and events. I had the opportunity to see many of the premier recording artist of the time because of my affiliation with the campus radio station,

WTSU. There is, however, one event that sticks out in my mind and actually kind of haunts me to this day.

Chandra Norman won the election to be the latest Miss T.S.U. It was coronation night. I went by Wilson Hall to pick up Sandra Baxter. Sandra was set to perform a poem at the coronation. I got to the dorm, met Sandra in the lobby, then escorted her to my car (my pride and joy first Z car). I opened the door to let Sandra into the car. I had noticed a couple on the lawn in front of the dorm who appeared to be in conversation. I did not give them much mind at first, but as I was about to close the car door, I noticed the male had grabbed the young lady by her throat, and had picked her up in the air. At the time, I kept a loaded .38 Special with a two-inch barrel in the glove box of the car. I told Sandra to stay put as I got my pistol. I walked over to the couple. By now, the male (and let me say, he was a giant. I'd put money on it that he was lineman of the Big Blue football team) had the young lady (she was the size of Olive Oil – go to Popeye for that reference) on the ground and was choking her. I walked over to the scene. I told the male to let go of the female and let her up. Without looking up, the behemoth told me "I'll reach up and pull you down here and do the same to you." I told him "You'd better look up first before you go to grabbing." I had my .38 pointed straight at his head. There was no way I going to let that giant get his hands on me. I saw him relax his grip on the young lady's throat. He allowed he to get up. I told her she needed to go back to her room in the dorm. I told him he needed to disappear. Both went their separate ways. Sandra and I proceeded on to the coronation, and she gave a stellar performance (as Sandra Baxter ALWAYS did). This next part kind of pours salt into the wound. When I got Sandra back to the dorm, we came up on the scene of multiple campus security officers, assisted by Metropolitan Police officers, handcuffing the giant I had encountered and were interviewing the young lady. Apparently, he had come back to the dorm and she had left her room, only to have the scene repeated. I was kind of hot, mostly with her, because I could have gotten myself killed coming to her rescue.

COX'S BOYS HAVE A NIGHT AT ZANIES

One evening, a tight group of my male theatre compadres who we referred to ourselves as "Cox's Boys" decided to go to Zanies on open mic night to heckle the comics. Understand, we were not your regular group of guys going to Zanies to heckle the comic. We were a group of young men trained and experienced in improvisation and ad lib. We were experienced in all manner of theatrical endeavors. On a lark we decided that we could go to Zanies and give the comic hell. We would verbally attack them like a pack of rabid hyenas. We gave the first few comics pure hell. During this time, we consumed a few drinks, and we were all half buzzed. I'm sure the management and other comedians had just about had enough of us. There was a break in the show. Then a new comic was introduced to the stage. The comic they introduced was Judy Tenuta. Judy hit the Zanies floor with an accordion, and being half drunk, it seemed like she was able to swing from the chandeliers. Judy was all over the place with that accordion, and loopier that fifty drunk servicepersons. I looked at my fellow hecklers and let them know if they wanted to engage this crazy woman, they had my blessings. I was going to keep my mouth shut.

After our little sojourn to Zanies, being half drunk, we decided to go by Mr. Cox's house since he didn't live too far from the club. It was probably about ten p.m. We rang Mr. Cox's doorbell. It took a long time before we heard a familiar voice say "Who is it?" We identified ourselves as best we could in our elevated state. Mr. Cox opened the door and allowed us to come in. We could see Mrs. Cox standing behind Mr. Cox, near the kitchen. The Cox's were gracious and kind to a bunch of socially inept young men that evening. Mrs. Cox excused herself to the bedroom and Mr. Cox gave us a tour of as much of the house as would be appropriate for this unannounced visit. We did get to see his dug out "man cave." He showed us his prized liquor bottle collection. I guess Mr. Cox knew we were just a bunch of socially inept young men, who in a misguided way just wanted to show him how much we respected him.

The Cox's Boys who rode that night were: Barry Scott, Washington Dobbins, Lee Summers, Johnny Hollingshed, John Stuart Williams, and Barry Bruce.

TIGERBELLES

I had the distinct honor; and honor that a paltry few people can say they had the same privilege. That privilege was to be able to sit in classrooms and attend other various social activities with some very beautiful young ladies. Although they were physically beautiful, the beauty I refer is the beauty of their personalities. These young ladies were members of the Tennessee State University women's track team, known around the world as the Tigerbelles. To me, these young ladies were literally legends walking the campus. These young ladies were so grounded and friendly. Had you not known of their incredible track and field talents and notoriety, you would have thought they were undergraduates no different than the rest of us. If they did not already have Olympic gold medals and world championships, they soon would. The ones who were in my graduating class included:

Debbie Jones (Bermuda)

Lauri McDonald

Brenda Moorehead

Brenda Fuller

Cathy McMillan

Chandra Cheeseborough (Chandra was actually a couple of years behind me)

When it came to the leaders, the pioneers, the innovators of women's track and field in America, it was the Tennessee State University Tigerbelles. The Tigerbelles went around the world and singlehandedly dominated women's track and field to the point that people could not believe a handful of young ladies from this teeny-tiny school named Tennessee State University. The Tigerbelles literally turn the world of women's track and field upside-down. Literally, there was no other program that could compete with them. The answer for many other young lady track and field competitors was to create "clubs" that allowed individual female track and field athletes to compete together outside of their university or high school settings. It was then, by way of these clubs, that colleges and universities were able to identify and recruit entire teams all at once. The world of female track and field was then able to do what major college football and basketball were able to do: identify, attract, recruit and financially take care of upcoming exceptional world-class female track and field athlete. These strong female track and field programs owe their very existence to the Tennessee State University Tigerbelles.

WILMA RUDOLPH

It was during my college career that I had the distinct honor and privilege to be able to be in the presence, and the company of greatness. I already had the opportunity to be a student "sitting at the feet" of the great William Dury Cox, Jr. It was in his office that other great people seemed to magically appear. It was in the office of Mr. Cox that I got to meet track and field legend, sprinter and Tigerbelle, multiple-gold medal Olympian, record setting athlete, Wilma Rudolph.

My first encounter with Wilma, and this was not any different than any of the other students who could be in Mr. Cox's office at any particular time, is that Ms. Rudolph was sitting on his couch just like any of us. When I walked in, Ms. Rudolph was engaged in conversation. I joined in the conversation right along with them. It was so easy and natural that you really didn't think about it. Then this gracious, kind, wonderful lady said something, then all of a sudden, I asked "Are you Wilma Rudolph?" With no hesitancy she said "yes." But in the same moment she turned right around and said, "I'm just regular. I'm just Wilma." It was the tone of her voice that led you to understand that "regular" was the way she felt about her personage. It was just amazing to have those kinds of conversations with people of accomplishments. There would be other times that Wilma would be in Mr. Cox's office. After my initial meeting with her then I just kind of acted normal and natural, like we were just old friends.

Ms. Wilma Rudolph was an amazing person, and she was like so many other people of high achievement/attainment that I have met. They don't think of themselves as being anything special, or being so unapproachable that you are not able to speak to them. They are very approachable (within reason), you just have to make sure you are not wasting their time. Throughout my book, when you read about people like Randy Savage, Dobie Gray, Dale Ernhardt, and some of the other celebrities that I've had the opportunity to come into contact with, they all seem to share that one very genuine quality of approachability. The exceptions are far, few and in between. I just wanted to mention that Ms. Wilma Rudolph was a very special person; especially in light of all her achievements. Ms. Wilma Rudolph was greatly appreciated by the students of Tennessee State University.

THE POWER OF ALPHA PHI ALPHA FRATERNITY, INCORPORATED / The power of Beta Omicron at Tennessee State University

I had a most interesting journey in the land of A-Phi-A. I was working as a technician in Live Entertainment at Opryland U.S.A. As things would go, I met and became friends with Tommy "Reb" Holston. "Reb" and I would see each other at the employee uniform location. We just kind of started having non-specific conversations. Then, after we both learned of our camaraderie as Tennessee State University undergraduates, "Reb" asked if I had given consideration to pledging any fraternity. I told him I had never really given much thought because I was so involved with my theatre pursuits and the Aristocrat of

Bands. "Reb" went on to say that Alpha Phi Alpha always had it's eyes open for upwardly mobile, success-oriented, career-minded brothers. "Reb" thought that I made a good fit. It is interesting to note, at this point, that attending Pleasant Green Missionary Baptist Church all the men I knew at the church who had fraternal ties were men of Alpha Phi Alpha Fraternity, Incorporated. After I became an Alpha, I learned that some men at church were Omegas, Kappas or Sigma's.

The year was 1977. Along with "Reb" Holston, I soon found myself being recruited by multiple members of Alpha Phi Alpha Fraternity, Incorporated. I submitted my letter of interest to the Beta Omicron undergraduate chapter (the same chapter that my uncle, Scott Saunders pledged), attended the 1977 Interest Club meeting, was interviewed, then selected to be a probate on the 1977 pledge line. I entered the initiation process. I was on line with Charles Govan, Tony Lyons, Herb (and others to be named) Tommy "Reb" Holston was the Dean of Pledgees. I had been on line pledging for about three weeks About three into the pledging process, "Reb", Edison Mosley, and chapter president Hoskins came to me and said there was a problem with my credit hours. They had discovered (as I already knew) that I had failed math. That failure left me one credit hour short of what was required to pledge. They told me to hang with the pledging because Dr. Humphries, Dr. Atchison, and Dr. George Cox, and State Alpha Chairman, Zenoch Adams were working to get this issue resolved. I hung with the pledging. About a week later, the undergraduate leaders came to me again, and gave me the sad news; I would not be allowed to continue the pledging process (I call it the pledging process, because there was no such thing as an "intake" process at this time). Bummer man! Not that pledging Beta Omicron had been a day at the beach, it still sucked that I had to watch the guys I had built relationships with go on and cross "the burning sands" without me. I had to watch them perform in the November 1977 Greek show without me. It was then and there that I said, "Oh well, that was an 'almost!'"

Well, I congratulated the guys on their accomplishment. In my own mind I thought perhaps if I were to pursue pledging Alpha again, it would be grad chapter.

The year was now 1978. I had accrued enough credits to pledge. The brothers approached me again about pledging. I told them, that now as a junior, my mindset was focused on my theatre and radio endeavors. Pledging would happen at some time in the future; just not now. I had been told by the prospective pledges of the 1978 line that the brothers of Beta Omicron told them that if they did not get me on that line, none of them may as well cancel their dreams of becoming

Alpha's through Beta Omicron. They asked, and they asked, and they asked. My answer was always the same. "No." I guess the brothers would not take "no" for an answer. A great move on their part…the brothers went to Mr. W. Dury Cox, Jr. They begged Mr. Dury Cox, Jr. to get me to pledge. Mr. Cox called me into his office one day. He told me that Beta Omicron was "chomping at the bit" to have me on the 1978 line. Mr. Cox told me that he informed them that he would try to intervene on their behalf on one condition: Any time I told them I had a theatre project I was to be excused from pledge meetings; but the decision lay with me. It was through the influence of Mr. W. Dury Cox, Jr. that I consented to the pledging process, and that I am an Alpha today.

I pledged Alpha Phi Alpha Fraternity, Inc. Beta Omicron chapter in 1978. I still have my original membership card and shingle. The line name was "Mystic Eight". My line name was "Invisible", because I could always find ways to "fade" when I did not want to be found. As pledges of various Greek letter organizations moved about the campus, in those days, we had certain protocols:

1. We had to cut corners every time we turned.
2. We were not to speak to members of the opposite sex.
3. We were not to consume foods with sugar content.
4. We were not to respond to people who spoke to us, unless they were a member of the organization we were pledging.

I must say, I broke all these rules every chance I got. That was part of the game, also. Two other things that played into this process was that I had two brothers on the campus who looked like me. The brothers found themselves in embarrassing positions more than once when they mistakenly stopped Carl or Ken. They got an earful about not stopping my brothers. It became so bad (good for me) that when the brothers saw me on campus, they stopped approaching me. I could see them looking from afar, but they would not approach me. Another by-product was that members of Kappa Alpha Psi Fraternity, Incorporated would stop me; thinking I was pledging their organization. I also learned early on, that if you wanted to get any rest, you'd better find places and times to "fade". I had a key to the green room backstage. There were several divans in the green room. I could turn out the lights and get a good nod. The other "fading" location was the WTSU radio station record library. I can tell you, during my pledging period these two locations saw a lot of me.

It was Friday night of Hell Week, AND Homecoming weekend. This night, the brothers had us pledgees drink an excessive amount of vodka. This was an all-night adventure. I had to get up early the next morning and perform with the band for the Homecoming parade, and the game that followed. I was still fairly inebriated by the time of the parade, but I guess I was able to march in a straight line without passing out. When the game started, and the time came for the half-time performance, I was dog-tired! The band took to the field. I was okay until we reached the dance routine. I've already said that I was dance/rhythmically challenged. I did wake up in the middle of turning the wrong way, and almost falling down. What a way to tell yourself "Wake your sorry ass up!"

It may have been November 16 of 1978. All the pledgees of the Greek organizations performed in what we called a "Greek" show. All the Black Greek organizations performed popular music selections of the day. I was drafted to lead Gino Vannelli's hit "I Just Wanna Stop". I tore it up! I had the ladies screaming and throwing the panties! Yeah! I had the men cheering (no drawers, though...thank you!)! We hopped. Yes, I could stomp with the best!

The next night they ushered us out blind-folded behind the original library building. There was a huge bonfire. Most Greek letter organizations had done the same thing. At this point we were ceremoniously tapped in and given our first fraternity tee shirt. It was a moment of supreme accomplishment. I was proud of myself, my "sands", and the entire Alpha-Phi-Alpha Fraternity, Incorporated.

William Dury Cox, Jr.
Willis McAllister
Landry Burgess
Inman Otey
Kenneth McKay
John Tisdale
Scott Saunders

ANOTHER EXAMPLE OF THE POWER OF ALPHA PHI ALPHA FRATERNITY, INCORPORATED

An example of the power of Alpha Phi Alpha is a time that I was working at Fisk University. My first son Washington, third was born. Right after his birth I went to Mrs. Edwards, who was the H.R. / Benefit person at Fisk to have him added to my insurance policy. Mrs. Edwards was an older lady, and somehow, she missed turning in the paperwork to include Tres' on my insurance policy. It happened to coincide that Dr. Bobby Lovett, who was the Dean of Arts and Sciences at Tennessee State University reached out to me in regard to coming and teaching at Tennessee State University. I had taught there before and I told Dr. Lovett that it seemed like a conflict of interest for me to be teaching full time at Tennessee State

University and at Fisk University, but Dr. Lovett assured me that professors did this all the time. Dr. Lovett said between Fisk University and Tennessee State there had never been a problem with this type of activity. So, I had to make some choices. My son Tres', we were told at his birth would have to have surgery when he turned about eighteen months. The insurance company deemed his condition to be preexisting and would not add him to the policy. I knew the operation had to be paid for some way. The only logical thing for me to do, it seemed, would be to start teaching at both universities. Later, it came to the notice of the provost of Fisk University that I was employed full time at both universities. This was something he did not like, and he immediately made a move to get me fired from Fisk University. Fisk president, Henry Ponder (who would later become the general president of Alpha Phi Alpha Fraternity, Incorporated) was the president of Fisk University. Dr. Ponder, along with noted historian Dr. Reavis Mitchell, Dr. George Neeley, Spanish and Foreign Languages professor Marcellus Brooks, the chief financial officer were all members of Alpha Phi Alpha Fraternity, Incorporated. The provost went to Doctor Ponder and immediately requested that I be fired from Fisk University. Doctor Ponder already knew that I was teaching at both Fisk and Tennessee State University. Dr. Ponder knew the circumstances that led to me having to teach at both schools. Dr. Ponder probably appreciated the fact that my first instinct was not to bring a negligence lawsuit against Fisk University because of Mrs. Edwards mistake. Dr. Ponder also knew that I was an Alpha. Dr. Ponder listened to the provost, but I know he was not about to fire me. Instead, Dr. Ponder called me and the provost into his office. Dr. Ponder asked me, in front of the provost, about my motivation for taking a full-time teaching assignment at Tennessee State University. I explained to him that Mrs. Edwards, for whatever reason, had neglected to put my son on my insurance policy there at the University when he was born. That was the only reason. I needed the money. That being said, Dr. Ponder turned to the provost and said "Mr. Dobbins knows what he has to do. He knows why he is teaching at both places. Mr. Dobbins will know when it is time for him to stop teaching at Tennessee State University." That's the way the meeting ended. The provost was madder than "a wet hen", but brother Ponder had spoken.

I also had the distinct pleasure to have served under the leadership of another great Alpha man, President Frederick Humphreys, who was president of Tennessee state University when I was first hired to teach there. Later president Humphries would become president of Florida A and M University, in Tallahassee, Florida.

***I know all of this sounds crazy to have gone through all this, but I would not change a thing.

THE IMPACT OF ROOTS

The year was 1977. The reason I recall the year so vividly is because this is the year that the miniseries ROOTS appeared on television. I think it was on ABC (if I'm not mistaken.)

The book had been out and available for several years. In high school many of us were either required to, or we had read the book ROOTS. ROOTS was written by my great fraternity brother, Alex Haley. Let me say this now, because I'm going to squelch right here at the beginning the fact that Alex Haley was accused of, and sued for plagiarism. I believe it was found that he used materials found in the sources he used to research ROOTS without providing attribution. The sections of the book ROOTS, which specifically corresponded to the historical information side, came from other books, including the highly regarded writer/anthropologist Zora Neale Hurston's book Barracoon: The Story of the Last "Black Cargo.", which is the story of the last group of African slaves bought to this country in Mobile, Alabama aboard the boat Clotilda.
But having said that, Alex Haley acknowledged that he had put in nine years of research, and additional three years to write a book that became known as ROOTS. ROOTS is still in my opinion, phenomenal. It should still be REQUIRED reading in schools. You could not make up the adventure of Alex Haley in pursuing the origins of ROOTS if you tried.

Many of my high school classmates; and I now many of my college classmates, had read the book ROOTS. We knew the contents of the book, but the mini-series was far more impactful than the book itself. The reason for this is that this was the first time that we had seen the treatment of slaves on a plantation. It was the first time we saw slaves get beat. The first time that we had seen something like Kunta Kinte having his foot chopped off with an ax. ROOTS was the first time that we had seen slaves captured and taken from Africa in the way that it occurred. Allow me to interject, a lot of people will say "oh, you know Africans assisted with the capturing of their own people." and all of kinds of things of this nature. Well, okay! That's all well and good. It was part of the slave trade, and it was by design. There is a nuance. Most African nations were like most "First Peoples" North American soil nations. I do mean Native American nations overtook other tribes; they overtook other nations. People/tribes/nations that had been conquered were assimilated into the new nation, tribe, or culture in very quick fashion. I'm not going to say that the history of events was all soon forgotten, but pretty soon they were members of one tribe or one nation. They were no longer slaves. Such was the same this same type of conquering of other tribe/nations occurred in Africa. So, I'm just gonna put all this on the table to quell anybody who would like to come back at me about that.

However, the power of ROOTS is that, even after graduation from high school, it led me and many of my white friends to get back into contact, and discuss all of the things that we never knew. It caused us to talk about things because that this was the first time, we had ever had visual imagery that anything like this had ever occurred. Let me tell you, also, that by today's standards, ROOTS is considered mild. The book and movie Twelve Years a Slave provides more visual imagery of the harsh conditions of slavery in the deep south. The play, A Woman Called Truth is also very insightful. There have been other writings and works of art that have come into existence since ROOTS. These offerings have been far more graphic and far more visually stunning and revealing than ROOTS in the actual, truthful horrors of slavery.

I bring up these things because there are things that I see going on in society today. There are levels of racism and hatred that exist today that have no reason to exist. Apparently, there are family lines and ethnic groups that have kept certain ideals and practices going. Everyone is SO selective about how we teach history, and how we teach particular portions of history. We really don't want to teach history the way history happened because we might upset someone. It's a double-edged sword: when you don't teach, somebody will make stuff up. It's like the book, Animal Farm, by George Orwell. When the pigs gained control of the farm they controlled information the over generations, they could tell the historical story of the way things happened on the farm any way they wanted because they documented it the way they wanted it to be documented. It was the way THEY wanted it to be told. That's the danger that I've seen. Why in the world do we still have groups of people that praise Hitler? Why do we still have groups that hate Jews and other races and ethnicities? We should teach history, but we shouldn't change history. We should not turn from the ruthlessness of Hitler and the Nazi regime. It is the same way in America. We try to "soft-pedal" slavery. We try to even act like slavery didn't happen. We want to use terms like "long-term indentured servitude" to describe the nature of slavery. We want to say that slavery wasn't as bad as we have made it out to be. We don't want generations coming along to know that even in very recent times there have been the hanging of Black. We don't want to be taught about Billie Holiday's "Strange Fruit". I might would a different perspective if we actually learned valuable lessons from going through that dark period of American history; but we haven't. When we don't know we can be told anything. That's one of the dangers of having governors like Santos, in Florida. They want the freedom to say that courses like African-American studies are not valid. The fact is Africans had great civilizations and kingdoms, even before the Europeans. To want the luxury to teach that these captured/kidnapped Africans were just wild heathens is totally incorrect. There were great civilizations of Mali, Timbuktu, Ashanti, Benin, Egypt, Morocco. All these civilizations existed on the continent of Africa, but the story the powers-that-be wants to be told is that these were just heathens and savages who were totally uncivilized. They just walked around the desert naked. Thank God that Americans of European decent (who, but the way, were escaping tyranny and abuse themselves) put Africans into slavery to save them from themselves.

The truth is that the vast majority of Africans were captured because it was a systematic process. The slavers did not care how intelligent, how sophisticated the people were that they were enslaving. There was a process to break them down and then bring them to this culture where they had to learn a new language and a whole new way they would have to exist.

The other disappointing thing is when as a teacher I would encounter young African-Americans, who don't care about education, and would throw education to the wayside for the "common" behaviors they see on television. Behaviors exhibited on some of these "Wive's" shows. Yes, I'm just gonna say the "Wives" shows, The Jersey Shore, The Bachelor, the Bachelorette, and some of those reality shows. Those programs give a distorted perspective of life. They are not normal, everyday ways of life. If you think it's normal, it's only normal because we let the pervasiveness go on over years in an incremental way. The behaviors have only become more outlandish and worse. What these young people know is what they gravitate to on television. It is what their parents and grandparents gravitated (and still do) towards. The behaviors of many young people come right out of these kinds of shows.

But there is hope! Africans, and people of African descent are highly intelligent. I see it now every day at schools like Martin Luther King, Jr. in Nashville. I believe it's the same way at a school like Hume Fogg in Nashville. There are lots of high schools that have pools of intelligent African-Americans students. There are, however, far too many schools where the overwhelming majority of the academic day is built around fighting, social media, and being a social type of influencer within the school. I believe that has been detrimental to a greater level of academic achievement. It lets me know that a lot of those conversations that my friends of various cultures and races had, and the better understandings of each other that we had gained have been totally set back generations.

I also blame our elected public lawmakers, and our church leaders for society's setbacks. Far too many of our leaders in society are basically thieves. They're trying to steal from the public in as many ways as they can without getting caught. by being elected officials or being church or government leaders. These are the examples that (along with some family members who have antisocial types of behaviors) are very disheartening, until you see large groups of students who put their lives and their perspectives on an elevated academic trajectory. My heart is warmed when I see the way that the Black students interact with the white students, the Asian students, the Indian students, the other black students. All these segments interact with each other, and kind of, in a way, warm my heart. We have a chance, but we have a great, great, great opportunity that I still think that we are missing.

THE NIGHT THE ROOM CHANGED COLORS

I thought this would be an appropriate place to bring in the discussion I had with Captain Moore. The whole of the story actually included his wife, Evelyn Moore and both sons: Stan and Randy. Randy was one of my Opryland mates, as I called him. Randy was a "righteous" guitar player. He played in several shows in the Opryland Theme Park. We were all close and had very good relationships. As our fashion modeling careers were winding down, Stan and I continued to work together as Stan begin getting contracts to film music videos. Stan was always kind enough to call me if he needed a versatile performer to create a character (did you like the way I phrased that?) and I was always glad to help out.

One night as we were shooting a video. This night was cold as hell. That night I was playing a pimp in the video, and we actually used my 1972 Buick Electra 225; that thing that they called a "deuce and a quarter." We were between my shots. Captain Moore owned a fleet of motorhomes that he rented out. We were using one of his motorhomes as the green room for cast members to relax between their shots. At one point Captain Moore and I happen to be the only ones in the green room. He and I embarked upon a fairly heavy conversation. I don't know if you've ever had this type of conversation. A conversation where the room literally changes color, everything sounds different, and even the smells are like something new. Literally, that conversation made everything different.

We really begin to get into a discussion about my friendship with Stan, and how that friendship came about. Captain Moore began to tell me a little bit about his life growing up in south Texas. He had never been around Black people. Even during his time in the Air Force, he had very little exposure to African-Americans. He told me his perception of Black people had been one, but that he began to see African-Americans in a different way after Stan and I got to be friends, and after he and I got to be friends.

After that conversation I got to thinking; my dad had the same type of mind-set as Captain Moore. My dad used to question me regarding the white friends I had made. My dad didn't grow up around white people (which, in it's own way is always interesting. A huge segment of my family happened to have been white. My dad grew up being African-American, and that's what he knew, and that's how things went. This was even after he had served in the Navy during the Korean Conflict. He asked, "why do you have so many white friends?" I would try to explain to him as best I could we were just buddies. My dad had always emphasized that we make good, solid friends. I just called myself doing that. I really knew I had friends who were white, Black, Gay - everything, but I really tended to look at them in terms of them being good, solid people. I guess I had that luxury. I always talk about the history of racism and Jim Crow. In fact, many Nashville historians will tell you that Jim Crow originated in Nashville, Tennessee, and that Nashville was the original model for Jim Crow all across the deep south. My dad grew up in Jim Crow. I grew up in Jim Crow in Nashville Tennessee, not really knowing that's what it was. But, looking back at history I now know that is what it was. It was Jim Crow, so I know it had to be worse for my dad. So, in that sense, I believe my dad and Captain Moore share an understanding of history that it would take their children's relationships to begin to unravel.

But anyway, back to Captain Moore. He and I embarked up on a deep conversation about racism, and how different races interacted. At that point, I think I had had those previous conversations with my high school friends regarding ROOTS. That's why I put this conversation behind the ROOTS conversation., and Stan told me his father's reflections of that conversation after his dad died, as Stan and I began to recall things sitting around "jawing" as old friends do. Stan and I talked about certain things after his father 's death, like that night, and how that conversation was life transforming for his father. How his father was always highly complementary of me. His father talked about how there were some things he could have; should have; would have thought differently had he allowed himself to have had a conversation like that one long before. The irony is: With whom and how would he have had that conversation? All I know is that it changed me as well. I can tell you it was profound. It is sad to say that we live in a time, that if entertainment media has done any good thing, it has opened the world to same-sex couples, and same-sex couples leading households. Entertainment media has exposed us to families that consist of multi-ethnic, multi-cultural, multi-racial compositions. We have come a long way, but sadly, there is still a need to have conversations like the one Captain Moore and I had that night.

W LAC RADIO DAYS

Even before I graduated from college, I had to distinct honor of being hired as an intern at one of the most prestigious radio stations in the world. That radio station was Nashville's own WLAC radio. My very first day at WLAC I was not given a key to the radio station. I knew I would not be receiving the key so I was told to tap on the front window and the overnight announcer would let me in. So, my first time at the station I walked up to the front glass as I was instructed and tapped briskly on the glass. No one came to answer the door and I continued to tap for several more minutes. Then I noticed movement in what is or was the FM side of the station, which was a rock radio station. The announcer who came to let me in. His on-air name was "H". I hasten to tell you that will be a couple of more stories about "H" before this section is over. However as soon as "H" let me in I looked to the AM side of the radio station. There, I saw a woman in lingerie straddling the overnight AM announcer. I would assume that they were having vigorous sex. "H" said, "That is "J". "J" was the overnight announcer. "J" had picked up a date at the rock event at Flannigan's. So, that was my first encounter with the overnight announcer; having sex with someone he picked up at the local bar nightclub. As things would turn out "H" was notorious for taking the requests of the drug dealers overnight, and in exchange they would bring him favors in terms of drugs. As things would go, on occasion, when I would go to my locker there might be some contraband drugs. There could be opium, hashish, marijuana, speed, or postage stamps soaked in Blotter acid.

However, let me back up a little bit… The person who hired me as an intern to WLAC radio was news director Paul Randall Dickerson. "PRD", as I would soon come to know and call him, was a very interesting man. He was very astute, very clever, and steeped in the ways of news. I was so young Paul Randall Dickerson referred to me as "Young'un", and that was a good name for me. Soon after I had finished my internship, I got a call from PRD asking me if I would like to come aboard on the news team full time. Of course, I did. It was at that time I was told that they were firing another person or letting them go, which they did right in front of me. Awkward! But even if I had said "no", they would have hired someone else; so, I said "yes". I was given a key to the station, and typically I was there before anyone else. When I arrived one morning I went to the newsroom as I usually do and sorted out the overnight news for the two anchors to come in to start the newscast. I started back to the break room, which was to the rear of the building. When I preceded to open the access door to the breakroom, I heard all manner of confusion; things which did not sound right to me, so I shut the door and went back to the newsroom. About 10 minutes later Paul Randall Dickerson walked into the newsroom. I told Paul Randall Dickerson what I had heard. At that point he reached into his jacket and produced a snub nose thirty-eight pistol. He said that there had been problems with people breaking into the station and stealing things. That is probably what I heard. Paul Randall and I decided to walk back there. Of course, I decided to walk with him under the protection of him and his trusty thirty-eight. When we got there the entire glass panel had been lifted from one of the vending machines, and the content of the vending machine have been totally emptied. PRD told me if I did not carry a pistol, when I heard or saw something that was out of place, I was not to engage it but to call the police immediately.

Paul Randall went on to tell me that he was from Buffalo New York. His father was a gunsmith, and on many occasions made specialty caliber pistols and other guns for mafia figures. The mobsters would want a caliber, or a type of gun that no one else had, that would be totally uniquely theirs. That was the work that his father did.

THE EXPRESSO CONNECTION

Going back to "H. My first experience with expresso happened at the hands of "H". I knew that "H" brewed coffee a special way. He put the grounds into a mesh cloth, poured searing hot water over the grounds and as they soaked down, they produced coffee. "H" said I looked sleepy one day. He asked if I would like him to brew me a fresh cup of coffee. Well, of course I did. "H" preceded to brew a large cup of his specially prepared coffee. Unbeknownst to me, "H" did not actually drink coffee, he drank the beverage expresso. "H" however drank expresso in large quantities, and if you know anything about expresso it is to be sipped in very small amounts. In VERY small amounts. Well, "Young'un" put sugar and cream into this stuff that he thought was coffee. I did notice the thick layer of oil on the top of the cup. No matter how much sugar, no matter how much cream I stirred in, "this" "coffee" never acquired that mocha coloring. I did drink the entire cup. About thirty minutes later it felt like my entire world was caving in on me. I began to perspire profusely, I thought that I was going to throw up, and have diarrhea at the same time. I actually turned green. Paul Randall Dickerson looked over and saw me in my distress. He said "Young-un" what is wrong with you?" I said "I don't know. I just don't feel good." He said, "well, what did you eat? What did you drink? "I told him the only thing I had was the cup of coffee that I had gotten from "H". PRD said, (with great enthusiasm) "H" doesn't drink coffee, he drinks expresso!" "Expresso!" I said! I knew I had been drugged! What kind of drug is that? Am I going to die?" You won't die, but you are supposed to only drink a small cup of expresso at a time." "It is like supercharged coffee." I learned a very valuable lesson that day. It would be a long time before I took another sip of the expresso.

During my tour of duty at W LAC radio I got to work with two of the great legends and pioneers of radio. When I went to Tennessee State University, I got to know Mr. Don Whitehead. Mr. Whitehead was a friend to two of my mentors and men that I respected highly: Mr. Danny Owens and Mr. Dury Cox. Don Whitehead was one of the members of a fabled broadcast team at WLAC radio: John Richburg, Gene Nobles and Hoss Allen. Don Whitehead was the only black member of the team. In fact, it was a misnomer about their racial identities. Hoss Allen, John Richburg and Gene Nobles were all thought to be black men. They were, in fact, white. Don Whitehead, even by his very name, was thought to be a white man, even though he was the Black member of the team. Don Whitehead did news and the other three men were the primary announcers at WLAC. I say I had the good fortune also of working directly with Mr. Hoss Allen. Bill, or William Hoss Allen was just affectionally known as the "Hoss Man". If you go back and study the history of radio in the United States, as well as the history of R and B- "Rhythm and Blues" and read broadcasting in the United States and influences for the Rock and Roll Hall of Fame, W LAC radio will appear. When I met Hoss Allen, I really did not know the significance of his contribution to radio and to rhythm and blues radio history of Nashville Tennessee, and to broadcast. Hoss Allen was more than approachable. Iin fact, Hoss Allen would approach you. The first time that I met Hoss Allen I was an intern at W LAC radio. Hoss came to me and he told me that anything I needed... anything. Anything I wanted to know about professional broadcasting. Anything. If I wanted to sit in with him in his recording sessions in the studio, I was welcome. If I wanted to know anything about writing commercial copy, the news business, I could always come to him because he always had an open door. I really did not know at the beginning the greatness that I was in the presence of. It took a while to really find out because Hoss Allen never acted as if he were some great guy to be worshipped and adored. He just always was regular.

We used to play the Hoss Allen overnight show on reel-to-reel tape players (Studer-Revox 12" reel to reel tapes). Hoss would record his shows and leave them in the studio for the overnight engineer. We would play the shows. Between me, my brother Ken, my brother Joel, and my brother Barry Scott, we played those Hoss Allen tape overnight; usually while doing homework or some other kind of work to keep ourselves alert and awake.

One morning when I went in to work at 3:00 a.m. to start the morning news. I entered the radio station and as I walked through the offices, I noticed that every phone line in the radio station was lit up. I didn't think much of it at the time because there had been a storm overnight, and I just figured this was just some sort of electrical "Tom Foolery" due to the storm. However, as I got to the news studio-which was connected to the engineering room- I opened the door, and as I stepped in and I said to Barry Scott, "What is going on? Did you know the phone line have gone crazy?" Scotty said "no" he said Hoss Allen is on the air with James Brown. At that point I paid attention and looked into the talk studio. I looked into the talk studio, and the lights were on. I always came in at that time of the morning. The lights of the talk studio were never on. Barry Scott said the lights were on because Hoss Allen was live on the air. I thought that was strange because I knew Hoss Allen was never there at 3:00 am. Scott said Hoss is interviewing James Brown. But what was even more strange than Hoss Allen being in the studio was that James Brown was actually in the studio. I said to Barry, "Where is James Brown?" Scott said, "he's right over there." I looked into the dimness on the opposite side of the table from Hoss Allen. In the corner and there sat the legendary James Brown - in person – live, in living person. People were calling in from all over the United States. They were calling in from Texas. They were calling in from Florida, from North Carolina, from nearly every state. I believe that's because listeners told relatives in other States. You really couldn't hear the station in some of the locations we were receiving calls from. I believe they told relatives James Brown was on the air live on 1510am, W LAC radio, and here is the phone number. That shows you the power of three things: 1) The power, the prestige, and the importance of W LAC radio. 2) The power of Hoss Allen's ability to command an audience, and 3) the popularity of a legend like James Brown…that people found out that he was live on the air, and that they can call in and talk to James Brown-even at 3 o'clock in the morning. Listeners (fans of both the station and Mr. Brown) were inclined to wake up out of the middle of their deep sleep to have the have a chance to have a word on the air with James Brown.

As things would go James Brown had to go to the restroom. I took a chance, and I ran out of the newsroom. I ran into Mr. Brown in the hallway, and of course I said "Mr. Brown, Mr. Brown I'm one of your biggest fans. I just want to say I have appreciated everything that you done. All the music that you have made." There, in the dimness of the hallway James Brown uttered something to me; and I know he uttered it to me because he was looking directly at me and I have no idea what he said. I may have been cussed out by James Brown because I slowed him down from going to the restroom when he had an urgent need. I don't know.

I remember when I was a fledgling professor at Tennessee State University. Having been employed at WLAC radio, I asked the legendary Hoss Allen if he would come to speak to a broadcasting class at Tennessee State University. He graciously said that he was willing to speak to these young people. What an opportunity it was for them to be in the same room with, and able to openly engage a living legend. Hoss was gracious, he was kind. Hoss spent time interacting, talking with the students, regaling them with stories from his experience as a record producer and radio pioneer. One of the most fascinating stories Hoss shared (I know it was very personal for me because I had met and become a huge fan of the late Jimi Hendrix) was how a great young guitarist had been recommended to him to play guitar on a blues session he was recording. They brought the player in. They told him that this was a "Delta" blues recording. They wanted to know if he was familiar with the guitar work they needed for the session. Hendrix told them he was able to play the style. Well, as Hoss tells it; the session started. Jimi proceeded to play some psychedelic "licks". Hoss said they stopped the session and explained again to Jimi what they needed. They rolled the tape again, and instead of "Delta" blues licks Jimi played the same sort of psychedelic material. Stopping the session, a second time, they fired Jimi off the session. Hoss remarked to the gathering of students "I had the dubious distinction of firing Jimi Hendrix off a gig." I believe that the late doctor Donald Page recorded that presentation. I know that he recorded that that moment in time. Somewhere there does exist a recording of the legendary William Hoss Allen talking to a classroom overflowing with students at Tennessee State University.

The other incident that I will always remember Hoss Allen for is when Barry Scott and I started our own theater company, the Black-Tie Theater Company. When many other art groups were starting up as not-for-profit, Barry and I chose a different path. We decided that we would start a for-profit black theater company in Nashville Tennessee. Part of the issue we understood was that no other theater company; except perhaps, Karamu House in Cleveland Ohio and The Negro Ensemble Company in New York City for doing Black plays or plays written by

Black playwrights, with black casts with black characters. Barry and I were determined that we were going to give Nashville this specific art form. In the process of building our company we sought the advice of the legendary Hoss Allen. Hoss was always willing to give advice, so we asked him if he would sit with us and allow us to pick his business brain. We wanted to know what his advice would be. We knew Hoss Allen would meet with us. We set up an agreed date and time to meet at an old Charlie's restaurant. Barry Scott, William Hoss Allen, and I sat and talked for about two hours. We ate a little he talked a lot, and when it was time to end our meeting Barry and I both pulled out our credit cards simultaneously. Hoss Allen, without missing a bit said, "Ya'll put your credit cards away. Your money is no good in this establishment. It took me a moment to realize what he was saying because, I thought we had insulted him. Hoss, in that ultra-smooth bass voice of his smoothly said "I am the voice of Charley's. I have open tab with O Charley's. You don't spend any money anytime you are with me." It was just another moment that revealed the graciousness- the goodness, and kindness of William Hoss Allen. This event reminded me that I lived in a special day and time.

BERNARD "SPIDER" HARRISON

Another highlight of my years of working at WLAC radio was that I would have the privilege of working with and getting to know legendary Bernard "Spider" Harrison. "Spider" "Spy" Harrison was a super cool guy. He was a superstar in his own right. His show was syndicated, and he was known coast to coast as "Spider", or the "Spy Who Loved Me" or any of the assorted names he was known by in the hey-day of W LAC am radio. "Spider" was the connection from the legendary R and B powerhouse radio station to the new R and B sound of the radio station. When WLAC-AM eventually become a talk radio station Bernard Harrison was able to keep his rhythm and blues show. As a child I was a big listener to, and follower of Bernard "Spider" Harrison. What blew my mind was when I was fifteen years of age, I took a trip to the Bahamas. I was in a taxicab going to the hotel and the driver had on the radio. This was at night. His radio was tuned to WLAC Radio in Nashville, Tennessee. The host of the show on the air was "Spider Harrison. It totally blew my mind because it sounded as of if I were in Nashville Tennessee and standing next to the transmitter of the station. It just blew my mind because the station came in so clearly, and here I was listening to Bernard "Spider" Harrison at W LAC in Nashville Tennessee (my hometown, and the place that I had just left.)

EDDIE PARKER

Another legend (and tremendous guy) I met along the way during my tour of duty at W LAC radio was the legendary news reporter Eddie Parker. I want to say up front, Eddie and I hasten to give homage to his counterpart at WSM radio. Her name was Drew Smith. Together, they were a pair; and I mean they got the "straight skinny" on the news. They were beat reporters. They will old school radio news reporters, and they were true "characters." I use the term "character" in terms of their personalities, and I would not have given you a million dollars to have had the experiences that I was able to have with them; especially Eddie Parker. Eddie Parker was from East Tennessee; up in the "buni's", and if you were to push me, I could probably come up with his hometown. He knew everybody-political figures and entertainment figures, you name them and it wasn't that Eddie know them but they knew Eddie Parker. And I guess the most impressive thing about Eddie Parker was his relationship with the late Chet Atkins. I believe they grew up together and had been long time friends. It was nothing for Eddie Parker bring Chet Atkins to the radio station to be on a talk show, or just for an interview. Chet Atkins is arguably one of the greatest guitar players ever. Many excellent guitar players: like Vince Gill, Steve Wariner were bestowed one the greatest honors any guitar player could receive – that was to be designated "Guitar Player" by Mr. Chet Atkins. I remember as a young news person a morning news writer producer they called me "Young'un." Edie Parker right there with them. It happened one morning that I was driving him to work at 3:00 a.m. to do my usual news production writing. Let me say, you see all manner of illegal activity going on at 3:00 a.m. as you're driving in to work. On my way in to work this morning I was pulled over, and I got a speeding ticket. I didn't think that I was speeding but I didn't dare argue with the officer either. I took the ticket and went on my way to the station. A couple of days later I went to the courthouse to pay my ticket. When I got to the courthouse, I stood in line to pay the cashier, and get this behind me. As I was standing there, I heard someone say "Young'un", what are you standing in this line for? I recognized Eddie's familiar voice (Eddie reminded me of Darren McGavan's Kolskack's character). I told Eddie what happened. Eddie's response was "Hell no! You work for WLAC radio; you don't pay any tickets in this city." Eddie pulled me out of the line. We walked back to the back, past the cashier, in into the judge's secretary's office. Eddie asked if the judge was in his office. She told him the judge was in. Eddie walked, with me in tow, directly into the judge's chamber unannounced. Eddie handed the judge the ticket. Eddie said "I want this ticket torn up. This man is a news reporter for WLAC radio. I know he wasn't speeding, and I want this ticket torn up." The judge called out to his secretary to find the hard copy of the ticket and bring it to him. The secretary was dutiful. In short order she brought him the hard copy version of the ticket. The judge surveyed the ticket for a moment. Then he said, "This ticket says the driver was going fifty in a thirty mile-per-hour zone." Eddie said "I know this man; and this man works with me. I know he wasn't speeding." With that, Eddie took the ticket from the judge and tore it up. He said, "Let's go Young'un." We left the judge's chamber, and Eddie began to chastise me. He said, "As long as you work for WLAC radio and know me, you never pay a ticket." That was that.

HARLOTS AND PUSSY WILLOWS / LYNETTE EASLEY

Eddie Parker, as I have said, was a "character". He put women into two categories: "Harlots" and "Pussy-Willows". "Harlots" were who Eddie perceived as loose, fast, women. "Pussy-Willows were "do-gooders" who would never get into any kind of trouble. The Pussy-Willows" followed the rules. Lynette Easley was the news anchor, along with Paul Randall Dickerson. Lynette originated from Paducah, or some other Kentucky city close to Nashville. Lynette was married to WSMV television executive Elmer Alley. Lynette was also a very kind person who took great interest in doing what she could to guide my fledgling career. To Eddie, Lynette Easley was a "Pussy-Willow." One morning Eddie called in as usual to send me a voicer, with sound bites. I took the call on the speaker phone. The first words out of Eddie's mouth was "When I finish sending this I need to speak to the "Pussy-Willow." Without missing a beat, Lynette calmly...almost nonchalantly said "I'm sitting right here Eddie. What do you need?" I had never heard Eddie stumble and bumble so much to try to produce an apology. Lynette said, "It's alright Eddie, I know that's what you call me." No more about that incident was ever spoken.

I LIKE WOMEN

Let me start by saying that my sister, Angela, ran the show. When we had not done enough to show appreciation to our wives, Angela would call or come be, and ask "When was the last time you did something nice for_____? Well, I think you need to go to the jewelry store, the travel agent, or some other luxury for your wife. If you can't figure it out, or you need me to take you, I can." Message was received loud and clear by those of us who had good sense. Angela was also the "go-to" for her friends who needed an escort for some special social event. With me (because someone labeled me the family "Lothario") Angela always had a special set of instructions: I was to return her friend to her home in the condition I picked her up. I wasn't stupid; nor was I about to cross swords with Angela, so, with her friends, I was always on my exemplary behavior.

There were lots of years as a young man, especially during after college and following the college years that I was in many ways unfit to be a human being. I was merely a "ho." A male whore. I loved women; and I guess as it went, women loved me. I would call on a lot of women. I will call it dating. I went through a lot of women, having sex, and I loved every minute of it. I would take young ladies' home sometimes. I will say I dated my fair share of strippers and other types of wild women. I think it was impressive to my dad. Not so impressive to my mother, and definitely not impressive at all to the young lady I was seeing at the time. My dad, in his own sense of perspective would always say "Well he's not dating them to marry them. He was quite right about that. I will say on my behalf; I was honest. I told the young lady's right up front "I aint trying to get married. This is basically sport-fucking. This is just some fun. I told them that to be clear from the beginning. For some of them it worked. For some… I don't know, they fell in love with me. They either didn't get the message, or there was a disconnect some kind of way, and hearts were broken. A lot of feelings got hurt along the way, also.

I like women. I mean; I really, really like women. I could say I like something else but that's not quite as simple as that. I like women I like attractive women, and I like women who have good personalities. I've always liked women, but when I got to college I had a larger range, or supply of women that I could interact with. My first little girlfriend in college was very nice. She was very sweet and innocent. We even talked about getting married.

So, as things would go, we became very close, and then we became intimate. It was really good. She was sweet. She was attentive, and she was devoted, but as I say, there was a larger pool of women to become involved with, and it seemed that I wanted to take advantage of that particular situation.

I guess it was a good thing I really did not know how good looking I was, or else I would have been infinitely worse than I was, but there was many a young lady out there who was really cute…who was really nice, and whether I could talk them into making themselves available to be with me or they made themselves available, I would be available. I'm not sure, but throughout the course of my college matriculation there were many young ladies who I found myself in sexual entanglements. I suppose I was very unapologetic.

THE MALE MODEL TAKES ADVANTAGE OF THE SITUATION

Another part of my life that came into being was that of being a model. Eventually, it got to the place where I was always around very attractive young ladies. Getting to know the young ladies sexually was just right up my alley. I was so dastardly I wasn't even up to the level of whore. I was so bad I was just a "ho". I could only be two letters because that was all I deserved to be. I never lied to any of the young ladies. I never pretended to be anything other the young man who wanted to get into their panties. They were extremely willing to comply.

I guess I thought I was good looking, and in very good shape; but now when I look back on some of my early pictures, I was a REALLY good-looking guy. It is good that I didn't know just **HOW** good-looking, or things could have been a lot worse than what they were. When I started modelling and knew that I could get paid because of my good looks, and that folk would hire me…clients would hire me because I was photogenic.

OPRYLAND SERVICE CALLS

The female servicing situation was not made any better when I started working in Live Entertainment at Opryland U.S.A. Theme Park. There were young ladies just ripe for the picking all over Live Entertainment, and in the park itself. It seems I had my share of dancers, singers, and other young lady entertainers. I was one of the few good-looking, seriously in shape, straight young men in Live Entertainment - even in the whole park. pretty much I had my choice of females. There were also the other young ladies who worked in the park - and I was twenty or so, and as they say, "I was just sowing my wild oats."

I will tell the story of one of my Opryland… I won't call it a conquest because it was more about mutual attraction and desire. The entanglement took place; or it started when I was follow-spot operator for the show "For Me and My Gal". I had gone for a couple days when I went to The Jemison/Pair family reunion in Birmingham. When I got back to the show one of the young lady performers ask me where I had been because she had missed me being on spotlight. I told her I have been in Birmingham. She asked what I had been doing in Birmingham. I flippantly responded saying I had been doing lighting a couple of porno films. I guess I should have seen the fireworks go off in her mind, because she wanted to know what kind of porno film? What happened? I just thought "Oh, my goodness," I tried to drop the subject; and said "no, it was not a porno film. I was just kidding." She would not take no for an answer this young lady (who I can say was a very kind person) begin to stop at the ranger station to pick me up to take me to my vehicle in the parking lot. On the way to my car, she would always have a joint ready to smoke. We would smoke the joint, and I would just expect I would either be going home or going to my girlfriends. One night she said why don't you come home with me and will get a beer, sit and watch TV and see what happens.

The thing is, we both knew what was going to happen. What we both knew is exactly what did happen. She and I ended up having wild, crazy, unbridled sex… and it was good!!! She and I would continue down our passionate super-highway for at least a year or two after that initial encounter. I would have to say she enjoyed sex just as much as I did… maybe even more; and talking with some of our Opryland cohorts in the cast of For Me and My Gal, the rule was that this young lady liked her sex…end of report… and if you were going to get along with her you did not interfere with that in any way shape form or fashion.

Things would go we felt open enough with each other to discuss our other sexual entanglements and I can say she was rather formidable and stood toe to toe with me in the number of sexual involvements that a person could find themselves in but neither one of us was jealous of the other and nothing that either of us did stopped us from seeing each other and physically it was just a good time to be had by she and I in the moment.

MY FRIEND AT WLAC RADIO

Another sexual entanglement that was noteworthy was when I worked W LAC radio. I was a talk show engineer. I quickly became friends with the young lady who worked in the news department. She and I were always rather friendly. One morning I simply suggested that when we get off from work that I follow her home and we see where things lead.

Well, I did follow her home that morning and things did lead to rather vigorous sex on her couch. Again, I can say that she held her own. We physically exhausted ourselves that afternoon in her apartment, and continued to exhaust ourselves on various mornings, various evenings, various weekends, and any other times we could find to exhaust ourselves.

In the midst of all of this exhausting I still somehow found time and opportunity to exhaust myself with my friend from Opryland. So, no one was complaining and everything was all good. I still, however, had the girlfriend that I had in college. We were contemplating getting married, but I can tell you no one would have deserved to marry me. No one should have had to be put in the eye of the storm that I continuously put her in. Whether she knew or didn't know I am not sure, but it seems that women do know these things, and nobody's fooling anybody.

I do recall one time I was doing a fashion show for Castner Knotts at one of the really nice hotels downtown. After the show I was connecting with the young lady from W LAC radio and my girlfriend happened to walk up (I thought she had gone home for the weekend). She wanted to know what was going on. I tried to play it off by introducing her to my W LAC friend, but I think my girlfriend was having none of that. And so, she said that she was going back to her hometown. I pretended to be mad and indignant, which of course I had no right to be. When my girlfriend left with the friend, she came with I proceeded to go over to my W LAC friend's apartment and have all the fun a person can have in one afternoon. It was later that afternoon that my girlfriend called one me to come to Clarksville and apologize and make up. I did, and we made up by exhausting ourselves.

Now I was a first-class scoundrel, and I am not afraid to admit to that. But I was at least an honest scoundrel. Now to say that I was an honest scoundrel probably did not make being a scoundrel any better, but it is the best I can do, short of apologizing to the one steady girlfriend I had at the time, but who I cheated on as if there was no tomorrow. I probably owed her an apology, but the other young ladies knew what they were getting into with me from the beginning because I made it clear I was not interested in a relationship, or anything long term, short term. The only thing that I was interested in was sport-fucking. That was it. I made that clear from the beginning to each one of them that I got involved with that I was still seeing my steady girlfriend.

Perhaps the one I do feel worst about…and I told her from the beginning that this was going to be sport-fucking…and that soon I would be moving to Denver, Colorado to pursue a modelling career, which is what I did. When I got ready to move to Denver (and I had made it clear that that was my goal). But I'll be danged if when it came time to leave she seemed that she was hurt. I believe that she really felt that she could have changed me and kept me from doing what I said I was going to do.

I got to know this young lady because when I was in graduate school. I was working on my master's degree. I was at the point where I was writing my master thesis. I really needed a professional typist. Let me hasten to say that people in modern society don't do things the "old school" ways anymore because of word processing programs, and copy and paste, and cut and paste. All those functions which make it infinitely easier to research and save your research; then pull out of your research what you want. Then pull out the evidence from your materials. Back in the old days you would have to sit down at the typewriter. When you made mistakes, you had to use either white out or whole loose-leaf paper. Then you would have to start a page again. That was the way I had to do it.

However, I got to a point where I realized that if I typed my own thesis, I would still be writing on it today. I would be revising and working on it today. There were five people or my thesis committee. I had to submit a copy of my writing to each one of the committee members. They, in turn, made it bleed red with ink and you had to make the corrections that each member asked you to make.

Well, I think it was my second go round with this editing. It was becoming such a nightmare that finally I turned to one of the ladies at church who I knew was an exceptional typist. I asked her if she would type my pieces for me. Well, she asked me to bring it up to Meharry Medical College, where she was a secretary. I took it, and she said that she probably could do it, but she knew someone who was fast, really good, and really thorough. She said the lady would charge a decent price. She would contact that young lady and forward my material to her.

While this young lady (whose name will not be mentioned here) agreed to do it. She was quick. No sooner that she had my rough copy of my thesis with all my edits and corrections in her hands, she called me to say that the job had been done. I was amazed how this could that be. But when I went to Meharry to pick up the corrected copies she had entered the entire thesis into a Xerox Memory Writing processing program. She also set everything up according to the MLA or the IPA format which was required. So, every time I submitted the revised copy of my pieces to my thesis committee, and they would send it back to me bleeding red. I would take them all to this young lady and she would make the corrections and literally hand me back the corrected copy.

THE THESIS AND MORE

Let me get on with the story that I started. The evening when I knew I had successfully defended my thesis, and I knew I would be recommended for graduation to receive my master's degree, I went to the liquor store and I bought a bottle of nice champagne. I want to the apartment of the young lady who typed my thesis, and who had provided me with so much help along the way. I still know that even though I paid her the rate that she had requested. Her talent and skills in helping me to get my document secure was worth every penny I had paid her.

When I get to her apartment, I told her know that my efforts and her efforts had led to success; and I was extremely appreciative of having been put in contact with her, and of her being monumental to my receiving that degree. I told her a bottle of champagne was appropriate for us to have champagne to celebrate this occasion. Then quickly I added; I really bought the champagne to get her drunk to take advantage of her. Well, she looked back at me and laughed. She said, "Did you really think that you needed to get me drunk to take advantage of me?" My heart jump for joy out of my chest, and I said, "well I guess not" and she said, "you guessed right." I guess I don't have to tell you what happened next. From there a good time was had by both. I would say the last couple of encounters that I had with her were quite nice. She was actually a very sweet person. Too nice for someone like the person I was at the time. I told her I was going to Denver. She says she couldn't believe it, and that she thought that I would have changed my mind. I told her that I could not change my mind. She seemed disappointed, but I had been truthful with her from the beginning.

AUNT MATTIE MIGHT SAY

It would probably really take my aunt Mattie to tell you about me. I was such a scandalous ho. Aunt Mattie came to visit us in Nashville from Los Angeles California. My steady girlfriend was the one who I allowed myself to be seen with in public. I wanted her to meet aunt Mattie, so I took my girlfriend by my parents' house to meet Aunt Mattie; and of course, they had a pleasant conversation. In about an hour or so, after they had exchanged pleasantries, I said I had to take my girlfriend home so I could go and get some rest, because I had a shoot the next day.

Well, everyone should have known that to be a lie. I took my girlfriend home and dropped her off. I made sure that she was secure for the evening, and then I drove downtown to the hotel where a young lady was staying. This young lady was a model. She was absolutely gorgeous. I will not mention her name, but she had the most stunning green eyes that you could ever imagine.

She was a light skinned African American sister. African American sisters can come in so many beautiful shades, and so many beautiful skin tones. This model did not disappoint. She was tall, leggy, and just drop dead gorgeous. I picked the young lady up, and took her by the house to meet Aunt Mattie. When I got to the house and did the proper introductions aunt Mattie pulled me aside and told me "That's not the young lay you just left out of here with." I said, "no ma'am." All Aunt Mattie could do was shake her head.

MY "PHILADELPHIA" FRIEND

One lady friend I had in college was strictly a "Philadelphia" type of relationship. I will not mention her name because she will know who she is. I think we were attracted to each other, but nothing ever happened of a serious romantic nature. We were just good friends. She had a beautiful "baby doll" voice, and I just loved to hear her talk because there was so much sweetness in the sound of her voice. Let me emphasize; we were just good friends.

My friend was from Alaska. It would happen that she was staying over the summer to go to summer school at Tennessee State University. She was here and I was a Nashvillian. I was working at Opryland U.S.A. theme park as a technician in Live Entertainment. it was my show's day off. I was running follow spot for the show 'For Me and My Gal" in 1979. I wanted to make sure that my friend wasn't alone in the dormitory and the city. I gave her a call and she assured me that she had no plans for the day, so I asked if she wanted to go out to Opryland Theme Park and enjoy the park with me on my day off. She gladly accepted.

That was during the time I had my little Datsun 200 SX sports car. I went to pick her up. We were in the line waiting to get into the parking lot of the theme park. My friend asked me if I smoked. I said, "Well, on occasion I have a cigarette." This precious lady was a member of the fabled Tennessee State University Tiger Belles. Once I confessed that I smoked she pulled out a very healthy-sized joint and asked if it was okay. I said it was cool. She lit it. Hell, we were in a long line! So, why not! We smoked our joint and we entered the park parking lot. I am going to safely say I have never seen the park so brilliant and vibrant with color as I did on that day. My friend and I had an excellent time. We ran into my brother Carl, who worked in The State Fair area managing the games. Later, I asked Carl if he could tell if we were high. He said, of course he could. It was quite apparent. Oh well, stuff happens!

After our trip to Opryland, we would get together from time to time to smoke reefer and drink beer. There was one night I took her out to dinner. As we were on our way to dinner, she purchased a twelve-pack of beer, which we began to consume it on our way to the dinner spot. When we get back to the dorm, we drank another couple of beers and smoked another joint. I will say we were attracted to each other. She told me she was dating a basketball player at Vanderbilt, so she and I could not a have romantic (being polite) entanglement, however she did let me suck her nipples. She responded quite appropriately. I think she appreciated it, but she still maintained loyalty to this mysterious basketball player at Vanderbilt. But it was okay with me because she was still a good friend of mine.

GRADUATE SCHOOL

Two years after I received my bachelor's degree, I was working at W LAC radio. I was working at the Barn Dinner Theater, and doing some work at Opryland U.S.A. Mr. Daniel E. Owens, who was the manager of WTSU radio, asked me if I had ever considered graduate school. I told him I had not. He asked me to come back and go to graduate school at Tennessee State University. Mr. Owen said all my expenses would be paid. I decided to take Mr. Owens up on the offer. I enrolled in graduate school. As I matriculated through graduate school, I had the opportunity to be assistant manager of W FSK radio, and to work closely with Mr. Cox and Mr. Brady in the theater department. I had the opportunity to write a master's thesis on the history and development of blackface minstrelsy in America from 1865 to 1895.

The matriculation through the master's degree program was probably as difficult a task as I had ever experienced academically. The process of writing a master's thesis required many hours of research, sorting and organizing information. Then there was the continual writing, re-writing, and editing the document. I had learned to type on a typewriter in high school and while writing news at WLAC radio. That is how I executed the first copy of the thesis. Each time I would hand it to the esteemed members of my thesis committee they each would return their copy to me looking like it had been stabbed to death. That's because they all made corrections in red ink. They could have easily invested in a red ink factory and made themselves rich.

The members of my committee where the highly regarded William Dury Cox, Jr.(the chair), Dr. Jamie Coleman Williams (department head), Dr. Bobby Lovett (history professor supreme and Dean of the College of Arts and Sciences), and Dr. Lawrence James. A young man working on a thesis could not have had a more august committee.

I got tired of the "red ink" expeditions. I engaged the services of my good friend Thyckla Johnson Gray to put me in touch with someone who could type this document for me, and make sure it was properly formatted. The lady's name was Janet Davis. I contracted miss Davis once Thyckla got the confirmation that Ms. Davis would accept the job. I would end up paying Janet Davis handsomely; but it was worth it. The revision process then sort of became a game, because every time I received the copy back with the irritating red corrections I took them to Miss Davis. Janet would call me back within the hour to say that she had made the corrections. I would go to Meharry, where she worked, to pick up the corrections and take them to the members of my committee. The members of my committee were equally astounded at the speed with which the corrections were made and returned to them for their further approvals.

Defending My Thesis : A History of Blackface Minstrelsy in America From 1836 to 1896

Then came the day that I would have to defend my written thesis to my thesis committee and anyone else that I wanted to be there. Anyone else who wanted to attend could. I successfully defended my thesis because that I was able to get my first master's degree. The names of people who were on that committee:

After so many months of writing, editing, and getting approvals came the time when I would have to orally defend my thesis. I can tell you I was as nervous as a cat in a room full of rocking chairs, but I was always told that I would know my thesis better than anyone else; including the members of the committee, so I should not be worried or anxious.

Perhaps the most profound question that came to me the day I defended my thesis was from Dr. Bobby Lovett. Dr. Lovett asked if I understood the differences between northern plantations and Southern plantations. Dr. Lovett suggested that perhaps that was the reason why the northern minstrels who made up the earlier Mistral shows depicted life on the plantation as something joyful recalled rather fondly. I had never thought of that aspect of the minstrelsy. The question made a lot of sense.

The other good thing about earning my master's degree and completing it in 1984 is that my sister Angela and I had the opportunity to participate in the graduation ceremony from Tennessee State University the same year. That truly was a highlight.

Thesis Committee chairman was Mr. W Dury Cox, Jr.
    Dr. Jamie Coleman Williams
    Dr. Bobby Lovett
    Dr. Lawrence James

I was fortunate to have had these super heavyweight intellectuals guide and direct me. Not only with obtaining my first master's degree, but also for guidance in life.

Doctor Jamie Coleman Williams was a powerhouse leader in the AME church. She was for many, many years the editor of the AME journal the publisher and editor. When the historic AME church was attacked in Charlston by a white supremist, Dr. Williams was on the podium with presidents Obama and Clinton. With Dr. Jayme Williams you got a "two for one". Her husband, Dr. McDonald Williams, was also an intellectual powerhouse, and her right-hand partner in everything.

Mr. W. Dury Cox, Jr. is the epitome of the term "genius". Mr. Cox had more theatre in his little fingers than most people would ever be able to gather in two or three lifetimes. No one was as well-versed in the history of the theatre as was Mr. William Dury Cox, Jr. It's one of those rare, rare opportunities that you ever get to sit at the feet of someone so knowledgeable, creative, and genuinely talented. The master's thesis Mr. Cox wrote while a graduate student about the technique of lighting the faces of African Americans was used a guide for Hollywood studios.

Dr. Bobby Lovett is one the most highly regarded historians in the state of Tennessee, and the nation. Dr. Lovett was chair of College of Fine Arts. During my oral defense of my master thesis Dr. Lovett asked me if I had researched the conditions of the plantations in the north. Dr. Lovett had exposed a weakness in my research. I had never dreamed about there having been plantations in the north.

Dr. Lovett reminded me that I had accurately described the white developer(s) of minstrelsy as a northern white man (men). Dr. Lovett's question centered on the fact that white "burnt cork" (and eventually authentic Black minstrels) may have originated with the idea that plantation life of the north was nowhere near as brutal as plantation life for slaves in the south…especially the deep south. Well; lesson learned! People don't have to be dogmatic in their efforts to get you to understand that thoroughness matters. That is one of the many lessons which has served me well during my academic career. Thank you, Dr. Lovett!

My fourth thesis committee member was **Dr. Lawrence James**. Dr. James was an excellent creative theatre artist. Dr. James was also an excellent play director. It was an honor to have him on my committee.

THE LIFE OF THE MALE MODEL

The way my modeling career started was through an introduction to movies, commercials and training film videos while I was an undergraduate at Tennessee State University. The first real introduction to commercial/professional show business came when it was determined that the movie "Wilma", based on the life and track and field success of Wilma Rudolph. Wilma wanted the movie about her life to be made on the Tennessee State campus, and the area surrounding the Tennessee state campus. Mr. W. Dury Cox, Jr. (my theatre mentor) was cast as "Pappy Marshall, the assistant track coach to Jason Bernard, who played Tigerbelle coach Ed Temple. Many of the young people in the theater department, like L. Warren Young, and Stacy Green got roles.

"Wilma" was Denzel Washington's first movie. Denzel was doing the television show "Saint Elsewhere." Denzel Washington was selected to play Wilma's boyfriend, Robert Eldridge, in the movie.
I auditioned but did not get a role. I do not know whether it's true or not, or whether people will even believe this, but Mr. Cox told me I did not get the role that I audition for because my name being Washington Dobbins was too close to the name Denzel Washington.

What happened after my initial foray into the film business is that I decided I might be able to make a little bit of money if I invested a little bit into getting some head shots done. I asked some of the people who I worked with in a training video the name of a solid, reputative photographer should I talk to about investing in getting decent head shots done. Armed with the information they provided; I settled on a photographer named Mitch Karam. I do have to give Mitch a lot of credit for the success that I had while I was modeling. After my head shot session with Mitch, he said he knew someone who was looking for male models. Mitch said they needed a good-looking Black guy. Mitch said they did fashion shows; and you might even get to be in the newspaper from time to time. I had already been doing some modeling assignments with Mitchell's Formal Wear, and Arzelle's bridal company. They did shows together, so I had already done a little bit of the runway thing for Mitchell's. It was during that head shot session with Mitchell that he turned me onto Carlana Moscheo. Mitch may have actually called her, and told her he was doing a session with a model she needed to meet. This was exactly the way you got to be "connected" in the business. People you meet, who you become friends with and consistently do good work with refer to other people and other jobs. The larger your network of contacts grows the more work you get. Pretty soon you find yourself working all the time and making good money along the way. Carlana Moscheo was the fashion Director at a store called Castner Knotts (which is no longer in existence). Mitch got me an appointment to see Carlana Moscheo. I'm just thinking "well, she probably is not going to like me and I won't get any work anyway, but I'll meet with her.

I got to Castner Knotts and found Carlana Moscheo's office. She was very nice, and at the same time very professional. She was also a really nice person. I also met Carlana's assistant, LaRaun Scaife. They both were really nice people. Carlana began to take my measurements. She measured me around the shoulders and then she measured me around the hips. Carlana looked at LaRaun and said "he has a twelve inch drop." I had never heard that expression. Being new to the modeling profession, I thought "twelve-inch drop? What does that mean? Carlana explained "you are forty inches around the shoulders, which is great. That's perfect size for the suits the models wear." "The perfect model size forty regular." Carlana said your arms are little bit longer. You would need a forty long, but you're forty. Your waist is twenty-eight. That's smaller than waist size of a lot of women. You have a twelve-inch drop." Carlana said you have a severe body contour. That was the first time anyone had ever told me that.

But, Carlana began to putting me in the fashion shows. I guess I did okay, because they didn't stop calling for me. Let me confess right now that I was never comfortable doing ramp shows; perhaps because I always felt so self-conscious, and because I never felt I had any real rhythm. Soon, Carlana began to call me about newspaper ad shoots. I appeared in newspaper ads weekly. I was in a Castner Knott television commercial at least once a month. Not bad for a young guy out of the Providence village of Nashville. I will say that I became a celebrity, but it's funny, I didn't feel like anyone ever recognized me. There were times when somebody would say "oh, aren't you in the paper? or something like that. I always felt very, very plain. I always felt very ordinary. So, that's really how I got into modeling. From the work that I did for Castner Knotts I could now take my tear sheets and go just about anywhere. People in other cities were very excited about the work that I had done. But I had "tears" because of my professional approach to this profession. I had, and still do have, a serious work ethic. I was always ready. I was reliable. I was rested. I was prepared. I could be counted on to be punctual. I would do the right things to get the job done. I had energy to do the shoot. It would look good when I was done. I talk with a lot of young people who tell me they want to be in this profession. I gave them a rundown of all the qualities I listed for you. I let them know that modeling is a business. It is not a pleasure cruise. Modeling and show business are just that - businesses. You have to treat them as a business.

It's also a business of attrition. Those who can do the job correctly and consistently are the ones who get the work. The ones who, for whatever reason, can't seem to get that understanding fall by the wayside - and that happens very quickly.

STAN "MO" and "DOBBINO"

Doing modeling gigs is how I met Stan Moore and initiated a friendship that lasted over 40 years. Stan was the only white guy I knew who could recite perfectly from memory Rudy Ray Moore's poem "Signifying Monkey." That was more than a notion. Stan would move to Dallas Texas. He and I kept in touch. I knew Stan had signed with Mike Beaty, in Dallas to see if I wanted to sign with his agency, Industry Dallas. I did go out to Dallas to meet Mikle Bailey to see whether I wanted to sign with Industry Dallas. Stan began to get contracts to create music videos. I would get call from Stan from time to time to have me come and create a character for a music video that he was shooting. I even sold Stan a sixteen-millimeter Bolex movie camera I had purchased from Dr. Donald Page. Stan said the camera worked perfectly. Stan said he used the camera to shoot B" rolls. ***It is important to remember that the original "Road Warrior" was shot on sixteen-millimeter film.

Later, I would meet Stan's parents, Evelyn and Captain Moore. They were the nicest people you ever wanted to know. I had a standing invitation to go to their home at any time. One time I was invited over for some celebration. When I got there, Captain Moore welcomed me with a warm, genuine embrace. Captain Moore asked me if I wanted a beer. It was a Pabst Blue Ribbon beer. I told him I would like one. Captain said Pabst was a white man's beer. I asked him if a white man had paid for it. He said that the answer was "Yes." I spoke. "For real? Then give me two!" Captain Moore was a decorated Air Force fighter pilot. Upon leaving the Air Force Captain Moore became a Captain for Delta Airlines. Mrs. Moore would become the fashion coordinator for Cain Sloan (the chief rival of Castner Knotts). Cain Sloan is now known as Dillard's. Mrs. Moore was a cool lady, and just "good people."

Another model I met and became working partners with was Jay Antos. Jay was the "big dog on the block." Jay was in the Washington Manufacturing ads. Jay seemed like he had the New York connections. Everybody was very helpful. We all tried to help each other. We gave each other pointers and contacts. Connections was the name of the game!

DENVER CONVERSION

I can say that the last encounter with "JD" was the beginning of a transformation for me. I want to say that it was because of "JD" because I know that at the same time and about the time that all of that happens. I have made up in my mind that when I went to Denver it was going to be strictly about business. I was not going to Denver to be a "ho." I was going to Denver to be a serious working model. I was going to Denver to further my career. I wanted to be very focused on my work. You begin to understand how temptations seem to come out of the woodwork. I knew I was a good-looking guy, but by this time, I knew I was a physical specimen. There was just no doubt about it at all.

When I arrived in Denver, I would be out riding my bike or walking. Women pulled over in their cars to talk to me. I don't mean to Kia's or Honda's (well, there were a fair share of those, too). I mean Mercedes Benz. I mean BMW. I mean Jaguar. I mean Maserati! I mean expensive cars!!! Practically all these women were white. That was another thing that caused a bit of confusion in my mind. If I had been my old self, I certainly would have taken advantage of all these opportunities (I might have wound up dead, also), but I was very focused and I was very different than I was before. But it was an interesting experience, nonetheless. I am glad I made that conversion, and I am glad I made the transition. I delved into my religion, my God, and became more spiritual in every conceivable way.

When I first moved to Denver I stayed' maybe two weeks with my brother, his wife and children. Then I rented one room in a building that was composed mostly of homeless tenants. I had to share a communal bathroom with everyone on the floor. A lot was left to be desired, in terms of hygiene. One had to hurry up and take care of business.

The first month or two in Denver was tough. First, because I did not have Colorado identification, I could not get a bank account. I had no place to deposit and manage my money. It was even harder to get a decent job without Colorado identification. There I was, a person with a college master's degree, having a difficult time securing a menial job.

However, I continued to persevere. Finally, I was able to get a one room apartment near Smiley's laundromat, which was in the downtown area on Colfax. I live about six blocks from the state capital. I also lived across the street from an artsy, trendy movie theatre. This part of Colfax was lazy and quiet during the week, but on the weekends, it turned into a jumping spot for the young, trendy set.

I never had to worry about hot water, because my apartment was directly above Smiley's laundromat, which was touted as the largest laundromat in the world. As long as Smiley's had hot water, so did I.

My mother help me to clean my first apartment, and get it squared away. After a while I talked to the people who owned Smiley's and the apartment building to see if they had a better one-room. They did. They showed me and allowed me to move into another apartment which was much nicer than the first apartment. Once I got it cleaned to my satisfaction it was a very nice apartment.

A day I remember most about that apartment is that one day I turned the oven on to put some food inside. The oven in apartment gas. I had never used gas before, so I was not aware of high gas operated. Well somehow, I turned the oven on. I did not think it had come on. I don't remember whether I heard the gas hissing or not. I remember opening the oven door, and I put my head inside. Stupid!!! There was an eruption, and I literally fell back all the way across the room. I was damn fortunate I didn't blow my stupid face off! But you live and learn.

NEW YORK CALLS FROM DENVER

So, while I was staying in my one Room efficiency over Smiley's laundromat, I had a great view of Colfax. I become close to the owners of the apartment building. They were impressed that I kept my apartment so clean and neat. The apartment looked way better than when I first rented it. They saw me in the hall one day and mentioned that they had a two-bedroom apartment which had just come available. They could rent it to me for the same price that I was paying for the present apartment. As we were negotiating my transfer of apartment, Jo Farrell, owner of J.F. Enterprises introduced me to all the major talent agent representatives out of New York City. Joe Farrell JF images was the largest talent agent in the West. she had an office in Denver and she had offices in Los Angeles, California. She was known as "The Red-Headed Barracuda" because she was a tough, shrewd businesswoman. She represented me out of her Denver office. I was in Jo Farrell's Denver offices' one Saturday. I believe I was there to meet with one of her talent representatives. I ran into Jo Farrell. After we had exchanged pleasantries, she asked who I was. I told her that I was signed to the agency. Jo Farrell said no one had told her about my signing. I believe that was because the talent representatives already had clients, they had established relationships with, and they more interested in getting jobs for. Jo Farrell went on to tell me about an event she was having in Boulder. It was a competition for new modeling, voice and commercial talent. Jo told me that because I had missed the sign-up deadline, I would not be able to compete, but she did want me to go to the event in Boulder and meet the representatives from the agencies in New York. I went, and met the representatives of Zoli, Elite, Wilhelmina, Casablanca's, Ford, all the big names in talent and modeling in New York. Every representative told me if I came to New York one of these agencies would sign me. It would really be my choice of the one I would want to sign with. They told me that if I had been female, the agency would have signed me where we met, put up in a New York apartment and provided with all kinds of perks. They told me that they did not do that for male talent. Armed with this knowledge, I immediately put in a call to my Aunt Louise and Uncle Robert White. They were so kind and supportive. They offered me a one-bedroom apartment above their garage. They told me that I would be five blocks from the train station. The train would take me into the heart of the garment district. That would be where I needed to go. They told me I was not to pay any rent. I packed my Datsun 200SX and prepared to drive to New York. Dr. Jayme C. Williams called me several times to come back to Tennessee State University to teach. I accepted that offer. I turned my little car in the direction of Nashville Tennessee. I believe Jo Farrell fell out with me because of my decision to not go to New York; especially after she had probably gone to bat for me with the New York talent people, then I reneged. I had heard that Marlboro cigarettes was looking for a new "Marlboro Man." They wanted the new Marlboro Man to be black, and my name was in the mix. I guess all that went down the drain when I came back to Nashville.

MY MENTORS BECOME MY COLLEAGUES

In August of 1984 Dr. Jayme Williams asked me to join the faculty of the Communications department. I became a faculty member and peer to the same people I had held in the highest regards as teachers, mentors, and guides. The first thing all these faculty colleagues TOLD me to do was address them by their first names. They did not want me to address them as Mister, Missus or Doctor. They now all insisted that I address them as Don, Herman, Jayme, San, and so on. Talk about culture shock! That took a long time for me to come to terms with. HOWEVER, with Dr. Jayme Coleman Williams the closest I could come to first name status with her was Doctor Jayme. I felt it was best to let that be that.

Again, I say I've been blessed in so many ways to have had the opportunity to learn from the great Hoss Allen, the great W. Dury Cox, the great Jamye Coleman Williams and so many others. To know people personally, like coach Edward Temple, coach John Merritt, the great Wilma Rudolph, and so many others.

Z-CAR HEAVEN

When I was a young man, I was fortunate in 1978 to purchase my first car. It was mine, all mine. Bought and paid for myself.

I want to say at this point, my mother did not want me to buy that car. However, I bought it before I asked her or my father about buying it. I bought it home and showed it to her and my dad. My mother freaked out. "I didn't buy good vehicle. I didn't know what I was getting into. It might fall apart on me. I just gave away all my money" and all this kind of good stuff. But I bought it anyway, because I figured it was better to apologize and ask for forgiveness than to ask first up and hear "no." That time I was 20 years of age. I was working in Live Entertainment as a theatre technician at Opryland U.S.A., so I was actually doing pretty good. I was a rising junior at Tennessee State University. The part that blows me away today is that the car cost me $1800.00.

That vehicle was a 1972 Datsun 240Z. The car was solid, and it drove really well. The salesman and I entered into the sales agreement. As we were finishing the paperwork another salesman came to the desk and he was very angry because he wanted to buy the car. I bought it before he could buy it, and that was that.

Well, as I came to love my little car, I began to really realize the car drove very well and handled really well. My little Z-car had exceptional pickup and speed. I just really liked my 1972 Datsun 240Z.

So, a day or two after I bought my car, I returned to work at Opryland. It was the end of our show day, and I was getting off. My Tennessee State classmate, my buddy, my pal Lee Summers was leaving his show (Showboat). I asked Lee if he wanted to ride with me up to Clarksville Tennessee to show my new car to my girlfriend who lived there. Lee was gracious enough to consent.

We got to Clarksville, pulled in my girlfriend's driveway. Her ride from work was just dropping her off. I showed my girlfriend the car. Lee and I did not even get out of the car. We backed out of the driveway and headed back to Nashville. I had heard stories of old Clarksville Highway and Old Ashland City Highway. I probably didn't pay as much attention to these stories as I should have. I have been on old Clarksville Highway before. I had ridden the bus to Clarksville. Anyway, Lee and I ended up not back on the interstate but going down Old Clarksville Highway. The fault was all mine. The twists and turns on that highway were countless, and the fog was so thick you could cut it. I began to have all those thoughts about how Fort Campbell had put Nashville off-limits to the soldiers because so many of them were getting killed when they came to Nashville to party, then attempted (unsuccessfully) to navigate Old Clarksville Highway back to the post. I was as afraid about being in this situation as I had ever been about any other situation I had ever been in. I was even more fearful because I was driving; and because I had gotten Lee into this mess. But you learn how to plough on through your fears and your anxieties and get the job done. As we continue to drive, I looked to my left, and I thought I saw what was interstate twenty-four. I was praying that I saw interstate twenty-four, because it was frightful being on Clarksville Highway. So, at that point I did trust my instincts. I came to a street where I could turn left and head back toward what I thought was the interstate. Surely there was an entry ramp to get on interstate twenty-four. It was interstate twenty-four. It soon became a much safer, much more comforting ride back to Nashville. Lee and I made it safely home.

My first Live Entertainment gig at Opryland Theme Park was the show "For Me and My Gal" (https://youtu.be/m90hoaOVloQ?si=tsPA18MlGP3KmdrG). The show drummer was Karl (whose last name I can't recall) also drove a Datsun 240 like mine. I had no initial idea of a good mechanic. When you are a young guy twenty years of age you don't really think about having a good mechanic when you buy a vehicle. Karl suggested a gentleman by the name of D.P. I began to take my car to D.P. Eventually I would come to know (because it was on the news) that this mechanic, D.P. had been stealing parts from his customers cars and selling them on the "black market" and making quite a good living doing that.

I can only imagine what parts may have left my Datsun 240Z. The history of the car made it pretty special. When I was in the process of purchasing the car I found out the car came from Vancouver Canada. It had a front air dam, louvers covering the back window, and an air spoiler across the trunk of the car with the letters BRE. I went for a long time not knowing what BRE stood for. Eventually Karl would introduce me to another mechanic. This mechanic became more than just a mechanic. He and his family became lifelong friends; actually, just like family. The Clark Crawford family became family to the Dobbin's family. Clark is to this day, perhaps the best that Z-Car / Nissan / Datsun mechanic I know. Above all of that he is just a super guy!

I learned that Clark Crawford raced Datsun 240-Zs on the IMSA race circuit. I took my car to his shop (which so ironically- and how you understand some things are meant to be) which was located on Straightway Street, in East Nashville. Straightway street is where my mother and father lived when I was born. The irony was huge. When I took my car to Clark's shop for the first time Clark began to look the car over. Clark is a very curious individual. He began asking me questions in regard to the car. He said, "where did you get this car?" "What is the background of this car?" "What do you know about this car?" I told Clark I had purchased the Datsun 240-Z at The Car Store on Lafayette Street. I told Clark they told me the car came out of Vancouver Canada. That was all I really knew about the car. Clark when on to say, "did they tell you that they sold you a race car?" I said "no, they didn't tell me that." Clark said "well, let me tell you how I know. "First of all, I race these cars. Clark said, "this engine is not a stock engine." Clark said, "this is a racing engine that's in this car." "You bought a race car." You have oversized pistons." That BRE stands for Brock Racing Equipment." I told Clark I had been trying to figure out what that meant ever since I ought the car. Clark explained that Brock was a Datsun 240Z race car driver who developed a line of high-performance equipment especially for the Datsun 240-Z. I could about fell through the floor. Every performance aspect of that car proved him right. There were no disappointments in the speed or the handling ability of that vehicle. It was a very singular vehicle. My Datsun 240-Z was a 240-Z on steroids, meant to be out on the race track, and I was the proud owner.

Through the years I would take all my vehicles to Clark Crawford. I was purchasing Nissan products, so Clark Crawford was always my "go to" mechanic. My family members began to purchase Nissan products. My sister, my brother; and Clark was our mechanic. He was our family. He was our friend; and that's just the way it is.

One day this race car started sputtering, missing, and just performing poorly. My mom, and of course a blew a gasket and said "I told you you should not have bought that car. You bought a piece of junk. You wasted your money." I was pretty upset, but it was my dad who came to the rescue. My dad said "there is nothing wrong with this car." He said, "you purchased a good car, but your car is in need of a tune up. Your spark plugs have fouled. They are not firing efficiently." He said, "take my car to work, and leave your car with me, and I will tune it up for you." I began to think, "Hell, I can't pull no fine chicks with your car; but okay." I did feel highly distraught over my decision to buy the car, but trusted my dad knew what he he was talking about. When I got home my dad informed me that he had completed the tune up, and took the car out for a test drive. He said that everything was good. There was nothing wrong with my car. It just needed new spark plugs and wires, which he purchased and install for me. Dad went on to say he could not adjust the dual carburetors because doing that took a special machine. If that synchronization was not done correctly the car would run out of sync and run about like a raggedy "nickel mop" as it did before the spark plugs. My youngest brother, Joel, told me that my dad had fixed the car and completed the tune-up. Joel pretty much told me the same story as my dad, except that my dad left out a few of the details. Elaborating, Joel said that once my father completed putting in the spark plugs and the wires he suggested that they go out for a drive. Joel said that they went way up Nolensville Road. Out passed Old Hickory Boulevard, headed into Nolensville Tennessee.

Nolensville Road turned into a two-lane highway and as they headed out. Joel says a car a Camaro Trans-Am, or some hot racing automobile pulled out behind my dad, and accelerated in pursuit to overtake or pass my dad in my little Datsun 240-Z. Obviously, they did not know my dad, because my dad didn't play stuff like that. Joel said my father downshifted, stepped on it, and before you know it that vehicle behind them was way in the distance. My dad had smoked him. I know my dad was truly impressed with that little Datsun 240-Z the same way he was impressed with his '57 Chevy, to which he had made many modifications. From what my father told us, the '57 Chevy would also run like a "scalded dog".

After that, there were many a-day, and many a-night that I took people's pride away from them in the cars that they were driving. These were supposedly hot cars: Olds 442's, Porsche's, just about any Camaro, Firebirds - just about any hot car of the day. I took their "lunch" from them with my little Datsun 240-Z. The only time things turned out bad for me was one night I was driving down Interstate-65, and a black vehicle went by me so fast it made me feel like I was standing still. I, of course, stepped on it. As I came up behind the vehicle, when it was getting off at the Harding place exit, I realized that it was a Porsche Turbo Correra. Well, somedays you're the windshield and somedays you're the bug!

I love that Datsun 240-Z and drove it until I paid for it, and then some. I noticed that it was rusting badly in both floor pans. I asked different people how I could resolve that issue. When I asked Clark Crawford about it I was informed that the rust was that bad because the car came out of Vancouver Canada, and had been exposed to a great deal of salt on the roadways. The salt really ate up the undercarriage and many parts of the body of the car. If I had any real sense I would have kept that car, fixed it up and put it away to drive later. It was already paid for. The car ran just fine, but I didn't keep it. I ended up trading it in for a Datsun 200 SX, a brand-new vehicle with a five-speed manual transmission. That was a pretty nice new car, but I should never have sold that first Z-car.

I soon realized how much I missed that little 240-Z. I started inquiring of Clark Crawford about the whereabouts of another really good to 240-Z. Clark suggested a car which was owned by Mary McAllister. Clark had done all of the service on it, and he would vouch for that car on any day of the week. Clark advised I needed to talk to Mary McAllister and buy that car. I immediately engaged in negotiations with Mary McAllister to buy her 1973 Datsun 240-Z. This car was a dark hunter green with the tan saddle interior. Mary McAllister's car was in immaculate condition and immediately I agreed to purchase the car. I did not regret it. One second after I gave Mary $3550.00, I fell in love with in love with that car. I stopped driving the car when I started working for the Boy Scouts. The Boy Scouts furnished me with a company car, so I didn't have to run up the miles on my Z-car. I parked the Z-car at my grandmother's house for about two years. When I finally decided I needed to drive that car again it wouldn't start. I had my little car towed to Crawford Z-Car, which now was owned and run by his former partner, Doug. Doug diagnosed the issue and told me that the engine had locked up from lack of use. My 240 would need a new engine. Doug told me he he had taken a stock engine out of his 240-Z that he had converted to a race car for himself. So, Doug head an engine just sitting on the shelf. Doug sold me that engine for about $1200.00. For about $300.00 more dollars he installed it. I thought, "what a deal!" A brand new engine with only 78000 miles on it for $1500.00. I begin driving my green Datsun 240-Z with the saddle interior proudly. I do have a picture of my oldest son, Tres' standing next to that vehicle.

As things would go, my fraternity brother and cousin needed a car. He was attending college at Jackson State in Mississippi, and his old vehicle had broken down, and he needed a good reliable vehicle. Why in the world would I sell him my Datsun 240??? I'm still digging my foot out of my ass over that one! I did tell him, "before you get rid of this car you come back to me, and you let me buy it back." He agreed to that, but he did not keep his promise. At some point I found out he had traded my Datsun 240-Z for a Jeep! I wanted to be hostile, but I couldn't. My calm demeanor. But, it is upsetting to this day to know that the Datsun 240-Z that I had invested maybe $6000.00 in would be worth close to $30,00.00 today. Also, the first one that I owned (the race car) would probably be worth more than that. That was a car I spent $1800.00 for. Having the first 240-Z would have provided the means for a comfortable retirement.

I think that it is appropriate to add at this time that my brother, Ken, purchased himself a Datsun 240-Z. It was a silver one that he named the "Silver Bullet." Ken had lived in Denver close to the Coors brewery in Golden. That's how he came to name his car the "Silver Bullet." I owned the green Datsun 240. Ken and I decided to go to the Volvo tennis tournament in Memphis Tennessee. Ken was living in Cape Guirado, Missouri at the time. He drove to Nashville, where we connected, and drove to Memphis; him, in his "Silver Bullet", and me in my little green to 240. We traveled on down to the Volvo. It was a great little trip. When it was over Ken took a course home to Cape Girardeau Missouri paralleling the Mississippi River and I came back to Nashville. The distances were about equal.

It was doing our tennis trip to Memphis that, among other players, we got to see the great Andre Agassi in person. Kevin Curren and his South African tennis partner. As Ken and I were leaving out after the final match through the crowd we saw that Kevin Curren and his partner were walking in front of us. Ken remarked to me that he would like to get Curren's autograph. He did not want to ask, so I yelled out "Mr. Curren, could we have your autograph please?" Very politely, he did stop and give my brother his autograph. That made it an even better trip!

I would also say that my first little 240-Z car came in pretty handy for the family. Not too long after I got that car Ken and and his wife, Gayle would had my niece Candyce. On several occasions I would let Ken borrow my car so that he would have transportation to get to the doctor or pediatrician, or so that he could get to work. I was then borrowed a car from one of my parents, or my girlfriend at the time would come to pick me up. It is safe to say that Z cars have had a very important role in our lives, and we are very fond of that particular vehicle. It is too bad we don't have the money to buy these fantastic little cars now, and that we didn't keep the ones we had.

OPRYLAND U.S.A.

I believe the year was 1977 when I first started working at Opryland U.S.A. theme park. My first job at Opryland was in a best food operation in the Rock'n'Roll area known as Chubby's Diner. When I'd worked at Chubby's for a while I was promoted from fry-man to back of kitchen lead. I met a lot of good people at Chubby's. The back of Chubby's Diner faced the Gaslight Theater. I would always run into theater people; performers and technicians, leaving their shifts at the Gaslight theatre. I would take time to talk with these Live Entertainment employees when they came to buy hamburgers at Chubby's Diner while they were on their breaks between shows. I especially let the technicians know that I was in the theater program at Tennessee State University and knew my way around lighting equipment, building sets and general electricity. One of those conversations yielded the opportunity to get transferred to Live Entertainment. One of the technicians for the show "For Me and My Gal" let me know that they would need a replacement spotlight operator or replacement stagehand. He told me who to go to speak with. I went to the Live Entertainment office, and they told me I would have to reapply with Live Entertainment specifically. In about two weeks I had the job. At this point I had worked at Chubby's for a season. An The year is now 1978. I transferred into Live Entertainment and began running the spotlight for the show "For Me and My Gal". I became known to the techs as well as the performers. I can say I had a great opportunity to meet many persons who went on to film careers or Broadway careers. Among those, one of the most well-known performers is Mary Elizabeth Mastrantonio. Mary Elizabeth created the character Mama Cohan, the mother of the character George M. Cohan for the two years that I did "For Me and My Gal." Mary Elizabeth was a sweetheart; just a wonderful person. I was very happy to see her in movies like Scarface, The Color of Money, Robin Hood: Prince of Thieves as Lady Marian, The Abyss, and the Perfect Storm. Mary Elizabeth was just a very nice person, along with others who, like I said, would go on to have really great careers, including: Lee Summers, Cindy Rhodes (who appeared in Flashdance and Dirty Dancing with Patrick Swayze). Cindy Rhodes was another very nice person. Cindy married singer/songwriter/ performer Richard Marx. I had the opportunity to run into Richard Marx in a restaurant in Memphis one evening. A very nice person. As I continue on the "Opryland trail" … I left the theme park in 1980 to pursue a radio career, but sometime about 1984 I returned to the theme park and teched shows such as "… And the Winner Is", "I hear America Singing", the horrible "The Big Broadcast".

THE CONCERT SERIES

The Opryland years discourse would not be complete if I did not include the opportunity to work with the amazing concerts that were held at the Geo Celebrity Theatre at Opryland U.S.A. We were a "crackerjack" crew. We were the best among the best. In 1993 our crew, Wilma and Fred (catering crew), Stan Stout (stage manager) won the CMA award for venue of the year. In beating out the competition (The Palace at Auburn Hills Michigan, the Big House in Branson Missouri, Radio City Music Hall in New York, and The Forum in Los Angeles California) our total crew provided the highest level of comprehensive service to the touring artists and crews of the country music genre. Members of that crew were me, my brother Joel, Kevin Varnado (crew chief), Richard Whitehead, Josh Thompson, Roscoe Shelton and others. The crew of 1993 did some really amazing things. Later, I would end my career working on the Opryland Concert Series, which was located at the Chevrolet Geo Celebrity Theater. It was while teching the concert series I got to work with many, many, great artists. already such as Billy Ray Cyrus, Alabama, the Oak Ridge Boys , Tanya Tucker , Vince Gill, Johnny Cash, Wiley Nelson, Restless Heart, Confederate Railroad and many, many others. Perhaps the greatest thrill of that was having the opportunity to be in the presence of Ronnie Milsap. It is the worst kept secret that I am one of the greatest Ronnie Milsap fans going. When I met Ronnie (and "met" is a VERY loose term) I had met Dale Earnhardt, and had a really great conversation with him, I had met all manner of celebrity at the Geo and could hold conversation with anybody. I also want to say that my high school classmate Pam Tillis had embarked on a successful recording career. She too, was one of the artists that I had the opportunity to work with while teching the concert series. When Pam walked into the theater she recognized me first from high school. Pam was very warm and embracing. She's just good people. Another Overton High School classmate I want to speak about before I go back to writing the Ronnie Milsap story is Dean Tubb. Dean Tubb is the son of country music legend Ernest Tubb. Dean and I met in high school and became good friends. You would not ever know that he was the son of such a celebrity, because he never acted that way toward me or anyone else that I knew. Dean was driving the bus for Charlie Daniels. I was on stage working the setup and I heard someone shout "Dhey Washington Dobbins!" I looked up and it was Dean Tubb, who immediately gave me a big hug. Dean invited me to come on the bus to see what Charlie Daniels' bus look like. Dean said that he and his brother had taken over a bussing company that his father started. Dean was the personal driver for Charlie Daniels.

Going back to the Ronnie Milsap story... I may have mentioned that I was a good friend to his producer, Tom Collins. I was at the wedding when Ronnie Milsap sang "Let's Take the Long Way Around the World for Tom and Jenny Collins. I always kept in touch with Tom Collins, and when the opportunity to work with Ronnie came up it was just an exciting moment for me. At one point Ronnie Milsap's chief piano technician (we just called him "Dude" , had escorted Ronnie backstage close to the technical office and I was standing right there. I wanted to speak to him but words just would not come from my mouth. It was perhaps the weirdest moment of my life. I just could not speak to Ronnie Milsap; not even to say "hi", not even to say I'm a big fan... nothing! when this occurred I immediately called Tom Collins and told him what happened Tom said hello just speak to Ryan he's a nice guy just say "hi". To make a long story short, I could not say "hi". It never happened and I never got to speak with Ronnie Milsap.

CONWAY TWITTY AND TAMMY WYNETTE

Two performers that I worked with passed away during the course of doing concerts with them. The first artist was "The Best Friend A Song Ever Had." Conway Twitty was a very nice man. It was good to have the opportunity to work with him . We were setting up for his show one afternoon. The stage manager came to us and said "gentlemen, there won't be a show tonight." The crew members asked what the problem was. Mr. Stan Stout informed us that Mr. Conway Twitty had passed away . That blew me away, because we had literally done performances with him two days ago. Conway appeared to be as healthy as a horse.

Another artist passed away not much longer after we had worked with her. This was Tammy Wynette, the artist who recorded "Stand By Your Man." When I had the opportunity to work with Miss Wynette, I really was shocked because she did seem very fragile, and I could not understand why a woman of her stature in country music was still touring. I suspect, that like all performing artists, performing is what you like and live to do, and that's why she kept on performing. But, I was really, really taken aback again by how fragile she seemed. In my opinion it would have been better is she could have been sitting at home on a comfortable couch watching television and enjoying her life that way. As I make that observation, I realized that watching television all day is not enjoyment of life for some people. Tammy Wynette was doing what she wanted to do.

MR. ROY ACCUFF

Another high point of working at Opryland theme park was getting to meet on many occasions and speaking with Mr. Roy Acuff. A theater had been built on park property which bore his name. A home for Mr. Roy Acuff was built in the park. Mr. Acuff could access that home near the Gaslight Theater. There were many opportunities where we would see Mr. Roy Acuff traversing in the cart driven by an aide back and forth across the park. It was not unusual for him to stop and actually hold conversations with young performers, or just young people in general who he happened to run into. He seemed like a really great individual. Mr. Acuff was a partner in a music publishing partner with the grandfather of one of my high school classmates, Fred Rose. Fred Roses' Grandfather was also Fred Rose. There was a publishing company in the Melrose section of Nashville, on 8th Ave which bore the name Acuff/Rose Publishing. Again, it is amazing to me to have been this close, or as close as I was to what many people considered "country royalty". "Country Royalty" might have been misleading, in a way, because the "Royals" that I came into contact with were just average, ordinary, regular, everyday people just like me.

Another high point in the Opryland years came in 1996. I think I had had just as much of the park as I could take. I was gearing up for the next concert series season. The first performance would be with the Johnny Cash. My dad was a huge Johnny Cash fan. When Johnny Cash was on television you dared not touch that dial, or my dad would probably kill you. I did the Johnny Cash set up, then the concert. It was when the shows were done, and we had loaded Johnny Cash out, I called the Live E. technical "brass" and told him I was giving notice. They asked why, and I just told them it was time to move on for. and that's what I did.

MY T.S.U. / OPRYLAND COMRADS-IN-ARMS

Once I was hired into Live Entertainment at Opryland, and I had established trust in management that I could do the jobs I was entrusted, they began to trust me enough to recommend others for technical positions in Live Entertainment. I was able to bring aboard my brother Barry Scott. It was also a high point for me when I worked at WLAC radio to bring in Barry Scott as a studio engineer. I was brought in as an intern, then given a job at the station. As I performed well, I heard of opportunities for others to work at WLAC radio. I was able to bring in Barry Scott, my brother Joel, and my other brother Ken Dobbins. We became known as the Dobbins Boys (sounds like old-west gun slingers) and Barry Scott. We receive as much notoriety on the air from the talk show hosts that we worked with. We worked behind the scenes, but we were well respected and well known.

Barry Scott - Barry Scott, at Opryland, worked primarily with the show "Cosmic Laser Explosion". Barry was a technician for the show. Barry learned about the operations of the Krypton laser and Argon laser units. Barry also got experience in pyrotechnics; how to set the charges, the different types of charges, and how to operate them safely. Later Barry would be connected with the first edition of the Concert Series located at the Theater by the Lake. It was there that Barry had the opportunity to meet and work with Travis Tritt. That relationship led to the opportunity to do music videos with Travis Tritt. Barry went on to do movies with Jim Varney. , Barry appeared in all of the "Earnest" films with Jim Varney. Barry became well-known and well-respected in the theater circles of the nation. Through his performances mostly with Black Tie Theatre and S.H.O.W. Productions, Tennessee Repertory Theater and Alabama Shakespeare Festival Scott established himself as a theatre force. Barry also made appearances in the television series "In the Heat of the Night" with Carrol O'Connor and Howard Rollins. While we were in college Barry went to Hollywood, where he worked with Norman Lear's Tandem Productions. That connection was made possible his association with Judy Ann Mason, who was a chief writer for the television show Good Times.

Barry Bruce – An Opryland alum, and college classmate. Barry Bruce was true-blue T.S.U. classmate and theater comrade. Bruce grew up in Lebanon Tennessee, not too far from Nashville. Bruce's father was principal of Lebanon High. Barry Bruce was one hell of a dancer! Bruce was also a "Triple-Threat", meaning he proficient as singer, dancer and actor. Bruce performed in the original Broadway cast of Dreamgirls. The story Barry Bruce told me is that when he arrived in New York, his real intent was to audition for a role in "The Lion King." Bruce said the line of auditionees stretched down the street, and around the corner (mind you, I am talking about a New York block). Someone standing in line mentioned that he might want to go to the audition for Dreamgirls. They said the line was much shorter, and that he could do that audition, then come back to this one. As fate would have it, Bruce got the role in Dreamgirls.

Leon Summers – Where do I start when it comes to Lee Summers, Jr. A Nashville native. A graduate of Stratford High School, in Nashville. Lee and I became running buddies and fast friends. Lee another one of those "Triple Threats". Lee is a singer extraordinaire! Lee and I graced the stage of the "A" building/Poag auditorium at Tennessee State University. Lee auditioned for the theme park a couple of times before they brough him aboard in Live

Entertainment. The rich baritone voice of Lee Summers brought the house down every show when he performed "Ole Man River". In 1980 Lee was honored at the Live Entertainment banquet with the Male Performer of the Year Award (Mary Elizabeth Mastrantonio was the Female Entertainer of the Year that season). Lee left Nashville and joined Barry Bruce in New York City. Lee also secured an audition for Dreamgirls and got the part. Lee is also well-known in New York for his show "A Piano and a Microphone". I had the opportunity to talk to the tour manager of Lion King on one occasion when the show came to Nashville. I asked him if he knew Lee Summers. He responded, "You mean Lee, who does the show "A Piano and a Microphone?" I said yes. The tour manager went on to comment on what a great show that was, and that everybody knew that show. Lee has also written, directed and produced several original theatrical works. Lee ultimately graduated from a college in New York, went on to get his Master's degree and became a college professor.

SUPER ATHLETIC YEARS

Joel Workouts

This is the place I talk about where my physical fitness just really took off. Later, I will talk about how Barry Scott and I got into training. We were training partners; and we pushed each other along the way to get better. I will talk about how Michael Berry helped to supercharge my workout routine. With Michael Berry's assistance I achieved what I call "Adonis One."

But, at the beginning I have to talk about my brother Joel. So, that's where this physical fitness section should really begin. You see, Joel and I were very athletic and super competitive. That's not to say that all the Dobbins boys were not athletic and super-competitive, because if you were a Dobbins boy, and Washington senior's son, these attributes just really came along with the territory. So, it does start there, Joel is the youngest of the five Dobbins children. Even with my sister, Angela, having transitioned on to her reward, Joel is the youngest. and Joel grew up following the three older brothers. Joel had to be tough, resilient, and competitive just hang in there with us. Joel and excelled in football, and track and field. From a young age the man of the Providence community called him "O.J.", in reference to O.J.(Orenthal James) Simpson, the great U.S.C. running back. I also believe O.J. Simpson played at San Diego state Community College before he became a U.S.C. Trojan. Joel was physically fit. He was the fastest young man on whatever athletic team that he was associated with (more football than baseball or basketball). Joel was well rounded in all sports, but he excelled in football and track. When Joel got to Overton high school and began to work out under the direction of coach Nick Coutras, Joel really developed himself physically. He became a physical specimen. In addition to that Joel ran track. His specialty was the sprints. Carl also ran track and was a superior high hurdler. Hurdles was a track and field event that just scared the living daylights out of me because I could never think of going over a hurdle and getting caught on one and going head-first into the track. Carl excelled in hurdles. I do believe that one of his chief rivals was a guy out of Mount Juliet Tennessee with the last name Majors. I do believe Majors was related to the older set of my grandfathers' brothers and sisters.

Before I began proceeding down this workout avenue Joel had already been a member AAU Junior Olympic track team. I think his coach was Jeff Tidwell. Other members of the team included Marcus Curry and Jeff Powell. Jeff Powell went on to become an outstanding wide receiver at the University of Tennessee at Knoxville. Dalton Grant. They were all "hard charging" individuals. I mean they flat put it down-all of them. They were a superior Junior AAU Olympic team. Many of them also had outstanding college track and field careers. I don't remember how the conversation began, but Joel and I began to get together at the Overton high school track. Not necessarily for him to train me, but Joel did begin working with me. I guess that's another testament to the commitment I had already made, in terms of physical fitness. Joel would meet me at the Overton High school track. He worked out a program for me to increase my endurance and stamina; as well as develop the techniques for sprint efficiency. We worked hard. Joel's program was excellent. He also included exercises to increase leg muscle strength and upper body muscle strength. I really did need a lot of help in my upper body strength. I was fast; especially when running the 220-yard sprint. Joel said I had naturally perfect form for running that event. I could show out. The times he recorded for me proved that I was more than just a notion. Joel would have me run up and down the bleachers, he had a program for me to hop up and down the bleachers. I can tell you it was because of Joel's workout program, his work ethic, and my work ethic that I literally blew the doors off my fitness program. You can ask anyone: you can ask Joel, you can ask my brother Carl, my brother Kenneth, or my mother. You can ask my brother Bobby what level of fitness I had achieved. This occurred somewhere between 1982 and 1984. Most people will never come close to the level of fitness I attained. They tell me I was all inspiring because those persons who knew me, and were around me wanted to achieve the same level that I had achieved, in terms of muscular density. I was an inspiration to a lot of people I didn't even know. I really didn't know how inspirational all of this was to others. I guess having multiple partners, varying workout plans, and multiple ways of increasing my endurance was a testimony that I was no joke. Coach McIntyre (head football coach at Vanderbilt) asked me to walk on to his team. I had professional football players like Reggie Hayden, who played linebacker for the Birmingham Stallions, to tell me that he could probably get me a workout or try out with the team in the USFL. The USFL is a League that was established by former president Donald Trump. Reggie, I guess, just recognized my strength and my abilities. When people believe you can perform at that professional level or collegiate level, and they have never seen you play a down of a sport that they have achieved success it says a lot.

BARRY SCOTT

This part of the book highlights the point where my physical fitness just really took off. Barry Scott and I got into training. We were training partners, and we pushed each other along the way to get better physically. Scotty was one of my best friends…really my brother. Scotty and I got to the place where we would run flat-out for about three miles. My brother Barry Scott and I started training together. We both had memberships to Cosmopolitan Health Club. When we worked out we pushed each other to go further, faster, and harder. Aerobically, we got to the place when we were on the track we could literally sprint two or three miles. Our conditioning was that good, aerobically. After working out we would generally go to Shoney's because they had a very good salad bar. We would get a salad - maybe a chicken parmesan, and ice tea. We would use the time to talk about theatre, other things, life…we were just good workout partners.

Bobby Workouts

My brother Bobby and I would go running. The spot was right of West End Avenue as the place where they were developing the Interstate 440 interchange here in Nashville. At one point they had carved and graded it out. I would go over to Bobby's apartment and then we would go down to this developing 440 Parkway area. We would run. It was intense. Bobby helped me a whole lot with developing endurance. I had multiple workout partners and multiple plans. I always kept a loaded gym bag in my car, and had multiple places I could just stop by, and get in a workout. I was no joke. Vanderbilt football coach McIntire actually asked me to walk on at Vanderbilt. I had professional football players like Reggie , who played for the Birmingham Stallions, to tell me that he could probably get me a workout or try out with the team in the USFL (which, by the way but was a league that was established by former president Donald Trump, I guess, just recognized my strength and . When you are invited to give it a try at that professional level or at major college level; have never seen you play a down of a sport that they have excelled it must be a good thing.

ROCK N'ROLL Express

Rick Morton and Robert Gibson were the Rock and Roll Express, a team of professional wrestlers who were in the middle Tennessee and west Tennessee area. Rick Morton was a graduate of Antioch high school and grew up in the same neck of the woods that I did. Rick knew many of the same people that I knew. Robert Gibson, as far as I knew, was from the Memphis area. I met Robert a couple of times, but it was Rick that I got to know well. Rick and I got to know each other well while working out at Cosmopolitan health club, at the Nolensville Road location, which was right up from Haywood Lane. I got to be friends with great Morton because I was always at the gym. I was already proficient at executing my workout. It's not like I was some hanger-oner, or that I was going to harass and annoy a celebrity. When we were in proximity in the gym one day, I just struck up a casual conversation with Rick about seeing him wrestle on television. The more I got to know him, and the more we talked, we ended up talking about his days at Antioch high school, where he was on the wrestling team. I can't remember where he had a career as a collegiate wrestler, but it was the collegiate wrestling that soon bought him into the world of professional wrestling. Rick Morton's dad was the referee of all the professional wrestling bouts in Nashville and Memphis. Rick and I got to be pretty good friends. He would even supply tickets for me to go down and watch the wrestling matches at the Fairgrounds arena when he and Robert were on the card. Sometimes he would get me tickets to other wrestling matches through his other contacts.

I went to the Nashville Fairgrounds to watch Rick and Robert wrestle one night. I remember this match the most because Rick and Robert had a match against a giant team called the Zambuwie Express. The match was one of those crazy, weird free-for-all contests. The Zambowie Express consisted of two giant Ugandans and I mean "giant" in every sense of the word. Because of their speed and cunning

Rick and Robert held on and made a pretty good show of it. At the end of the bout I think everybody was just happy to walk away alive; especially Rick and Robert.

It would be a couple of years later. I was working at Opryland theme park. I think the show I was working at that time was "… And the Winner Is." I was a part of the stage crew on the deck. I become friends with many of the cast members including a young lady named Meg. One day between shows, on our long lunch break, Meg and I were walking through the park toward the cafeteria. We noticed a mob of young people gathered in the park. Meg and I just kind of looked at each other and rhetorically questioned each other about what we thought was. This, actually was not that odd of an event because there were always special events in the park. There were always "pop-up "celebrity appearances in the theme park. As we got closer, and we were able to look over the top of this pile of young men (maybe some little girls) we saw over in the corner a guy with blonde hair and two big, fat, huge diamonds in his ear. Megan turned to me and asked, "Is that some kind of rock star?" I looked and I looked, and I thought. I said, "I know him." I said, "that's Rick Morton." Meg said, "who is he, a rock star, or something?" I said "no, he's a professional wrestler. He lives here in Nashville. I work out in the gym with him." Meg said, "you know him?" And I said "yes, I know I know him well." I yelled "Rick Morton!" Rick looked, "Washington Dobbins! What's going on, man!" Rick said, I need to sign a few autographs." "It looks like you are handling your business. Carry on, brother!" Megan and I walked on to the cafeteria. She asked, "do you think those studs in his ear are real?" I said, "they're real." You can't believe the amount of money he makes. They're real." It's not the flashy ending of a story that you would normally like to have, but it's a true story, nonetheless. I would imagine that if you would ask Rick Morton if he remembered me from those days in the gym, he would probably tell you "Yes." It was Rick Morton who advised me to stay away from "Chief", one of the other wrestlers who worked out in Cosmopolitan on Nolensville Road. Rick said Chief would whack you. He doesn't play like other wrestlers. He wants everyone to believe wrestling is real. I avoided Chief, except the times to acknowledge him when he was in my general workout space. I would also see another wrestling legend in the gym, Tojo Yamamoto. He even had those wooden clog shoes that he wore everywhere. During a match, he would bust the opponent's head open with one of those wooden shoes.

OTHER PEOPLE AT COSMOPOLITAN

Even before I worked out at Cosmopolitan Spa in Green Hills I worked out at the location on Nolensville Pike. There was also another gym that I worked out in Gallatin Road in Madison. I was a "gym rat". I was a staunch workout person. I met so many people during that period of working out. Read people like Mario Ferrari, who owned one of the finest restaurants in the city, Mario's. We just kind of started talking one day. We struck up a conversation and I found out who he was. He would tell me about keeping his boat down in Clearwater, Florida doing against the off season.

Another one of the guys that I met who I really was impressed with was Dobie Gray. Most people don't know who Dobie Gray is, but Dobie Gray was actually a stage musical performer before he became known as a songwriter. Dobie was a singer and dancer. Dobie Gray was in the Los Angeles cast of the musical HAIR. Dobie wrote the song, "The In' Crowd", but the song he would be most remembered for now is "Drift Away." The radio in my house, growing up, often woke the household up to one of these two songs. I happened to be in the gym doing my workout thing, and I heard someone call out "Hey Dobie", and then they said something about music. In my mind I thought "well, the only person they could be referring to is the great Dobie Gray." I looked up and expected to see a white gentleman, but I looked up and I saw someone who was as brown as I was. Once I got over that initial shock, I walked over to him and I said, "Excuse me sir, are you Dobie Gray?" And of course, he said "Yes, I am." And I said, "I know your music, because every morning the radio in my house woke us up to the strains of Drift Away, or "The In' Crowd." "It is a pleasure to finally meet you." Dobie Gray was courteous. I hope I was very respectful of him, his time, and his generosity. I would continue to see Dobie at cosmopolitan health club as he and I continued to work out there. It happened that as I was the manager of WFSK radio. WFSK brought in many very special guests over the period that I was the manager. I was there for eight years. One of the station announcers interviewed someone who knew Dobie's manager. I thought it would be great to interview Dobie Gray. It was through his management that I was able to finally get the contact for Dobie. The interview was arranged, and Dobie Gray come in for the interview. We had a really nice interview. I used to play that interview for my public speaking classes. I presented the interview in the context of preparation for an interview. I used it as an example of having your questions ready for the subject. I emphasized doing your research and preparing questions based on research. But I also emphasized the importance of having a conversation, and being ready to ask those questions that arise during the context of having a very spontaneous conversation. It was doing the course of the conversation that Dobie Gray and I reflected on the son "Drift Away." Not the Uncle Kracker version, which has a piano playing the riff at the beginning, but the original version (Dobie Gray's recording) that Dobie Gray recorded with a guitar riff at the beginning. It is a complex piece of guitar work (if I might say) and it was Dobie who said "many an excellent guitar player have put their guitar aside based on never being able to play the opening riff to "Drift Away." That interview, and that musical insight occurred because of having a gym membership at Cosmopolitan Health club. I did have a recording on tape somewhere (it will pop up somewhere). I'm not sure what I've done with it, but I have one.

Another gentleman and his brother than I had the pleasure of meeting and getting to know somewhat through working out at Cosmopolitan Health Club in Green Hills was Randy "Macho Man" Savage, and his brother Lanny "The Poet" Poffo. I guess Randy Savage's real name was Randy Poffo. "Macho" was very good athlete. He started out as a catcher for a minor league baseball team. Later on, his claim to fame would come when he became a professional wrestler known as the "Macho Man." His superstar ring persona was made more readily identifiable by the loud, rough, gruff, gravelly voice that he spoke with. I was in the gym working out and I noticed these two guys come into the gym. They pretty much kept to themselves. During that time, most of us who were in the gym pretty much kept to ourselves. So, it was not unusual that they did. I looked, and there he was in person. He was that guy that I saw on television every Saturday. Randy "Macho Man" Savage and Lannie, "The Poet" Poffo. Once you kind of get used to seeing them in the gym working out you know from being a gym rat how to kind of maneuver your way around to meeting and engaging people. When you are near someone who is working you just get in a quick "Hi", checking out their temperament and personality, that kind of thing. So, I knew Randy and his brother were very cool people. The brief, initial conversation let me know he was very approachable. He liked to talk about the condominium complex that he owned in Sarasota Florida. He was nothing like he was on television. He was a very calm, clear thinking, even humorous person. We got to know each other well. We got to be pretty good friends because I didn't bother him or Lanny during their workout. We all knew we were serious about that workout. Again, I say, you never know who in the world you will meet; and these were great guys that I met in the gym.

I talked about working out at a gym on Gallatin Road (I had multiple memberships, and always carried a loaded gym bag). Steve Turner, a motorcycle officer who was stronger than a horse's ass, and I worked out there. Guys would come in there from the WWE or the WWF. I remember the time the "Horsemen of the Apocalypse", "Maxx Payne", "The Undertaker" came into that gym. It was kind of cool to see "The Undertaker" walk through the gym, because he was so tall, he stood head and shoulders over the equipment. I would love to say I really knew or engaged "The Undertaker", Maxx or the "Horseman." They actually came in in so sporadically, or when they were wrestling in Nashville, that I never got to know them well enough to say "I see you guys wrestle on television", but they did come into that gym.

John Payne

John Payne and I worked out together at cosmopolitan John Payne worked out in the gym with me a lot. John was a natural body builder and competed in numerous competitions which were free of steroids or human growth hormones. John eventually went on to own his own jam a opened his own, naming it Marathon Fitness. Marathon Fitness is still located off Joe Johnston Avenue in the old Marathon Automotive building. I would work out at Marathon and John would contribute programs to me to work on. John didn't have to do it, but he did. I appreciate that. Marathon is where I met Eddie George. John and I met at Tennessee State University. John went on to become a Nashville firefighter. I salute all first responders! I value our friendship and all the help John gave me along the way. He was not my personal trainer, but he took an interest in my efforts and a gave me exercises programs which were very effective.

Tony Rowland

Thinking back on those days and years of working out, another person who comes to mind is Tony Roland. My first remembrance is of Tony Rowland was from my days at Overton High School. Overton High School and Maplewood High School. Would have an average rivalry. I knew many people at Maplewood. Some of my best friends in church went to Maplewood. They were my partners in crime, even though they lived all the way on the other side of town. There were players like Big Ronald Hale, Preston Brown, E.J.Junior, Jr. I was familiar with many of the players at Maplewood. Let me say I was in the band, I was not on the football team when all of this happened, so I do want to be clear on that. This particular Friday night Overton went to Maplewood for a football game. Coach West Elrod was the coach of Maplewood. This was a big game. Maplewood's star was well-known in the media. Preston Brown was a murderous running back. The big goal of John Overton was to stop Preston Brown. In fact, Preston Brown was probably held to minus four yards in. John Overton got beat rather soundly that night, because Overton head coach Nick Coutras and the team focused on no other player except Brown. No one accounted for a player named Tony Rowland. The big goal of John Overton was to stop Preston Brown. In fact, Preston Brown was probably held to a minus four yards in rushing. But, John Overton got beat rather soundly that night.

I am not sure that the coaches knew that Tony was a top level, even nationally ranked collegiate wrestler. Tony took the first kick off and ran back a touchdown Overton. Tony went on to score three more touchdowns against John Overton. So, John Overton held Preston Brown to a minus four yards and still loss to beat Maplewood. Tony Rowland was a player who went totally unaccounted for. Tony wreaked havoc on the Overton defense and special teams. That was my first introduction to Tony Rowland. Tony went on to wrestle at the University of Nevada Las Vegas; one of the premier collegiate wrestling programs in the country.

Tony returned to Nashville and began teaching aerobics at one of the gyms that I belonged. This gym was located at the corner of Murfreesboro Road and Thompson Lane. The gym was located in a strip mall shopping center. I don't remember the name of the gym, but they also had a location out on Gallatin Road and Due West. Depending on my demeanor, I would go to either one of those locations or I would go to Cosmopolitan. I had memberships with both, and I just kept a loaded gym bag ready to go so I could just go get a workout anywhere.

One day Tony was teaching aerobics at the Thompson Lane Murfreesboro Road location. Tony started telling me to come and do the aerobics class he was teaching. I told him I was not coordinated and could follow the routines. Tony kept encouraging me by saying "Come on Wash, you can do it. It'll be great for your fitness plan!" I am not good at step routines. I am not a dancer. I am athletically coordinated, but totally dance routine uncoordinated. That was the real reason why I did not want to venture into aerobics, not because I couldn't do it but because I would probably embarrass the living daylights out of myself.

But, one day I decided to venture into Tony's aerobics class. I bumped into a lot of people along the way of trying to learn the routine (but, I believe some of the young ladies bumped into me intentionally) but once I learned the routine I became pretty good at actually doing it. The thing that came next was I seemed to be the only person in the aerobics class whose name Tony knew. Every other second Tony was like "come on Washington, you can do it! It was Washington this and Washington that. By the end of every class everyone knew my name, because of Tony. What can but I can say, my footwork and coordination got much better because of Tony. Tony and I actually are still pretty good friends.

You couldn't write a script for the way life works. My son Joshua ended up in enrolling at Tennessee State University. Josh became quite involved in many activities at the university. I was very proud of his involvement at the radio station, WTST, the Chicago Club, pledging Beta Omicron chapter of Alpha Phi Alpha Fraternity, Incorporated. Along the way Josh met (and I had told him several times that Chris Rowland was the son of friends of mine, Tony Rowland and Ingrid Smith Rowland. I always told Josh to get to know Chris, because Chris came from good people. I told Josh I know his parents, and they are good people, so I know Chris is good people. Chris and Josh did get to know each other. It was just one of those turns of fate that how can't plan or try to make happen. As a further note, Joshua ended up pledging Alpha alongside Eddie George's son, sho was at Vanderbilt. It is ironic (and I did mention this to Eddie George when we worked out at Marathon – that I have a picture of Eddie George signing Joshua and Tres' jackets when they went with me to a Titan's game, and we were down on the field). You couldn't plan that your children would become friends of the children of persons who you were good friends when you were young. To add to the story, Tony's wife Ingrid, became a flag girl in the Aristocrat of Bands. There has to be something about connections in the universe. My daughter, Kaellyn became a flag girl in the Aristocrat of Bands and actually got to know Ingrid Smith Rowland.

Nick Coutras / Cosmopolitan Days

One of the men who became a constant gym companion was my former football coach, Nick Coutras. Coutras, and I say former football coach with a grain of salt, because when I first wanted to try out for the team at Overton. I was in the band, but I approached coach Coutras about playing football. Coach told me that there was way that I would ever play football for him. I asked coach why. He said "because you didn't try out for my team when you came as a sophomore. Coach Coutras made it clear that he only allowed those persons who played for him as a sophomore to continue on into their junior and senior years. I felt I had a fairly decent shot at playing, and a fairly decent amount of talent, so I told coach I would like to try out anyway. Coutras said "you can try out as much as you want but you won't play. I won't allow it. I guarantee you won't play."

At the appointed time that football practice began, I joined the group of young men out on the field. I began to submit my best efforts. Coach Nick Coutras held true to his word. He gave me an opportunity to do absolutely nothing. In fact, he took every opportunity to make it so bad that I would quit; that I would walk away. One of the things that happened is that in practice coach wanted us to use a particular kind of block. In my exuberance I threw the wrong kind of block. Coach Coutras immediately noticed this and questioned me heatedly about why I had thrown the wrong block. Coutras told me to start running the hill. There was a hill adjacent to the practice football field that led up to the tennis courts. It was a formidable hill. Coach Coutras told me to run that hill until he got tired of looking at me run up-and-down. I was determined not to quit. I was in full football gear, but I fixed it in my mind I was going to run that hill and was not going to quit. So, I knew I would have to run up-and-down that hill a few times, but it turned out I ran the entire practice without stopping. As tired as I was, I was determined not to let coach Coutras have the satisfaction of making me quit. So, as I ran the hill practice came to an end. All the other players were headed back inside. It was then that one of the coaches remarked to coach Coutras that Dobbins was still running the hill. What do you want him to do? Coach Coutras said tell him to come on him with everyone else.

Another memorable practice was the day that we were practicing a running/tackling drill. Well, this in this drill two combatants laid on their back and waited for the whistle to be blown. While you were on your backs a football was laid close to one of the players. When the coach blew the whistle both combatants rolled over. The one who had the football closest to him would try to pick the football up and run around or run through the player coming in his direction. Well, as it turned out coach Coutras, coach Pat Graves, and coach Griffin all orchestrated what the next episode to make me quit. They got the biggest man on the team, Timmy Shockley, to line up across from me. I know it was intentional because when I lay down on my back Tim Shockley was not the person who was across from me. The coaches switched persons, and intentionally put the football near me. When I rolled over Timmy Shockley was moving toward me with considerable pace. That can only mean that he had been standing up waiting for the whistle. By the time I tried to grab the ball in my best efforts of determination,

Timmy Shockley, who weighed about 300 pounds (and I probably weighed 142 pounds, carrying two rocks and in full football uniform) was pancaked by Timmy Shockley. Let me put 300 pounds in perspective: that is Tony Saragusa pancaking Steve McNair. I hope you get the picture. Well, needless to say I most likely had a concussion because the lights went dim grey, and then dark. I couldn't see anything, but I could hear the coaches saying, "Is he okay, or is he dead." The other players were asking the same question. Coutras, Graves and Griffin knew the dirty trick they had pulled on me. Even if they wanted me to quit it was a dirty trick, and even after that, that wasn't the day I quit. That day did not come until coach Coutras; I guess weary of my determination, went to Mr. Golden, the band director, and worked out a scheme to get me a brand-new instrument if I would come back and join the band. Mr. Golden said "after all, it was a waste that he needed me as a musician and coach Coutras would never allow me to be a football player at Overton.

But coach Coutras became a member of Cosmopolitan Health Club after he retired from teaching and coaching in Metro Schools. As things have a way of happening, we became good friends. Those crazy days of football at Overton were never mentioned, even though we both knew what had happened. I would see coach Coutras, we would have decent conversations. Coach Coutras told me he had been hired to reestablish the football team at Cumberland University. I was very happy for coach Coutras because I knew that coaching was his joy. I did respect coach Coutras because I knew the positive impact that he had had in the lives of so many young men.

As a postscript: Coach Coutras did go on his words more than once during the time that I was at Overton High School. The fact is, he recruited young men in the school who he felt should be playing football but were not. He recruited Timmy Shockley, William Eddy (who played at Vanderbilt after high school). And Thomas Gilbert (who also played for Vanderbilt). So, Coach Coutras did recruit those players against his own rule when he felt it was advantageous.

Michael Berry

When I first started working out I always considered myself to be a "ninety-pound weakling". I mean, I worked hard on things like pushups, sit-ups, and dips. So, in that regard, I was okay, but I was not strong. But the good thing about all of it was I had no body fat. In terms of building strength, the only way I could have gone was to making muscle, because I didn't start out with a lot of muscle. I kept working in the various gyms (I had about four memberships) and little-by-little I could see my strength improving. I could tell my confidence in the gym was increasing, and my self-awareness was not quite so high anymore.

But, I have to say, the person who really supercharged my workout was a guy named Michael Berry. Michael Berry and I worked together at Opryland theme park. Michael was a swing dancer for three of the shows in the park, which meant that he had to know practically the entire choreography for three shows. Michael had to be prepared to step in on a moment's notice on any show and do the choreography for the role of the missing person. Michael Berry was like all the other performers I worked with at Opryland. He was just a super-talented guy who could do all of the things that were asked of him; and then some. I wouldn't call Michael Berry a tremendous singer, but I will say that he could hold a tune. Michael's greatest talent was his ability to come in on a moment's notice and do a show.

So again, I will always say that fate is both funny and fickle. When you saw Michael on stage from the audience, or from the spot rail, he looked like he was 6 feet tall and weighed about two-hundred pounds. But then you would walk upon him after the show, and you realize Michael may have been five feet-seven inches and weighed about one-hundred and fifty pounds. What was the reason for that optical illusion? The reason was Michael Berry was cut to within an inch of his life. By cut, I mean that his muscle definition was so perfect that it has made him look like an awesome imposing super large figure when you looked at him from far off. I put myself on serious workout goal because I knew my present physique was nowhere near what I desired. My first real physique I called "Adonis One". I was working out at Cosmopolitan Health Club, in Green Hills. I saw Michael Berry on the weight workout floor. I thought, "that's that dude from the park." Leave it up to Washington Dobbins, I just walked up to Michael and started a conversation. I said, "Hey, don't you work at Opryland Theme Park?" Michael said he did. I said, "I just notice you came by as a swing for "For Me and My Gal," Michael was appreciative of my comments, and I said, "you are really cut up, can you give me some pointers?" I noticed Michael Berry did one handed pull ups. His form was perfect, and he was on top of his game. Michael Berry began to give me pointers; and he even spot me and coach me to help me with my workout. I have to give Michael Berry real credit for supercharging my workout. And he spent time with me to help me to get myself together to the point that in an even-handed manner, literally with each arm I could do one handed pull ups. I could do sets raps of about 15 one-handed pull-ups or dips. Michael Berry gave me pointers on doing sit-ups and crunches. Michael Berry gave me a lot of advice on correct form and technique for each exercise. I can tell you nothing pays off quicker in the gym that correct form and technique. Working out under Michael's tutelage, I saw immediate and dramatic results all the way around. My biggest regret remains that I never had a lot of pictures made while I was in that ultimate state of fitness. I had my diet was down to the science, my exercise program was down to a science. Those were days that my weight room intensity was through the roof!

Steve Turner

Steve Turner was a good friend, and Metropolitan Nashville police officer for probably 30 years. It was his job out of college. Steve recently retired from that career and was doing some additional work for the Metro/Nashville court systems. Steve attended Tennessee State University. Steve was a running back on the Tigers football team. I'm not sure if he ever played in the NFL, or another professional league, but Steve was one hell of an athlete. Steve really started out as my sister, Angela's friend. I believe they were undergraduates at Tennessee State University at the same time.

Steve was an officer who rode motorcycles. If you were fortunate enough (or, unfortunate) from time to time you might see Steve along the roadside somewhere doing his police officer thing. You would not forget him if you ever saw him. Steve looked like Superman, and that someone had spray-painted his uniform on him. Steve was a physically imposing figure.

I remember time (I saw this on the news) Steve, and his partner had apprehended some drug traffickers on the interstate. When they were bringing them to the courthouse retention area downtown the female suspect turned around and kicked Steve's partner. Steve's partner went flying down the steps in the stairwell in the back of the Criminal Justice Center. The television cameras were there taking in all of this activity. Steve reached up and grabbed the young lady. I think he may have thought for a moment that she needed to take a trip down the stairs behind his partner, but Steve resisted and retained his composure. Steve and I talked about that later. He just laughed about it, which was typical of Steve.

The thing I want to mention about Steve; at this point, is because this is a part of my gym rat lifestyle story. Steve, I worked out at one of the gyms in Madison on Gallatin Road and Due West. I would go in and I would see Steve. We would talk, and on occasion Steve would ask me to give him a spot while he was lifting. I was a pretty imposing physical specimen myself back then, but Steve wanted to get in a set of benches. He had about (and this is not exaggerating) 500 pounds on an Olympic bar. I believe for sure he had three of the forty-five-pound plates on each side od the bar. The bar itself was forty-five pounds. When Steve asked me to spot him. I just looked at the way the bar was bouncing up and down. I looked at Steve, and said "If you can't get that bar back up I won't be able to help you out. We will have to bring some of the big boys over here to lift that up off you." Steve said "It'll be OK. You just spot me." I just want to say that when the bar came off the rack with so much weight on it, the whole rig started jumping like it was on a trampoline. Steve held it steady and got his reps in. I just helped make sure that damn bar got on the rack, because there's no way a person could have let that much weight fall on their chest without losing a sternum. Steve got in his reps, and I realized at that point that he was almost a superhuman individual. But I also want to say that Steve been a great family friend. He was a great friend to my sister, my mother and all of us brothers. He's a great guy. I see him and his wife from time to time in their retirement exploits on Facebook. You couldn't ask for greater guy, or a better friend than Steve Turner.

Oooops!!!

I love telling this story, because it is a true story. It is a story that should be included, fittingly, at the end of my great gym escapades stories.

In the midst of my workouts when I was doing my perfect form sets of one-armed pull-ups, my perfect form dips with thirty-five-pound barbells in my weight belt. I was working at WLAC radio the coach of the Vanderbilt football team, coach George MacIntyre, was doing his coach's show at WLAC. I had gone into the studio control room. Coach Mac was on the air doing his coach's show. At the end of the show coach McIntyre left the talk studio and came through the door to the control room. Coach Mac looked at me and said, "Washington where did you play ball?" I said "Coach, I played a little bit in high school, but I didn't play in college." Coach responded "You say you didn't play in college" "Well, I'd like you to walk on the Vanderbilt. I know if you walk on, I can get you the scholarship." "Coach, I've graduated from college." He said, "Did you play ball?" I said "No." Coach MacIntyre said "Well, you still have four years of eligibility."

Well, right around that same time some of the guys that worked out in the gym we're playing in the USFL and the NFL. Some of them started telling me they could get me a tryout with the team they played for, or the league itself. If they could, would I be interested? Of course, I was interested. I'm thinking money I could make as a professional athlete.

Well, things are not meant to be.

I suppose if it had happened to me all my life, I had prepared to have had a promising career as an athlete, or if I had already been playing a sport at a very high level, perhaps I would've been disappointed. But, as things were to go, I was in the gym one day, working out by myself- which was not unusual. It was not unusual for me to be lifting as heavy as I was. I was doing a set of behind the neck presses with heavy weights. When I finished the set, I was, as usual maneuvering to put the weight back onto the rack. I missed the rack on my left-hand side. I didn't realize it until I felt the weight keep dropping. I tried to compensate and push the weight back up, but instead the weight, with me still holding on, flexed out at an awkward angle. I could literally hear the muscles in my shoulders tearing. It took a long time to come back from that injury. For a long time, I could not even lift my arm above my waist. I didn't have surgery or anything, but what I probably should have done was to go to Coach Mac and let him know what happened. I might have got Vanderbilt to get me some physical therapy to get the injury squared away. But again, I always kept several irons in the fire, in terms of career options: modeling, acting, technical theatre, radio production and writing, academia, the Navy. I believe it was having so many life direction options that allowed me to have the luxury/penalty to let some things go to the wayside without following through. That was the "double-edged sword" that happened to me.

It Slipped His Grip

There was another friend; and church member who worked out in the same gym. Many of the heavy lifters in the gym, in order to conserve energy and strength, did not wrap their fingers around the bar, especially when benching. The more desirable technique was to cup your hand around the bar. Then you got your reps in. My friend from church was doing this appropriately, but as things would go the bar and weight that he was lifting slipped off the cuffs of his hands and fell him onto his chest. I don't know how he managed to get it off his chest. He really should have broken his sternum. I don't know anything because I wasn't there. but my friend told me the story. For several weeks he could not do chest work because of the injury. Even I got hurt lifting weights. If I can get hurt in the gyn then you can get hurt in the gym lifting weights.

Irish Billy Collins, Jr. (Extra)

I'm going to throw in the name "Irish" Billy Collins, Jr. right now; not because I knew him but because I knew of him. Billy was a hero of sorts in the boxing community. I venture to say that growing up in Nashville, everyone knew about Sheriff Fate Thomas's "Punching Posse". I followed boxing closely for many, many years. In fact, I may as well say decades. I knew the name Clint Jackson. I knew the name Jerome Coffey. I knew the name Johnny "Bump City" Bumpus. Eventually, I would get to meet all of them because I became good friends with Ricky and Jackie Beard. Ricky and Jackie were from Jackson Tennessee, but they took me around to all of the boxing training spots in Nashville. One name that I mentioned because of the situation that occurred is the name "Irish" Billy Collins. Billy Collins, Jr. was a guy, who like Rick Morton, attended any Antioch High School. Billy Collins, Jr. quickly rose high up in the ranks of middle-weight boxers. Billy's father was his trainer. I watched many of Billy Collins fights on television as he was coming through the ranks. I was watching the night that Billy had a fight against Luis Resto (and manager Panama Lewis). Billy took a savage beating. I could not believe it. I knew boxing. I knew of the boxing skill of Billy Collins, Jr.. I knew his capabilities. I just could not believe what I was seeing playing out on television. I had watched many of Billy Collins fights on television as he was coming through the ranks. Each time Billy went to his corner after each round, he told his father it felt like electricity was going through him each time Resto hit him. He also mentioned that Resto's hands were moving with exceptional speed. Following the savage beating Billy took, his father went over to shake the hand of Luis Resto. When Billy Collins, Sr. grasped the hand of Luis Resto he realized there was no padding the glove. Billy Collins, Jr. had been getting hit with what amounted to a bare fist covered by a sheet of leather. There was not padding, whatsoever. At that point, the referee came confiscated the gloves. Boxing officials and the court examined the gloves and determined that the gloves had been tampered with. Yes, Luis Resto had essentially been hitting Billy Collins, Jr. with bare fists. The ultimate end was that Luis Resto and Panama Lewis received prison sentences and banned from boxing for life for this underhanded action.

After the court trial Irish Billy Collins, Jr. did win a settlement. But who knows what goes on in the mind of a person after suffering such a humbling defeat. Billy Collins suffered a cracked eye socket, and a detached retina. Billy Collins began to go blind. I can't say what happened on this night, but Billy Collins, Jr., at high-speed drove, his car into an interstate bridge support and was killed. As I say, I never met Billy Collins, Jr. in person, but I followed his career very closely. I know boxers. It put a lump in my throat to recall these events; to think about what the future held for this young man's life. Sometimes things that enter our lives enter our minds. Our thoughts cause us to do things that we would never have otherwise done. I just want to say, "I remember you Irish Billy Collins, Jr."

I BELIEVE I CAN FLY / I WANTED TO BE A PILOT

I was working at WLAC radio as a Morning News producer. During the course of a station buy out and changeover I became friends with Lieutenant Kerry Newman. Lieutenant Newman, in my past, had been sort of a mythical character. Lieutenant Kerry Newman was the person who was designated to start the Metropolitan Nashville police motorcycle division. This unit was known as "Newman's Raiders". "Newman's Raiders" were highly feared (and I do mean feared) by everyone in Nashville. Lieutenant Kerry Newman also started the aviation division for Metropolitan Nashville police. I met Lieutenant Newman at WLAC radio. I was a morning news producer. When we switched to an all talk and news radio station. I became a board operator and midday engineer. I met Lieutenant Newman and realized who he was and what he did. I asked if he would allow me to go flying with him sometimes. Lieutenant Newman was gracious and consented immediately. Lieutenant Newman told me to meet him at Cornelia Fort Airport at five a.m. I believe that was my first test. If I really was serious about this flying thing, I would be there. I was as good as gold. Pretty soon I was meeting him every morning and every afternoon. Immediately, I found myself climbing aboard his plane. After the first trip, just about every day that I would I flew with Lieutenant Kerry Newman as he did traffic reports over the Nashville area. Progressively, the more I flew with Lieutenant Newman the more he allowed me to man the controls of the plane. He would advise me about the areas we should avoid - mostly the Harding Mall area, because he said that is where the large commercial airliners were making their final approaches. Newman said you haven't lived until you get caught in the downwash from one of these big jets. More and more I would fly with Lieutenant Newman until the point in between traffic reports he would take naps, and I would be left to my devices flying the plane. One time I remember we were flying, and Lieutenant Richard Thomas was flying about two-hundred feet below us. Lieutenant Newman had taken one of his famous naps and opened his eyes in time to do his traffic report. When Lieutenant Newman woke up he immediately grabbed the control of the airplane. He realized that he had been asleep, and that Lieutenant Richard Thomas was flying below us, but coming at us from the 12:00 o'clock position. All was good after that. When I started flying with Lieutenant Newman he owned and flew a Cessna 72. That was the first plane that I actually got to lay hands on and control in the air. The second plane that Lieutenant Newman purchased and began flying was a Mooney. Mooney was a high-performance aircraft. Lieutenant Newman told me the Mooney would handle far differently than the Cessna. The responses that I had gotten used to with the Cessna aircraft caused very clumsy reactions with the Mooney. The Mooney aircraft required a far more deft and skilled approach in handling. It was with the Mooney that I began to understand that you had to have far more finesse instead of a manhandling approach with maneuvering the aircraft. To be perfectly candid, Lieutenant Newman allowed me to fly the plane once we were in the air. And it was his thought that I should take formal flight lessons and get my pilot's license. Lieutenant Newman told me the only thing I needed to really get a grasp on was the takeoff and the landing, and to complete the written test. Lieutenant Newman also went on to say further that I should join the military, (and I interpose at this moment that Lieutenant Newman and my father were both Navy men, Korean Conflict veterans.) That is the direction that Lieutenant Newman pushed me. Had I been able to get into the Air Force, the Navy, or the Marines; and into their pilot or aviation programs he would have been happy. As things would go, I did take the Naval ASVAB test. I took the officers Commission test as well as the naval aviation test. I felt pretty good about myself because the Navy informed me after the test there, I scored high enough to go into the aviation program and sit a second seat. I took the Air Force exam. The Air Force did not even call me back. After the test with the Air Force, I had such a bad headache (and the test took all day) that even if I had passed the test I don't think I would have cared if they had never called me back. I did pass the Navy officer candidate side of the test, as well as the aviation component of the test. I consider it a huge, missed opportunity to have had the chance to receive naval aviation training. The reason I did not accept the navy's offer is because I wanted to be a pilot. The Navy told me that I could enter the pilot program after five years of service to the Navy, at which time I could reapply to try to achieve pilot status. I would have to commit an additional five years as an officer and as an aviator. That would have been a total of ten years right off the bat. I did not want to wait the five years and I declined. This is one of my first missed opportunities to have done something with my life that would have yielded tremendous results, but you can't always look back. You must keep looking ahead.

I believe it is because I was talented in so many areas that when the Navy did not immediately come forward with the option that I desired I simply moved on to something else. I was a physically specimen; and I knew that I had opportunities in modeling, and actor. I knew I had opportunities in amateur and professional sports. I had an earned master's degree. Therefore, I had an opportunity as a professional educator, the opportunity to secure a PhD or terminal degree. Perhaps too many opportunities and too many options led to not taking opportunities I should have.

WFSK DAYS

In my career in radio perhaps the craziest thing that ever happened was that I built the radio station at Fisk University only to have it taken away from me. My mistake is that I built a station that could operate itself. It goes back to my first day at Fisk University; where I was hired in 1990 to teach public speaking, theater arts, mass communication, and history of mass communication. I believe it was the fall of 1992. The radio station was housed in the administration building (a Carnegie building) that sat in the middle of the campus. This building had an open a atrium, a skylight type of roof. The radio station was housed on the second floor. A fire occurred in the radio station area. I was not the general manager. I wasn't even connected with the radio station at that time. The general manager was D. W. when the fire occurred. Most of the station sustained substantial water and smoke damaged. The then general manager decided that he would just leave and go back to California. This left the administration with a burned-out radio station and no one to get station going again. I was asked by Marcellus Brooks, who was chair of by Foreign Languages and Humanities, if I would accept the challenge and rebuild the station. My counter was that I could not rebuild the radio station AND teach classes. It was then determined that I would be relieved of my teaching load while I committed to reestablishing W FSK radio. I agreed to do this, and this begin a one-year journey - along with engineer, Wayne Miller, to reconstruct W FSK radio. We had to send out all of the equipment to be rehabilitated due to smoke and/or water damage. This included the antiquated W FSK analog transmitter. I really wanted them to refurbish or to purchase a new transmitter so that the station would have a decent transmitter. However, the university administration decided that we could simply clean up the transmitter and continue to use it. With great effort, engineer Wayne Miller was successful in that goal. However, I must note at this point, the old analog antiquated transmitter was equipped with a gold-filament tube. Depending on the price of gold a tube could cost anywhere between $1200.00 to $1500.00. We generally replaced tubes twice a year. I also had to get into contact with the Federal Communications Commission to get permission for the station to be silent doing the period of reconstruction. The Federal Communications Commission granted that permission. Within one year, engineer Wayne Miller and I had WFSK back on the air. I was asked, at that point, to resume my teaching responsibilities. I said fine, but I can't run the radio station and teach. The provost, S. S., suggested…no, told me I could just absorb the radio station management with my teaching responsibilities. I told him no, because the radio station was a full time responsibility, not part time. I certainly was would not absorb management of the station with the full-time teaching schedule. That ended that particular tenure with W FSK. At this point they simply hired another general manager; never mind that I was willing to maintain management, and all they had to do was to add the general manager salary to my teaching salary.

Of course, it is my second-go-round at W FSK radio that was the most important; and in many ways the most painful. I was finishing up a teaching obligation with Metropolitan Nashville Public Schools (at Hunters Lane High school). I had not done enough work to have my temporary teaching certification renewed. I knew I would not be returning Metro Schools as a teacher. God always has a "ram in the bush". I received a call from senor' Marcellus Brooks. Senor' Brooks asked if I would come, just for the summer, get WFSK radio squared away a second time. Of course, I was not in a position to turn down this request. I agreed to come and resurrect the radio station. I went to the Fisk campus and met with committee comprised of faculty and administration. I asked what particular issues they were having at the station. I was informed that a group of outside volunteers had commandeered the radio station location space on the Fisk University campus and would not allow anyone from the University, specially the administration, to come to the radio station area. "Well, that's a challenge I thought" but I felt up to the challenge. The second time around came with its own particular set of circumstances, the group of people play engage at the radio station we're all members of a rather large church in Nashville TN and felt like that they had business skills and management. I quickly found out several things: first of all this group of people we're actually selling advertising time on a not-for-profit radio station, and from what I could gather they were making a rather handsome profit and would monthly come together and hand out the prophet checks from advertising. I went about the business once I found out who the major players were, oh removing them from association with radio station W FSK and replacing them with other volunteers whose goals visions were more in line with what the radio station actually needed. I began to include more students in the programming of the radio station, and at the same time expanding the programming offerings of the radio station. I installed three business programs, one self-help type of program, a Latin jazz in Latin pop rock program, a program that featured Haitian music, and then Clement it the cool jazz programming that WFSK is using to this day, secondly I received a call from an anonymous supporter informing me that WFSK was operating without a license from the FCC. the caller went on to say that his station license and Kentucky right outside of Nashville had applied for the 88.1 frequency was and was set to erect a very tall transmitter oh with much more power than WFS K had. With this information in hand, I immediately contacted the Federal Communications Commission again. I informed them that I had just been hired as general manager of WFSK campus radion station at Fisk University. I told them that as I checked the files, I found no copy of our license to broadcast. I asked it they would be kind enough to provide me with a duplicate license to broadcast. The person I was speaking with put me on hold. When they came back to the phone they informed me that they could not find where the WFSK license had been renewed. I assured them there had to be some oversight, because I had been assured the license had been renewed. I would end up talking with several folk at the F.C.C. To make this long story short, I negotiated with the F.C.C. for one whole year. WFSK campus radio station, located at Fisk University was finally granted the official license to continue broadcasting. This marked the second time I saved the radio station for Fisk University.

December of 1998 it also proved to be pivotal moment. it was during that time that Nashville suffered an epidemic it seems of tornadoes. there had been a very bad tornado in Alabama two weeks before they have been very bad tornado in Clarksville about a week before and it was during this time that a tornado tore across Nashville and what meteorologists it turned was a mesocyclone that had three component tornadoes within it. one component tornado came directly over the radio station. I was told by engineer Wayne Miller, and the adjuster for the insurance company that the transmitter had taken a direct lightning strike, which "fried" the transmitter, rendering it useless. I informed the administration of this discovery. The first response from the administration was to have engineer Wayne Miller rebuild the transmitter. I informed them that it would take far more money to restore the damaged transmitter than it would for the university to purchase a brand new solid state transmitter, which would be reliable, and not continue to broadcast using an antiquated, unreliable rebuilt analog transmitter. I told the administration that their insurance should cover the cost of a new transmitter due to lightning damage. All parties agreed and signed off on the purchase of a new transmitter. Engineer, Wayne Miller, selected the transmitter which would be both cost effective, and capable of meeting the future needs of the radio station.

There would be other innovations to WFSK during my eight year tenure as general manager. Dr. Jerry Plummer, the host of Financial Empowerment, was also a computer genius. Dr. Plummer became the station technical guru. Dr. Plummer is responsible for the incorporation of the first automation system, allowing WFSK to realize the twenty-four hour capability our broadcast license allowed us. Very soon, WFSK was broadcasting programming overnight, which included music, syndicated programming, and programs pre-recorded at the station. I also created staff/personnel manuals, as well as general station operations manuals. I established a connection with the engineer at Vanderbilt University's campus station. That person ended up giving WFSK it's first real components of radio station studio furniture. Before this generous donation WFSK was using makeshift particleboard furniture, which messed up several really nice ties and suits that I had the misfortune of wearing to the station.

The Time Had Come For the End / My Steve Jobs Moment / M. L., K. W.

The year was 2004. I had been general manager of WFSK radio for eight years, at this point. The university administration had changed several times since my return in 1997. I have already survived one station take-over attempt by another mid-level administrator. The next takeover attempt came when Hazel O'Leary was the president of Fisk University. K.W. had been hired as the public relations officer for the university. K.W. and his minion, B. _. Started coming to the station, and showing a more than healthy interest in the operations. K.W. and I met with M.L., the director of human services on day. M.L. informed that a decision had been made to place the station under the umbrella of public relations. I said that I did not agree with this decision because campus radio station, WFSK, had always been a "stand-alone" operation that supported all campus activities and events. It was not necessary to be placed under public relations. Despite my arguments, the station became a subsidiary of public relations. Pretty soon K.W. and his minion began to ask me for reports and any and all reference materials, contacts with record labels and syndicated programming. Every time I complied with their wishes they were not satisfied; and told me I had not submitted what they had requested, and that I had not submitted this material in a timely manner. K.W. and B._. were determined that leadership was unsatisfactory. I believe the day was October 5, 2005. K.W. and M.L. came to my office and told me my services were no longer needed. They gave me one hour to clean out my desk and leave the station. This "canning" really sucked, because Deyanne and I had just got married, and were working to get our lives on the road. So much for building a station that literally ran itself. My services were no longer needed, and I felt my dismissal was a product of my own success. I know how Steve Jobs felt. Steve Jobs built Apple, only to be fired from the company when the board of directors executed a "power play" and told him his services were no longer needed at the company Jobs had built. In Job's case, Apple CEO's and management soon learned the company did not run without Jobs, and he was reinstated as president of Apple. I could not have been that lucky. I had rescued this station not once, but twice from losing its license and not being able to broadcast and be the voice of Fisk University in the Nashville area. I had, in a sense, taken the station from its infant state to a station that could stand on its own. Then, this station that I had spent eight years of my life developing was unceremoniously taken from me for no good reason – except that it practically ran itself_ - and was turned over to someone else to be the general manager. I will tune in to 88.1 FM from time to time. With a couple of exceptions, WFSK sounds just like the station I built. I also want to point out that I was never fired from the university. I was still allowed to teach the classes that I had been teaching.

BARRY'S FATGHER DIES / MY FATHER DIES

It was Super Bowl Sunday 1987. Barry Scott and I were supposed to watch the Super Bowl together. Barry was managing the Mr. Gatti's pizza restaurant on Gallatin Road, in Inglewood. After work, Barry brought two pizzas to my house, and then went to his house to change to come back to my house to watch the game. So, as Barry prepared to come to the house and I prepared to watch the Super Bowl with him, I received a call from him saying that he would not be able to come watch the Super Bowl. I asked him what was going on. He told me that his father had just died from a heart attack. He said that he was going over to be with his mother and his brother who were already there. I told Barry I would ride across town with him because I did not want him to go by himself.

I proceeded to get ready. During the course of time that Barry arrived at home the sun had gone down, a powerful ice storm swept across the city. The heavy layer of ice caused everything at night to glow silver. The tree lambs, the foliage, everything glowed silver. The roads were black and slick. So, he and I drove over to his parents' home. His parent's home was on Dove Place. We got there and we sat with his mother, his brother Raymond, his sister Doris and Chandra Norman. My brother, Ken and his wife, Gayle (who is Barry's sister) arrived in town with their children. We attended the funeral at Kayne Avenue Baptist Church. The burial was at the National Cemetery on Gallatin Road in Nashville Tennessee. Life went on. I could never say back to normal, because when family members so close to you transition life moving forward is NEVER really normal. But our lives went on.

It was about three weeks later; my brother Joel and I rushed my father to the emergency room of Southern Hills Hospital because he could not get his balance together. Dad was very disoriented, and his speech was slurred. When we got him to the hospital, he was adamant about not being sedated. However, we made the decision (along with the medical professionals who were there in the emergency room) that he would be much more comfortable if he were sedated. From that moment my dad never regained consciousness; at least not consciousness as we most often tend to establish what consciousness is, from our perspective. My dad was diagnosed with a stroke. My dad had come through a lot of difficult situations, and we actually thought he would come through this one. He was a man, who the 29 years I had known him, chain-smoked Pall Mall filter-less cigarettes. That red pack. My dad "religiously" drank "boilermakers" whenever he got off from work. Please don't take this to think that my dad was a slacker, and not a hard worker, because he was a diligent, hard-working individual who many times worked multiple jobs after his regular workdays to make sure his family was taken care of. My dad was exceptionally bright, in terms of just being smart human being. The thing that I always recognized about him was that he had this kind of absolute memory. In other words, if you showed him a process one time; if you told him how to do something just one time, he remembered it in detail. I believe that having a mind gift of that nature is a blessing, but it is also a curse. All minds work differently. I believe when you have certain intellectual gifts of talents it affects your mind in a different sort of way that most of us will never understand. Let me say that I believe my oldest son, Tres', received or inherited this intellectual gift/curse.

We called my dad's sister, Tommie to let her, my grandmother, and the rest of the family know what had happened, what was going on, and the prognosis. At this time, my grandmother was living with my aunt Tommie in Chicago. In true Uncle Scott Saunders fashion, they immediately left Chicago and drove to Nashville. They were soon walking into the intensive care unit. I have to say, I guess I do look like my dad a lot, because Aunt Tommy told me that when she entered the ICU, she thought her brother had made a remarkable recovery, because she saw me standing next to his bed, and thought that I was him. Quite a compliment. I just wish that things had turned out differently.

Doctors are a different kind of people. Doctors gave families and patients their diagnoses and their prognoses, however, they refuse to give patients and families the FULL scope of their medical expertise and insight. I knew there had to be more detail to the information they gave us, so I called Doctor Luther B. Adair, Sr., who was my former wife's uncle, and asked if he would do the family the honor of coming by and examining my dad and giving the family insight and enlightenment about his true condition. Dr. Adair was chief of Radiology at Meharry Medical College, and the hospital. Dr. Adair also had a sub-specialty in neurology. Somewhat hesitantly, and I can certainly understand why (because hospitals and doctors are squeamish about having another medical professional coming in from the outside to check behind their work). Doctor Luther B. Adair, Sr. also voiced that hesitancy. But Dr. Adair went further on to say that if Southern Hills Hospital would give their consent for him to examine my dad, that he would do it for the family. We certainly appreciated that. Southern Hills Hospital did consent. Dr. Adair came to the hospital and examined my father, looked over his chart and history. He then proceeded to share his observation and insight with us.

Luther went on to explain that my dad had suffered a stroke in his brain stem. He went on to describe how the brain is a pretty fascinating organ of the body, because in most occasions when a stroke occurs in the brain, and that part of the brain is damaged, the brain has this unique capacity to teach other parts of the brain to take on the responsibilities of the damage portion. Dr. Adair went on to say however, in the case of my father, the stroke had occurred in his brain stem. Dr. Adair said the brain stem controls consciousness. There is no other part of the brain that can be taught to control consciousness. Thus, my father would never resume consciousness in the sense that we understand consciousness. He may have involuntary movements that we might perceive as being awakeness, awareness or consciousness, but it really would not be that.

We thanked Dr. Luther B. Adair, Sr. for his insight, expertise and honesty. My dad would remain in the ICU for ten days before transitioning on to the next world. To make a long story short, my dad transitioned exactly one month after Barry Scott's father, which meant that my brother Ken and his wife Gayle lost both fathers in a period of one month's time. In a very ironic twist to this entire event/story, a couple of month's following Dr. Adair's examination of my father, Dr. Adair was taking a shower, preparing to go to work. As he got out of the shower (this is being reflected in the words Dr. Adair actually said to me) he asked his wife, Claudia, to get him a particular medical reference book. She asked why he wanted the reference. He told her he thought he was having a stroke. He wanted to look up the symptoms. Dr. Adair was indeed experiencing a stroke. Feeling himself getting weaker, he told Claudia to call an ambulance. He was taken to the hospital. Dr. Luther B. Adair, Sr. survived the stroke, but was never able to return to work at Meharry. Dr. Adair's vision was affected, and he was unable to accurately read radiological images. Dr. Adair suffered some paralysis to his hand and arm, as well. Dr. Adair did live quite a few years following his stroke but did transition on to be with the ancestors.

A FATHER'S SACRIFICE

I wanted to take a few moments and talk about the sacrifices my father made. It's an interesting thing when people give up huge parts of themselves, their dreams, their aspirations and goals to make things better for others. The person I'm really talking about is my dad. There came a point when I had an epiphany; where I realized the tremendous sacrifice that he made in giving up Is his own education, aspirations and dreams to raise a family. I believe my dad held on to education because he knew education would be the thing that would help get him to the next level of his life. Working through this life is hard; and I know it was hard for my father because my dad's father (my grandfather) passed away when my dad was nine. I look at my grandson now and I know he's about the age my dad was when his father passed away. I realize how much my dad missed having a father in his life because of the things I hear my grandson say. My grandson also made statements that let me know how impressionable children are at that age. I guess it really made me have thoughts about my own parenting; too. I am always reminded of my own parenting decisions. Despite believing you are doing the best thing in the moment, I feel like I didn't always make the best decisions, but non-the-less, let me progress. My dad enlisted in the navy right out of high school. I am going to say this right here… I have been to the battleship, Alabama. I have been all over that ship. I have been below decks. I have seen where the men slept, ate, and worked. I have been deep into the belly of the ship; into the engine room. I have looked up thought the little windows that may be your only view outside if anything happened to your ship. I imagined being an eighteen-year-old young man; straight out of high school, taken from a little place like Providence and shipped out to San Diego, California. Imagine yourself in a loud, hot, and smelly engine room about eight floors below the deck.

That was He enrolled into Tennessee State University, where he and my mother got together. He and my mother got married. They start having children, and Dad immediately left college and took a job with the Nashville Veteran's Hospital. There were a couple of things that I found out. One thing I learned quite by accident, and the other thing came me in an epiphany.

The first thing is that a few years ago I requested transcripts from Tennessee State University of all my scores. In the process of them sending me my transcripts they also inadvertently sent the transcripts of my dad. Of course, we were both named Washington Dobbins. I'm junior. I have a different social security number; but I guess that name – Washington- appears so infrequently that they just sent everything they saw that had Washington on it to Washington. When I ended up with my dad's transcripts, I noticed on that there were a bunch of "D" s and "F" s. I would have expected to see "A" s, some "B"s, but when I started seeing "D"s and "F"s it really confused me because my dad was not a "D" or an "F" student. Further, my father was on the line pledging Omega Psi Phi (I remember my dad being a "Lamp". The more I thought about it the more it perplexed me. Finally, my mind settled on something that I have always known…and because I knew it, I don't know why I didn't figure it out in from the beginning. I said my mom and dad met at Tennessee State University. Almost as soon as they met, they got married and started a family. Well, my dad quit school to support his family. In the process of leaving school and supporting a family my dad gave up his own education. He sacrificed his own education for the benefit of his family. Daddy was on the pledging line for Omega Psi Phi, Rho Psi Chapter. He gave that dream up completely, without hesitation or reservation. Now I always say, and I hold to it: My dad was a really smart guy. I mean, really smart. And he knew he was smart. I think the people around him knew that he was smart. The people of Providence knew he was smart. I remember that he would go help give vaccine shots to the livestock of various community members. One time, in particular, he was giving vaccines in a syringe to some hogs on one of the farms. There was hog that they could not get a hold on to give it the inoculation. My dad actually took aim with the syringe and needle, and threw it like a dart, striking the hog squarely and accurately. My dad was not only a smart guy, he was also a VERY capable guy.

So, I guess even sometimes when I wonder maybe why my dad was seemed to be very angry about things, I know that we have to walk a mile in someone else is shoes to understand what is going on with them. I may understand everything fully and completely, but what I say is this: My awareness is way better than what it was, and I appreciate the many sacrifices that my dad made. My dad almost made the ultimate sacrifice for the United States of America during his service in Korea in the Navy. My dad sacrificed his own wellbeing for the wellbeing of his wife and children. I am sure the sacrifice weighed heavily on his mind. Everything that he was, and everything that he didn't accomplish... everything that he could have been. On top of all that I know my dad fought his own special "ghosts". Every one of us have our own particular ghosts that we contend with. I am no exception. My dad was one tough guy. He had to be. I know that toughness is in the DNA of all Dobbins. My dad was a serious chain-smoker of Pall Mall filter-less cigarettes in the red package. All the smoking, and all the drinking would have killed a lesser man much sooner than when God saw fit to call my father home. All of that adds up and I am sure that weighed heavily on his mind. You see, none of the Dobbins are stupid children. My sister was not stupid. My sister was very smart, and all my brothers are very smart and talented, just like our parents. A lot of that smartness I give to my dad.

This is the second thing that happened. I teach Cinema Studies at school; and during the class Cinema Studies, I have the class watch movies. One of the movies I had selected for us to watch was the Illumination Entertainment feature SING! I don't know how many times I've seen the movie SING! but it has been a lot; and the last time I was watching it with my class something dawned on me. It hit me like a ton of bricks! Maybe that's why all of the pieces came together - the transcript, the struggles my dad had... there is a scene at the beginning of SING! where the father purchases a theatre for his son who has aspirations of owning the theatre and providing entertainment to the community. Well, the father koala, as it turns out, used his body to wash cars in order to earn the money to buy the theatre for his son. and it answers the father sacrificed his own goals his own aspirations his own dreams to meet the dreams of his son. Seeing that, and again I say I've have seen the movie SING! countless times, and that was the first time that that scene has resonated with me like that. It caused me to have an epiphany regarding my father's own sacrifice. The sacrifice of the father koala was a stirring, emotional moment; and as I was standing there near the front of my classroom all I can think is "Dobbins, don't you cry. Don't you cry in front of these students." I held off, and held up, and I did not cry. But I think it's important that we all make sacrifices. Our parents made sacrifices for us. It's important that we carry that on; that we make sacrifices for our children, our friends, the people we love, the people that we care about. It goes even further because my grandparents, my great aunts and uncles sacrificed for the generations that were yet unborn. It is vitally important for us to continue.

There is another "whammy" that came to my mind in the midst of these revelations. The awareness of how broken relationship; especially due to the death of a parent at an early age really leads to a break in the continuity of the chain of life. Parents are the first teachers for their children. The guidance and leadership of the parents are critical for the development, learning, knowledge, and instilment of family culture within the children. My father had a critical link of his life broken…taken away from him…was robbed of. This is not to be taken lightly… Please understand that I am not wishing history would have been changed. I, my brothers and sister are all products of the development and evolution of the lives our parents were dealt. Without our parent's histories having taken their particular paths, none of our lives would be what they are today…as we know them to be. Decisions made along the way could have led to other directions being taken, and ultimately, any other way that life could have gone could have perhaps even led to my father's death, and there may have been no marriage to my mother; our father may have been influenced to select another mate, leading to another totally different outcome. I am saying that some valuable life components were not passed down from my grandfather to my father. My father did not receive certain knowledges and awareness's that he could pass along to his children. My father did not even have a father to example for him the way a father treats his wife; or the kinds of advice, training and other examples of things a young man learn intuitively, by osmosis, or direct learning/training from his father. My father missed out on so many of the psychological, emotional, financial, and wisdom benefits that would have been passed along to him by his father. My father's children missed out the advice that only a father could have passed along to us. My brothers and I; in terms have done much better by our children. I know we have all talked more to our children. We have been more of profound mentors and advisors to our own children. We have done much better than our father; but imagine how much better, in some sense, we could have done had we not missed one, but two generations-worth of mentorship missed. A family chain that is broken takes so much to repair regenerate.

There were times that my dad was not there and did not see some of the things that we accomplished. He was not there for some of the plays that I was in; for some of the football games we marched in. It is easy to think he wasn't there, or he didn't come because it didn't mean much to him. I don't believe it was because he didn't care. I think it was because it reminded him of how much he had missed out on with his own life; of the accomplishments that he had sought. I believe it reminded him of the things that he had given up for us and I think it was kind of painful for him even though he was proud of his children, and our accomplishments. His children were his prides and joys that made it possible for him to stick his chest out; but the idea and the fact is that our accomplishments were not his. But I think they had a bearing on his thinking and the way he was, and the way he responded to his children's successes.

Dreams are also funny things. Most of us have dreams, aspirations, goals. I'm convinced the dreams that God gives us we are supposed to have, and sometimes the dreams we receive are the seeds for the fruits of our children's labors. God gives us the dream to plant in our children. It then is up to our children to water, feed, nurture, and prune these dreams into fruition.

So, this whole discourse referencing this part of my life was generated by mistakenly being sent a transcript that was meant for my dad. I am glad that I have it. Watching the scene SING! Reminds me that God does work in mysterious ways.

THE SONGS OF OUR LIVES

In "my day" there were songs of inspiration for everything that might have been affecting our lives at the time. There were songs that seemed to write the script for our lives. I came about this thought because one week I was standing in for a Health and Wellness teacher at Martin Luther King Magnet School. The subject for the week was relationships. Good relationships, bad relationships and when might be time to end a relationship. The subjects also included possible healthy ways one should end a negative relationship. As I interacted with the students that week what came to my mind (and I told that to them) is that growing up we had songs that helped us to break up, make up, and express ourselves. It was kind of easy for us as we were guided through the process because the words of the songs really expressed things, and provided the script that we were not able to express through our own vocabularies. Also, the ideas and thoughts of artists make them some of the most honest, some of the most clear- and deep-thinking people of our society. Why would we make up the whole script when part of it was already given to us. These thoughts were part of our popular culture. They were part of our everyday world, and so we had healthy ways, through the music especially that we listened to navigate through difficult parts of a relationship, such as breaking up. I am not going to give you the whole song or all the words, but I am going to include the titles of some of the songs that we used in my generation navigating different aspects of relationships. We would play these songs repeatedly to help ease the pain.

WE'RE ON BREAK

My wife and I had a discussion one night about how young people break up in the most cavalier ways. I'm one to talk, but cavalier best describes the nature of many Gen-X/Millennial relationships. We came down on the side of how the music they listen to doesn't discuss breaking up or relationships in any responsible way. Personally, I believe the music is disrespectful to women. My wife and I were watching some of those divorce court and paternity court shows. As we watched, we started asking ourselves "What is wrong with these young people. They're hardly ever married. The couples refer to themselves as sort of a family unit thing. Then they break up or call themselves going on a "break". The first thing they do when they go on a break is have sex with someone else immediately. They talk about going on breaks like some people change underwear. While they are on a five-minute break, they're out having sex with an assortment of other people that they hardly know. A baby is produced, and they don't even know who the father is. When they realize that they don't care for their "break" partner, they just kind of come back together and act like they want are a family unit again. I was kind of appalled, even considering my own past, I was kind of appalled. I really don't even know how I could be appalled, with the stuff I did, but the couples on these shows put the stuff I did to shame. My wife and I determined they didn't have the same musical compasses and guidance's that we had. They didn't have the same scripts and words that helped navigate difficult moments. Sex was at the heart of all the music and entertainment they have in their culture. There was nothing compassionate, no scripts about feelings. There was no discussion about how you will feel in the moment.

MAKING LOVE / MAKING BABIES

When it came to making babies, I think that some of the best artists included Marvin Gaye, Earth Wind and Fire, Barry White, and Teddy Pendergrass.

When it came to making love, I don't think anyone actually said it any better than Earth Wind and Fire, The Isley Brothers, Jackson Five, Jeffrey Osborne, Peabo Bryson, and Marvin Gaye.

Teddy Pendergrass – Close the Door

Frank Ocean – Thinking About You

Ginuwine – Pony

Marvin Gaye – Let's Get It On / Sexual Healing

Donna Summer – Love To Love You Baby

Isley Brothers – Between the Sheets

Barry White – Can't Get Enough of Your Love

Rose Royce – I Wanna Get Next To You

Nina Simone – I Put A Spell On You

Prince and the New Power Generation – Cream

Earth, Wind and Fire – Reasons / Love's Holiday / Fall In Love With Me

BREAKING UP

When it comes to breaking up, I think artists like The Chilites, The Temptations, The Manhattans, Dolly Parton are great examples. I also have to throw in there Taylor Swift (I know some of you may not be "Swifties", but Taylor Swift has some really good breakup songs that come out of her own experiences. The Jackson Five "I'll Be There" is one of the greatest break-up songs ever. Again, all these songs taught us that some relationships were just going to end. They even taught us that some relationships were like rubber bands. They had that rebound element.

Taylor Swift – All too Well / We Are Never Getting Back Together Again

Toni Braxton – Unbreak My Heart

Chilites – Have You Seen Her?

The Jackson Five – I'll Be There / I Want You Back

Barbara Streisand/ Gladys Knight – The Way We Were

Dolly Parton/Whitney Houston – I Will Always Love You

Whitney Houston – I Have Nothing

Gloria Gaynor – I Will Survive

Bonnie Raitt (Mike Reid) – I Can't Make You Love Me

Marvin Gaye/Gladys Knight/Credence Clearwater Revival – I Heard It Through The Grapevine

Al Green – How Can You Mend a Broken Heart?

Bill Withers – Ain't No Sunshine

Carole King/Isley Brothers – It's Too Late

The Platters – The Great Pretender

Earth, Wind and Fire – After the Love Is Gone

Smokey Robinson – Tears of a Clown

Temptations – I Wish It Would Rain

MIND EXPANDING/ THINKING SONGS

Earth, Wind and Fire – That's The Way of The World

Temptations – Ball of Confusion

Marvin Gaye – What's Going On?

Grand Master Flash and the Furious Five – The Message

THE FIRST MARRIAGE

No one enters a marriage to get a divorce, and yet statistics show that fifty percent of all marriages end in divorce court. No one wants that but that is the sad statistical reality. An even sadder reality would be to have no parents. By that I mean that one parent could be in the grave the other one in prison.

I met the mother of my children when I was in college. We knew each other and we were quasi friends, but we weren't close friends, hanging buddies, or anything like that. But we knew each other. I knew of her prior romantic entanglements, but still, we were not anywhere close to being involved.

As things were to happen, I did move to Denver, Colorado. I was signed to the modelling agency owned by Jo Farrell, J.F. Images. Before I went to Denver, I was probably the biggest "ho" going. I went to Denver. It was pretty amazing because I had countless women straight out hit on me and try to pick me up. They wanted to buy me drinks in bars - all that kind of stuff. I was pretty tame because at that time I had made a promise to myself that I wasn't gonna go around hoing anymore. I was going to be focused on my work, because it was either work or don't eat. As I lived in Denver, I had a transformation of sorts. I did not want to be the old way that I used to be. I quickly determined that the constant running of multiple women was not how I wanted to live my life.

I came back to Nashville from Denver and begin teaching at Tennessee State University. I made a call to the woman who would become my first wife and we went out. We kept going out. It was an interesting dynamic because even then I knew that the relationship was simply physical. There was no friendship. It was simply physical. There were even times where we both erupted in fits of violent temper. In reality, we never should have got married because we didn't get along with each other. I say again, it was just a physical attraction. There were times, even after we got engaged, that there would be a blow up. I would leave her home in a totally violent rage. That should have told me something right there. We did, however, get married. Counting the year of divorce proceedings, we were married for sixteen years. But it felt like we were never really married it all. We were just kind of going through the paces as we lived together. I can say, with all honesty, that the best things to have come out of that first marriage were the birth of our three children. Even though we had been married for about six years when the first child came along, we were still never very good friends. Then the second child came along, then the third child (the baby girl) came along. It was by that time we were pretty tired of each other.

Sometimes it's hard to say to your children that your parents are not going to stay together, or even help them to understand the reasons why you're not staying together. But I will say that sometimes it is best for the safety of everyone. There comes a point where you shouldn't be together because it's not only dangerous for the married couple but is also dangerous for the children. One parent could harm the other; or both parents may harm or even kill each other (I'm not exaggerating). If one parent kills the other parent or harms the other parent they'd have to go to prison. The children will be left with no parents. So, I do say that there are times when parents must separate themselves from the other. That time comes when you are sleeping in separate bedrooms with doors locked because you both fear that either one could possibly harm the other. It's time to go your separate ways when trust is no longer alive in either of you.

I made the decision that the marriage should end. It was not a decision that I made lightly, but would great deliberation, a lot of tears, and lots of praying. I was just wishing that somehow; I was making the right decision. There were plenty of times I was just wanting to be sure I was making the right decision for me and my spouse. I wanted to be making the right decision because of the affect it would have on the children, and the potential harm that divorce stood to inflict on their lives. The last thing I wanted to do was wreck the lives of my children. It was tough. It is hard; and as much as I would have had things to be any other way, it ended the way it did - in divorce. After that, sometimes you can only hope to pick up the pieces; to salvage the broken parts and to move on as best you can with whatever you have left.

It is hard; and as much as I would have had things to be any other way, it ended the way it did - in divorce. After that sometimes you can only hope to pick up the pieces. To salvage the broken parts and to move on as best you can with whatever you have left. I've come to learn that children don't really grasp that concept (it is not even really important to them why you made decisions that you made) they just know that they want both parents in their lives, and they really want both parents under one roof. My sons can remember can recall the arguments, the fussing, the fighting, the feuding. That even with all that; every day they would still rather have both parents under one roof.

It's easy to judge other people. It is easy to judge yourself. All any of us can do is the best one can. I hope that that is what I have been able to do; and that somehow, some way, my children will actually understand that about their dad.

If there is a bright side to the first marriage, and the subsequent divorce, it is this. My ex (and her husband) and I are probably better friends now than we ever were at any time as a married couple. Perhaps it has something to do with distance, or just the fact that we now longer are creating a toxic environment by being together. Whatever it is, we can speak and act civilly and friendly when we are in each other's presence. I believe that's actually a win for us both.

The Green Mile Revelation

One night my buddy and I decided, quite randomly, that we would go to see the movie The Green Mile. My ex and the children were visiting her parents in Tuskegee Alabama. I had no idea what the plot of the movie would be. I did not even know the movie was written by Stephen King. The Green Mile stars Tom Hanks as Paul Edgecomb, and Michael Clarke Duncan as John Coffey. I think it should be remembered that John Coffey's character was an extraordinary human being who was gifted by God with the ability to heal and rejuvenate lives. There is a scene in the movie where John Coffey is being prepared to face his execution. Tom Hanks asks Michael Clarke Duncan's character what he wanted him to do. In the movie Paul Edgecomb was prepared to assist John Coffey with an escape from the prison. If Coffey wanted an earthly freedom Edgecomb would make sure he was successful. Michael Clarke Duncan's character asks Tom Hanks character why would he take a chance like that? Edgecomb (Tom Hanks) tells Coffey (Michael Clarke Duncan) that when he stood before the Lord and had to give an accounting about why he took the life of one of God's special creations, he had to know what to tell Him.

I sat there, and in that moment all I could think of was my own dilemma. If Karen and I got divorced I did not want it to hurt the children, and I also knew for my own life, what was I going to say to the good Lord about getting a divorce. I knew, I too, had to stand before my Maker and give an accounting for my action. Hell, it was a powerful moment, and I knew as soon as Tom Hanks began to let the question come out of his mouth; when he began to express that thought, I knew exactly what he was going to say. I don't know if you have ever had that moment where you know you were on the tracks and you know the freight train is bearing down on you, and you know that you are not able to get off the tracks. My emotions ran all over like that freight train. I knew I was going to cry like I had not cried in a long time. I boohoo sobbed openly and bitterly in that movie theatre. I know Bobby must have thought what was wrong with me; and so did everyone else. But it was a moment I couldn't help. I'm still looking for an answer to that question. I still understand that if Karen and I had stayed married there was a possibility that neither one of us would be in the lives of our children. I do believe that is how bad things had become.

I still know that you cannot predict the future. The only moment you can be sure of is the moment that you live in right now. I also believe it does no good to "Monday Morning Quarterback" because everyone can "Monday Morning

Quarterback". If you watch enough sports, you realize that "Monday Morning Quarterbacking" is all it is… a bunch of talk. You can't go back and do that play over again as if it were entirely new the first time. You can't redo the past and you certainly don't have a crystal ball to predict the future. So, you do the best that you can. I would tell you to live every moment the best that you know how; making the best decisions that you can possibly make based on your knowledge, your experience, and your wisdom. That's all you can do.

I want to take a moment to speak in regard to divorce. Many people say that when you get divorce you should not, cannot be able to marry again. That divorce goes against everything that God has put forth. I also know been told and understand that the only sin that is unforgivable is the sin of suicide. Because God will bring you through anything; deliver you from anything, including being a murderer and taking someone else's life. Just like Saul, who was converted to Paul murdered Christians on a regular basis, was not only forgiven but Paul was used by God to bring others to Christ. An amazing example. So, I have to believe that if you earnestly seek forgiveness for having a broken marriage and reuniting or uniting with someone else that God will forgive even the sin of divorce.

It's easy to judge other people. It is easy to judge yourself. All any of us can do is the best one can. I hope that that is what I have been able to do; and that somehow, some way, my children will understand that about their dad.

DEYANNE AND WASHINGTON BREAK UP

I never tend to call any decision we make in life a "mistake". I have always believed we have to be very careful about that expression. The reason I feel this way is because when you feel like one thing is a mistake it has the "ripple effect" in your life that everything else that came after was a mistake. I would never feel like our four children were mistakes. I would never feel like our grandchildren were mistakes. I believe one of the deepest movies I have ever seen that addresses this thought is "Spiderman, In the Multiverse." The lesson for the young Spiderman was that once he embarked into the multiverse and saw an event, he felt he could go back and change, because he had foresight that it would occur, the leader of the multiverse showed him the vision of how all the multiverses would be affected negatively because he had changed outcomes in one parallel plane. I also said at the beginning of this rather long-life history that the only thing we know about our present position in this life is that we are here, and that we are still alive. We know that if we had changed any little thing, that EVERYTHING that would come after it would be drastically different. We may have even had events that might have led to us being dead. So, as I venture down this road in history, I share the thought that IF Deyanne and I had stayed together, we have no idea of the events (positive or negative) that our lives would have led to. All we know is that we are together by the grace of God. We have been together. We've had our ups and downs, but we get along together very well. Now, on to the story…

For the rest of Overton High School years, I think you could have written a headline that would have read "Deyanne and Washington Break Up." As I reflect and enter into this story, it was Washington's fault that the breakup occurred. There was no reason for us to break up. What happened, and precipitated the whole thing is that Washington was sixteen. I always say, "stupid is as a sixteen-year-old boy does." Stupid had my name and picture written all over it. If you had looked up "stupid" in the dictionary, or sixteen, it would have been my picture that would have appeared next to it. No one, except Washington, can take the blame for a breakup that should not have ever occurred in the first place.

The event that led to us breaking up came when a friend of mine introduced me to a young lady who I thought would "put out." Deyanne and I had been together for a year, and she was just not about to jump into bed irresponsibly with me. Again, I say what is on the mind of a sixteen-year-old boy is getting between some young girls' legs. Well, let me say I did not end up between the legs of the other young lady, because the other young lady was not the person, I thought that they were. I probably wasn't the type of person they thought I was at the beginning.

I remember quite vividly the day that Deyanne and I met for me to say that our dating days were over.
We literally met on the football practice field. Deyanne had cheerleading practice at school. We had talked on the phone, and obviously I had told her there was something I wanted to talk about, and she could meet me at the practice field, in between her practices. Now, the worst-kept idea in the world is when you tell someone on the phone that you want to meet them in person to tell them something. Deyanne came with her friend, Jackie White. Washington just kind of spilled the beans that he was no longer interested in continuing the relationship, and that was kind of "it". Deyanne asked me a couple of times if I was sure that that's what I wanted to do? I said, I was sure. After that, she and Jackie turned and went back to practice. I'm sure that she was clearly upset by that incident, because in truth, there was no need for it. Deyanne and I got along "super well." We never argued; we never fussed, we never fought. and that was kind of the way we were, even at the end of the relationship.
There are some things that you say, that once you say it, you know you have made a bad choice. I knew that at sixteen, but I thought there was no way for me to fix it. Either my parents didn't know (and they knew Deyanne's aunt and uncle very well) or they didn't want to get involved. They never talked to me about it, questioned me about it, or anything. Maybe they were just happy that I would have the opportunity to see someone else. I that was true for her aunt. Her aunt was happy that we were seeing other people, and not all up under each other. I just knew that I was stupid. Every time I saw Deyanne in the hallway with someone else it just broke my heart again. But, when I would think about it, I didn't have anyone to blame but myself. I didn't blame her, or anyone else. I blamed myself. Deyanne did call me one afternoon after school to see if we could rekindle a friendship, which might have led to rekindling a romance. I had just smoked a joint, and I was high right at that moment. I was not a pleasant conversationalist at that moment. Deyanne and I did not speak after that.

So, for us to have gotten back together after about thirty years (as far as I was concerned) was nothing short of a miracle. In another sense, I don't know how she lost track of me because, as I said, I was in the Tennessean newspaper every week for Castner-Knotts. I can't believe that she was not reading, at least, the Castner-Knotts ads in the Sunday paper, or watching their commercials on television. How come she did not realize that her former boyfriend was featured in the ads and the commercials. Deyanne said she didn't know. She said that she didn't pay attention. It is hard to believe that one time we lived literally around the corner from each other, but that we never ran into each other, or saw each other. But the biggest miracle is that in 2002 God actually provided the plan to bring us back together as a couple. I learned from the first time. I'm not about to let her go again.

DEYANNE AND I GET BACK TOGETHER

I was working at Fisk University, managing campus radio station WFSK. I made the point to attend all social functions and gatherings that were university related; whether these events occurred at the academic level or the administrative level, I just made it a point to be a part of those gatherings. One day the United Way held a silent auction to benefit Fisk University. The silent auction was held in the Fisk University cafeteria. The cafeteria had been transformed into a very nice show place, and we all gathered there for this event. One of the partners there to help bolster the amount of funds generated through the silent auction event was the Federal Reserve Bank located in Nashville Tennessee. I had a fascination to the Federal Reserve Bank because as little boys my dad would take us to work with him. He would take and receive cash and secure bank documents to the federal reserve bank. My dad was never asked for identification or anything along those lines. He simply walked up the steps past the front counter (he was always cordially greeted by the receptionist) and on to his destination in the Federal Reserve. It did not matter if he had his kids in tow. They still let him pass freely, so we got to see many of the processes that took place to money when it is taken out of or put into circulation. This memory is what became the germ or kernel of thought that would lead me back to dating Deyanne Bridgewater.

During the silent auction, I struck up a conversation with a lady who worked at the United Way. I am a "talker", so there's always going to be a conversation somewhere that I can become involved. The lady told me that she came to the United Way from the Federal Reserve Bank. Immediately, I asked her if she knew Mr. John Bridgewater. Of course, she said she knew him well. I asked her if she knew how Mr. Bridgewater was doing; or whether he was still alive. She said he was still alive, and she knew that he had been pretty ill. She did not know the status of his health at the time of our conversation. I asked her if she knew of a way that I can just get in contact with him. I just wanted to know how he was doing. She did now know how to contact him directly; but she believed his niece was responsible now for seeing to his well-being. Of course, I remembered Deyanne and I said "Well, let me call his niece and I will find out how Mr. Bridgewater is doing."

Again, to complicate things, I didn't know how to contact Deyanne, and I knew it was going to be a challenge contacting her. She could be in the Bahamas…she could be anywhere in the world. Then I thought, "Let me see if I can contact Jackie White." I really did not even know how to contact Jackie White. I just knew that perhaps that was my best bet to contacting Deyanne. I can't tell you the number of sources I may have gone through JUST to reach Jackie White. When I was able to talk to Jackie White, she reminded me of the way that Deyanne and I had broken up in high school. Jackie was right there when I broke up with Deyanne. I wanted to get in touch with Deyanne. I said I was just wanting to call to ask about her Uncle John, and to see how he was doing. I did not want to disturb her life, interfere with her life, or create any type of tension or friction in her life. I just wanted to know how reve was doing.

I would say about a month… maybe two, passed. I hadn't heard anything back from Deyanne or Jackie, so it's safe to say I pretty much had forgotten all about the phone call that I had made to Jackie. I was sitting in my office at the Fisk University radio station with my telephone rang. I answered and there was a very cryptic, distant-sounding-feeling type of voice on the other end. Then a voice said this is Deyanne. I understand that you wanted to speak with me. Well, to tell you the truth, I could have fallen through the floor, but I tried to remain very professional and very unexcited about this call. I never thought that I would be hearing this person's voice again. I immediately told Deyanne the nature of my request for a communication from her. I pulled myself together and asked how her uncle was doing. We made only a few minutes of small talk. We concluded our phone call and hung the phones up.

What still gets me more than anything else is that I just couldn't leave it the way we did. I thought to myself, this is once in a lifetime, and you need to call her back and just ask how she is doing- how is her life -if she is married, dating, or anything of that nature. I picked up the telephone and I called Deyanne back at her work number that she called me from. I told her I did not want to interfere in her life or anything of that nature. If she was seeing someone or if she was married, I certainly was not wanting to interfere in that-but I just wanted to know how she was doing; maybe what had gone on in her life since we broke up in high school. We talked for a moment, and I asked her if she were married. She told me that she was divorced. She told me that she had just ended a relationship, and that she was not seeing anyone. I asked if maybe there was a time when we could get together… have coffee, or sit and talk, go to a movie or out to dinner. I want to know if she would she be open to that. She told me she didn't know. She would think about it. I said "that's fair", and we hung the phone up. It was, probably, a couple of days later that she called me back and asked if I still had the offer on the table. I told her "Of course". As things turned out we talked for nearly a month on the phone before we even met. We spent hours catching up on things that happened in our lives. We spoke very honestly and candidly about everything open. Deyanne suggested that perhaps one evening I could come to her house. We could have a sit down together meeting…talk…get to know each other kind of thing.

Of course, it's safe to say that she pretty much was interviewing me, and I did have the opportunity to interview her. From us just speaking over the phone for a month, if there was anything that was going to adversely affect us I think we pretty much would've known.

I do believe the biggest thing for each one of us is that since we both had children that we were protective of our them. We just did not want our children to be in the presence of anyone or invite someone into our lives who would be detrimental to the upbringing of our children.
 I would say that pretty much we were successful in that effort, although nothing is absolutely perfect- nothing goes absolutely the way everyone things to go, but what Deyanne and I found out is that we both really wanted the same things. We both were going in the same directions, and our temperaments were pretty much the same. Deyanne and I are not the yelling, arguing types of people. We are very much settled. Now, that is not to say that we don't have disagreements. That is not to say that there have been problems along the way; that there been stumbles and other obstacles to come up on our radars, but for the most part we try to handle our situations as rationally as possible with as little anger and as little frustration is possible. We always try to do that with no yelling, screaming, or drama. We are both pretty calm even when we are lividly mad or upset with each other.

Deyanne and I dated for three years. The first month of our re-dating Deyanne's mother passed away. That October Deyanne flew back to the Bahamas to attend her mother's funeral. From time to time, I had the opportunity to speak with her sister Patsy on the phone, when her sister Patty would call from the Bahamas, or when Deyanne called Patsy. Patsy was the first person to say that Deyanne and I were going to get married. Patsy was pretty much on target. It was the third year that we dated that Deyanne, and I were married. Patsy passed away not long after we got married. It was pretty upsetting, but it was also good to know that Patsy had been able to realize her vision that Deyanne and I would get married.

Right at our first-year marriage anniversary Deyanne was diagnosed with lung cancer. I know the diagnosis was devastating for her, but it was equally devastating for me. I was just getting to spend my life with the love of my life, looking forward to a long, fruitful, happy marriage. To get that diagnosis was just draw dropping. It was that just took your breath away. It knocked you down. I was actually in Louisville Kentucky when Deyanne called me and gave me that news. I was working for the Kroger company, in management training. I was on a lunch break when I have received a message from Deyanne to call her back. When I called her back the message, she gave me was upsetting. Immediately I went to my training supervising team with Kroger and told them what was going on and I need to return home immediately. Of course, they were gracious and kind and understanding and told me I immediately need to get in the car and head back to Nashville. I did and subsequently Deyanne was able to receive her cancer the surgery. The surgery and lengthy recovery and recuperation were successful. Again, it was a rough moment, but I am thankful to God that we were able to come through that moment, and that He allowed us to be able to spend many, many years together.

OUR TRIP TO THE BAHAMAS

It was a trip that was about thirteen years in the making. I know that we wish we had done it much sooner, but we decided that we would go ahead and go because if we didn't go we might never go. So, Deyanne and I planned and executed a trip to the land of her birth. It was a very intentional trip wherein we meant to go to the island where she was born. This trip was meant for me to see the beauty and the splendor of the island of Exuma Bahamas. We spent time in Nassau Bahamas because that is where all of her brothers and sisters now reside (well, except Obadiah- he does live on Exuma). Nassau is the capital and the center of activity, and the best place to be employed.

As we made our way out of the state of Tennessee, and eventually our of the United States I became somewhat confused by the United States does not handle a concrete immigration policy. It seems to me that the United States is selective in the way immigration is carried out. First of all, it takes an act of Congress to leave the United States - just to even leave Nashville Metropolitan airport to fly to Charlotte North Carolina when they know your final destination is the Bahamas. At the ticket counter we had to show our passports and our American identification just to check our luggage. Going through TSA we have to show our American identification and our passports in order to go through. In order to get on the plane, we have to show our American identification and our passports. To planes in Charlotte North Carolina, we had to repeat the process over again, even though we have done this just to get on airplane. We never even left the secure area, but for us to go from one plane to another the identification process had to be repeated. Of course, we knew that the process would be repeated once we arrived in Nassau, but that was understandable. The big thing was why would we have to continuously be subjected to this process when we were Americans in an American airport trying to leave the country. We were not trying to get into the country. I am perplexed at how people can walk into this country from our southern border but people from Haiti or people from the Bahamas and other Caribbean nations are not allowed to just come into this country. Additionally, the rules which govern their being in this country are exercised "to the tee". There is no concern about what people from the Bahamas, Haiti and the Caribbean What causes them to want to be in this country. Anyway, I digress a little bit and stood on a soapbox.

When we were on first final approach to Nassau the captain was waved off, which was fortunate for me because as we were approaching that first time I looked down and saw the beautiful, spectacular waters of the Bahamas and the land and everything below us. I was reaching for my camera phone. I could not get to my get to my phone and I was so disappointed that I had missed some extremely gorgeous shots. However, we kept going past the island and I knew that we were circling and bypassing the airport. So, the second time around I had myself together and I snapped picture after picture of this beautiful approach to this beautiful island.

When we set down in Nassau, of course, we had to go through customs and do the passport and identification thing. Going through customs at the airport there was a band playing many of the tunes I was already familiar with because I have several CD's of Bahamian music, so I was very familiar with many of the songs that they were playing. That was all good and Deyanne's brother Martin, and her sister Esther picked us up at the airport. Martin gave us the mini-tour. Martin gave us an idea of some of the things that were going on the island. They took us downtown to the Fish Fry. When you go to the Fish Fry there's local entertainment nightly. The food is tremendous! Martin and Esther took us to a restaurant (I think it is called Twin Brothers) The Conch salad that they brought to our table was mine-bendingly good! As we drove the city, Martin pointed out many of the newer conveniences being built by representatives from many countries. Atlantis Resort was constructed by a corporation from Dubai, where the mirror-image of Atlantis exists. Martin showed us many locations of the James Bond movies. He told us Ian Fleming (the creator of James Bond) actually has a home on Nassau; as does Sean Connery, the original James Bond.

Deyanne and I spent three nights at the Melia Nassau Beach, hotel which was right next to a huge hotel called the Baha Mar. In fact, Baha Mar in Spanish actually means shallow sea. This is where the name Bahamas comes from. I am told that there are places where the sea is so shallow that literally you could walk from one island to another. The water would not be much more than waist deep. Our three nights at the Melia Nassau Beach were great! Everything was all inclusive, so we could eat any time we wanted; and the food was really good. I was a little disappointed because there was no Bahamian fare on the menu but all the alcohol, all the liquor you could drink. They had a good dance floor/disco as part of the main lobby area. I could only imagine what the Baha Mar must have been like on the inside. I do know it had a casino, and we could have gone to visit the Baha Mar, but we did not.

This also was my first opportunity to get to meet, in person, Deyanne's brothers Roger and Nathaniel and their wives. I met Deyanne's oldest sibling, Prescola, and her daughter Lynne. When Prescola found out we were going to Exuma, she wanted to make sure I realized I was going to be standing exactly on the Tropic of Cancer.

As we drove around, we were constantly on the search for sweet genips. There were many places where individuals had set up little tables along the roadside, and said they had sweet genips for sale. You must be careful with genips because they are loaded with tannic acid. If you get the juice on your clothes, it is near impossible to get the stain out.

THE THIRD OR FOURTH DAY IN THE BAHAMAS

 So that third or fourth day we boarded the plane, along with her sister Esther and our niece Lakira and flew to Exuma Bahamas. We flew Bahamas Air. The equipment was ATR-600 turbo-prop airplane. It was a beautiful flight from Nassau to Exuma. The sights as we flew over this part of the Bahamas archipelago was stupendous. It was very exciting, on so many levels, to see Exuma International airport. It is a small airport, but it does take international flights into Exuma. We took a cab to our hotel. The best thing about the cab ride is that our driver was actually Deyanne's cousin. We stayed at the Augusta Bay; a very nice place right on the ocean front and had adjoining rooms with Esther and Lakira.

We immediately realized we wanted to see more of Exuma. When we landed on Exuma Deyanne said she had not been to Exuma in nearly 50 years. It seemed like everywhere we went Esther would make a connection to a relative or longtime friend of theirs who they hadn't seen, like I said, in close to 50 years. Pretty soon we would be getting a ride to the hotel from Georgetown. They met up with their God-sister Aileen. Aileen was an air traffic controller who directed flights into Exuma. Aileen directed our plane to a safe landing on Exuma. Aileen, on her days off (or maybe she took days off) drove us around the island two days. In fact, and she drove us down to the Tropic of Cancer, a location Deyanne's sister, Prescola wanted to make sure I understood the geographical location. I took pictures directly on the Tropic of Cancer. Aileen drove us around the island to Barra Terre, to Rolleville, and other memorable spots.

THREE SISTERS

As you travel along Queen's Highway on Exuma, which skirts the outer perimeter of Exuma, one of the most stunning views that you're told about long before you go to Exuma is the rock formation Three Sisters. As Aileen drove, she said "be sure and look to your right as we go down this stretch of highway because you will see the rock formation Three Sisters. It is one thing to hear about these types of views, these types of natural formations and sites, but it is another thing to actually see them in person. When I looked to the right the rock formation came up dramatically. It was stunning! There is a story about the Three Sisters Rock Formation. I will just give the thumbnail version: The story is that a sea captain had come to Exuma. This captain met three sisters and dated them all. All three sisters fell in love with the sea captain. As he went back to his ship and proceeded to depart Exuma it was said that each one of the sisters jumped into the water swimming after the ship as far as they could until they drown or perished. At each location where a sister perished a rock formation rolled up out of the water. Hence, these rock formations became known as the Three Sisters. It is a beautiful story, and an even more spectacular natural formation. It is one of the things that you will have to see when you choose to visit and explore the island of Exuma.

SEA GRAPES / COCO PLUMS

As My Baby and I walked from the Augusta Bay with Esther and Lakira we walked along the side of the Queen's Highway. Deyanne and Esther began to pick a white skinned fruit off the bush on the roadside. They said these fruits were cocoa plums. They picked a couple ate them, and then gave some to Lakira and I. They were very good. They had a different type of sweetness and texture about them, but they were very good. I did not suffer any ill effects from eating them, so I know they are "eater-friendly".

Another fruit that just grows wildly on the island of Exuma are seagrapes. Seagrapes, of course, grow wild all over the Bahamas, and I would suspect most of the Caribbean. Seagrapes were just coming in or coming of ripeness when we were in Exuma. Some were actually pretty good, but again, having the opportunity to eat Seagrapes, a fruit that I was totally unaware of, was a great experience. Other fruits that you will see growing naturally on the islands include bananas, mangoes, and sweet and tamarinds.

The beauty of the water of Exuma is also something that is hard to describe. There are so many varying shades of blues and greens that not even a very good camera can capture all the colors that you will see at any one location. One of the public beaches that we went to several times when we were in Exuma the water was so crystal turquoise clear, and the sand on the bottom was so pure white, it gave the impression that you were just swimming in a giant salty swimming pool. Again, there are not many places in this world where you can have that type of experience. Water that is that clear, majestic and warm.

BIG BAY / LIL BAY

Big Bay and Little Bay! What can you say about these areas of water that jut into the land mass of Exuma! These areas are just absolutely pristine and beautiful. You could be there on these stretches of beach and never see another human being the entire day.

REGATTA TIME ON EXUMA

October of each year they have the Great Exuma/National Family Island Regatta on Exuma. This is more or less a huge homecoming event as well as a spectacular sailboat racing event. The big thing about Exuma Regatta is that people who are from Exuma, from the Bahamas, come home from England, Canada, the United States. They also come from other places in the Bahamas just to be there for the regatta races. It is quite a spectacular moment. Regatta takes place near Barra Terre. The water and the beach all are set very low to the beachscape. You get a clear view for miles of the routes the boats will race in the area. Spectacular is a expression that comes close to describing the scene.

THE ROLLE COUSINS

COMING BACK TO THE UNITED STATES

TRAVELING WITH MY BABY: Retirement to the rest of our lives

It is interesting that Deyanne and I have been together for nearly twenty years at the time of this writing. Twenty years goes by really, really quickly, so my advice is to be vigilant and seek to select a person who you can spend the rest of your life with. A person that you get along with; that you don't argue with and settle down with that person.

This is not to say that there will not be some moments of disagreement, some moments of resistance by one, the other or both. Maybe quiet verbal combat. I do say quiet verbal combat because there will be times where you disagree; even with a person that you really get along well with, that you like spending your time with. Disagreements are just part of the deal of relationships. You have to be able to get over it and get on with your life together. That just kind of seems to be the way that Deyanne and I handle moments of debate. The times that we have disagreements are rare, and we like to, or we prefer to keep them that way.

TO KEEP THEM THAT WAY

Deyanne and I have really thought about is the amount of traveling that we will do when we retire. We've also discussed that when we both retire we want to move to Pensacola Florida. Pensacola sports a sunny climate filled with beaches close to the ocean. Pensacola seems to a climate and location that we both prefer. So, that is the immediate plan.

We also would like to travel. We both like to travel and see new places. Among the places that we would probably like to travel to is Las Vegas Nevada. We've always said we wanted to go there, and just never had the opportunity to go (we actually got to Las Vegas October of 2022). I think another place that we would like to go is back to the Bahamas. That just seems to be a place that we will always want to travel. Mostly, we would enjoy traveling to the outer/family islands. I will always say that Nassau is nice. It is a great place. It is pretty commercial, but there are beautiful places even in the capital of the Bahamas. Deyanne and I would actually prefer to explore the outer, or the family islands. The family islands are less commercial, and still many are, in terms of infrastructure and development, much the same as they were fifty or sixty years ago. It is very cool to see the native vegetation, the native scenery, the people who live simple lives. That's not to say that some lives are not difficult; but they are relatively peaceful and relatively simple, to the point that even many of the young people are choosing to depart the outer islands to move to Nassau, Grand Bahamas or to other countries to try to make livings.

For those of us who come from very busy, noisy places here in the United States, the calmness the serenity of those islands are ideal for United States citizens, especially older persons. I know it is simplistic, but the plan is to travel and see places while we're both still able to get about. We hope retirement is enjoyable, and as I usually like to say "uneventful".

by JALYNN DODSON

As we prepare for the upcoming move to Lawson High School, *The Topper Times* looks back at the history that brought us to where we are today, with staff writer Jalynn Dodson interviewing our own Mr. Dobbins on his experiences growing up in Nashville and as a student in Metro Nashville Public Schools during a time when segregation was widespread. *The Topper Times* would like to thank Mr. Dobbins for sharing his story and Adrian Torres for his assistance recording it. This interview has been edited for length and clarity.

JD: Hey Mr. Dobbins! Thank you for giving us the opportunity to share your story.

WD: Thank you for taking the time to sit with me and talk. I think it's a great opportunity for the student body to realize that life not so long ago looked very different here in Nashville.

JD: Tell me about your early years. Where were you born? What part of Nashville did you live in?

WD: I like to tell people I was raised in a village. That village was at Harding Place and Nolensville Road. It was, it is, called Providence. There's a historic marker there that indicates that the village was settled in 1868, right after the Civil War, so I grew up in a very rural area. I mean, it was more rural than Mayberry if you know about Andy Griffith, but it was probably the best experience a young person could have growing up, seeing all of the season changes and the life cycles of all of the animals and things like that. It was a very, very cool place. So, we were pretty much self-contained in that area. All of the people of the community held everybody accountable. So, if at any point I did something wrong, I was fair game for any elder in that neighborhood and so they would tell my parents or my grandparents what had happened.

JD: As a child, do you remember noticing the effects of segregation in your neighborhood?

WD: I do. A lot of times I recall the words of my mother because she would go and take my great aunt to places like the laundromat. My great aunt looked white. My ancestors were mulatto, but the mulatto ones looked white, and they would go to these white only laundromats and, and if my aunt acted just like she was white, or when they would ride at the front of buses and the trolleys and stuff like that they could basically pass.

JD: Do you remember the white, colored water fountains, anything like that?

WD: The strongest memory of the segregated nature of Nashville at that time is when my father would take us to the movies, and this was downtown. The Lows or the Crescent or the Paramount. Those were huge theaters, downtown show places, really. But my dad would go to the front box office and he would buy the tickets, but we couldn't go in the front. We had to go around to the back, down in the alley, up a flight of stairs to the balcony because we weren't allowed to, you know, downstairs, we weren't allowed to go into the front.

JD: What elementary school did you attend and was it segregated?

WD: Yes, it was. The first school that I attended was Providence Elementary School where Southern Hills Hospital is now, on land owned by Reverend Maxwell. Originally, he donated the land to have a school built there, for the children of that community; the black church. To have a school in their neighborhood. The school was built in 1951. I think somewhere around 65 or so when I started there, but I went there until third grade and that was when segregation was settled here in Nashville. There was Brown vs the Board of Education, and then there was a case here in Nashville and Alexander Looby was the lead attorney on it. So, it took time for this desegregation to be implemented. It wasn't just overnight. It was implemented in state and at the very beginning, and that may have been 1957, Hattie Cotton school was actually bombed because they didn't want the black students and the white students to go to school together. So, they thought, well, we'll just take the school out.

When my school community was desegregated, if you lived on the west side of Nolensville Road, you went to Providence, Tusculum, McMurry or Overton, but if you lived on the east side of Nolensville Road you went to Haywood, Apollo Middle School and then Antioch High School. So literally the desegregation, which is always a two-edged sword, divided our little village into two parts, but it always made it an interesting sporting time. You may have been at Overton and the other half may have been over at Antioch, then you had to face off against each other. It was a really different type of experience.

JD: Ms. Rosa told me you attended a new school after schools were desegregated. How were the schools different?

WD: The books we received had already been written in, already been marked up, pages torn out. We did get the "hand me down" educational material, in terms of desks, things like that. The other physical things are probably even, but I also think that the nurturing atmosphere of Providence was, you know, much more conducive than Tusculum.

JD: Do you remember historic national events?

WD: I remember those, yes. And we would mostly watch them on television and, see things on the news back in the day when they shot film. People who worked in the news were minor filmmakers because that was the process. We saw things on television every night, but I think the thing that sticks out most in my mind is that when something would happen in terms of civil rights, whether it was national, or Birmingham or Detroit or Chicago my mother would just, just break out into this boohoo crying, and I knew. Something had happened. The day that Dr. King was assassinated, I knew.. I didn't know what, but I knew something happened. The Sunday that the 16th Street church in Birmingham was bombed and the four little girls were killed in that bombing. I knew something had happened.

That is my most vivid memory from those early days of civil rights—my mother would just break down. She was from Birmingham, but she also worked at American Baptist. They called it Seminary then. She knew Reverend James Lawson. She knew Congressman John Lewis who wasn't a Congressman at the time. Kelly Miller Smith, who was good friends with Dr. King and Dr. King was always in Nashville. So, my mother had a close connection not only with the individuals, but also the locations and when something happened, because she was so connected, it really hit her. It hit her and we knew. We didn't know what happened, but we knew something had happened.

JD: Did she sit and talk to you guys about it?

WD: Not really, you know, they don't have conversations about it because it's hard and I'm saying this because that's a generational thing. My dad didn't talk about his service in the Navy being in Korea until much later. He didn't tell his mother anything. He didn't tell me anything. And my mother was kind of the same way. I didn't know and learn much of what was really going on with her. I knew on the periphery that things were happening but the closeness she was to the situation didn't come out until much later. We were probably adults when we really had those conversations, but we knew we knew things had happened.

JD: How do you think this impacted black communities all over Nashville and more broadly?

WD: This. I think integration is a double-edged sword. It had to happen. It was going to happen. But when it happens, it's not easy. There are going to be changes. And just like I said before, I left a nurturing school and went to a rather sterile environment. All of the people I was in the third grade with—when we were phased over to Tusculum Elementary School, all of us were separated. It was one black face in each classroom full of twenty white students. It's always a double-edged sword. And so, you get some of the, some of the bad with the good and some of the good with the bad. Change causes chaos. It does. And then hopefully, it settles down.

Right after high school, 1976, the miniseries *Roots* came out. The book had already been out for maybe two or three years, but then they made the miniseries and many of my white and black friends, we had never witnessed or visually saw things connected with slavery, like chopping off a foot or hanging or whipping. Things we may have heard about, but to see it on the screen. And it caused a lot of us to have some very, deep conversations. But also let me say, I hung around old people, my elders, my grandparents, my great aunts and uncles, and many of them have witnessed firsthand things done by the Ku Klux Klan and Jim Crow laws. And they told me stories and I made it a point to try to draw as much from them as I could, in terms of their knowledge, the things that they had seen and had experienced. So, for me, it was a big part that they that had seen a transition to where I was going to school, with white students interacting with them. And my best friend today is someone that I met in junior high and we were like brothers and he's white, but you know, our family.

JD: Do you think those conversations you had with people after, integrating schools were good? Like, do you think it helped or do you think it made things harder?

WD: I think it helped at that point. I think I've seen some regression, but I think at that point it helped. At some point, if you feel like, "well, this white person doesn't like me" or "that black person doesn't like me," you had the conversation. Then it's over and you kind of find your common ground. I think that's what we did at one time. And I'm not sure what's going on today, but in a sense, I feel like there's been some regression and some of those conversations we had, we might need to have again. I think we do. Our generation is working on having those conversations. I think your generation is at a good place and primed for it. Same sex couples and blended families—we're seeing a whole lot more and things we didn't see in the sixties, seventies, and even the eighties. We're seeing some things that I think mirror more, what our society actually looks like. So we stand a better chance of doing better.

JD: How can we honor and continue to celebrate the accomplishments of the civil rights leaders and the movement as a whole?

WD: I think we need to engage in honest conversations with each other and there should be no anger, animosity in those conversations. Certain things that happened in history, they happened. It's history, it's gone, it's past, but we have golden opportunities now to engage in meaningful dialogue and meaningful activities with each other.

JD: I think we honor them by doing that. How can we continue to uplift and educate our black communities and young people?

WD: Just by continuing to educate ourselves. As Malcolm X, and W.E.B. Dubois really said, education is the key. Yes. And education takes shape a lot of ways, informally and formally, but that we need to read more. We need to find out more about this world in which we live, and even as Malcolm X had once been told that all white people were the devil, but then when he went on the Hajj to Mecca and worshiped with "blue-eyed blond" Muslims, devout Muslims, true Muslims, he found out the world was much bigger and things were much different than he had been told, but he had to have that experience himself. And so sometimes when we don't open up to each other, when we don't allow each other to come into contact, and have these interactions, we lose, we lose, and we have to have these conversations. We have to open up our world to what's out there and to other people.

Made in the USA
Columbia, SC
11 February 2024

31281672R00102